The New Politics of Di.

The New Politics of Disablement

Michael Oliver

and

Colin Barnes

First published as *The Politics of Disablement* in 1990
This edition published as *The New Politics of Disablement* in 2012

Published by
PALGRAVE MACMILLAN

Palgrave Macmillan in the UK is an imprint of Macmillan Publishers Limited,
registered in England, company number 785998, of Houndmills, Basingstoke,
Hampshire RG21 6XS.

Palgrave Macmillan in the US is a division of St Martin's Press LLC,
175 Fifth Avenue, New York, NY 10010.

Palgrave Macmillan is the global academic imprint of the above companies
and has companies and representatives throughout the world.

Palgrave® and Macmillan® are registered trademarks in the United States,
the United Kingdom, Europe and other countries

ISBN 978-0-333-94567-4

This book is printed on paper suitable for recycling and made from fully
managed and sustained forest sources.

A catalogue record for this book is available from the British Library.

10 9 8 7 6 5 4 3 2 1
21 20 19 18 17 16 15 14 13 12

Printed and bound in Great Britain by

CPI Antony Rowe, Chippenham and Eastbourne

Contents

PART III   AGENDAS AND ACTIONS

*To Vic without whom this book would never have been
started, let alone finished*

Introduction

Background

When the first edition of this book was being prepared the capitalist world was emerging from one of its periodic economic crises which had given rise, in the United Kingdom at least, to a couple of major political confrontations resulting in the police being used to crush the legitimate protests of a group of workers and rioting on the streets of many of our major cities over the poll tax. Other groups too, including disabled people, were protesting over a whole variety of legitimate issues, and despite the rhetoric of cuts in public expenditure, considerable concessions were being wrung from capitalist societies all over the world.

Coincidentally when we were preparing this edition the capitalist world was undergoing another of its periodic crises accompanied by yet more rhetoric about cuts in public expenditure. While there have been a few mass demonstrations in major European cities, these have been about the scope of the cuts rather than their legitimacy and there seems to be an all-round consensus about reducing public expenditure, whatever the difficulties this may cause to marginalized groups, including disabled people. The 'end of ideology' predicted by one commentator (Bell, 1960) more than fifty years ago now seems to have arrived with a vengeance. The new politics that is emerging from all this seems more consensual and less confrontational than when we were writing the first edition.

The outcome of this is that we have written this book in a very different political environment. The optimism of the 1980s seems now to have disappeared and the tone of our current work is more pessimistic though, we hope, not depressing. We still believe that capitalism can be replaced by a more inclusive form of social organization and that this still has to be fought for by marginal groups, including disabled people. We do, however, recognize that this struggle is a complex, long-term project and we hope that this book can make a contribution to this endeavour.

Personal Biographies

The decision to write the new edition of this book as a joint enterprise was an easy

1

one. Although the first edition was written by one of us (Mike Oliver) we have worked on a number of joint projects both before and after it was produced and have continued to do so for many years. Additionally we are both professional sociologists and between us we have spent nearly sixty years working within that discipline. And like Comte (1987), we believe that sociology is the 'queen of science' and that sociological insights are to varying degrees evident in all academic disciplines. This is especially so with reference to analyses and debates about impairment and disability. Finally we both have impairments, though our personal journeys to self-identification as disabled people are obviously different. Thus it seemed entirely natural that we should collaborate on this edition as we work well together and our views on the production of disablement in modern societies are broadly similar, if not exactly the same.

Writing the New Edition

The first edition of the book began with a moan and a challenge:

> The issue of disability and the experiences of disabled people have been given scant consideration in academic circles. Both the issue and the experience have been marginalised and only in the disciplines of medicine and psychology has disability been afforded an important place. Unfortunately this has, itself, been counterproductive because it has resulted in the issue of disability being seen as essentially a medical one and the experience of disability as being contingent upon a variety of psychological adjustment processes. Hence there is an urgent need for other disciplines such as sociology, anthropology, history, politics and social administration to take these matters seriously rather than to merely offer descriptive and atheoretical accounts which leave medical and psychological approaches unchallenged.
>
> In order to counter the medical and psychological dominance in this area, ultimately nothing less than a 'social theory of disability' will be necessary, but such a theory cannot be produced until the various academic disciplines begin to take both the issue of disability and the experiences of disabled people seriously in their own right rather than as marginal to both theoretical developments and empirical work. (Oliver, 1990, p.x)

There is no doubt that since 1990 many disabled and non-disabled academics have risen to this challenge and we have seen the growth in published work across many disciplines, the development of disability studies courses at undergraduate and postgraduate levels, the establishment of centres of excellence and the creation of professorial chairs in the subject. The exact role that the first edition of this book played in these subsequent developments is perhaps for others to speculate on but there is little doubt that it came out at 'the right time'. What is clear is that some twenty years after the first edition we now have a group of academics working within an area that can be described as disability studies which we believe has the potential for producing meaningful social changes.

Accordingly the new edition will not be just an update of the first but will also address and incorporate new theoretical developments, changing social policies and contexts and emerging understandings about the nature of disablement in society. Overall the revised edition will seek to make an ongoing and original contribution to our understanding of disablement in society in the light of changes that have occurred since 1990. These include globalization, environmentalism, the end of Soviet-style communism, a succession of deepening crises within capitalism, the growth of religious fanaticism and bio-genetic medicine. Within this context, the overall aim of this book is to suggest ways in which the lives of disabled people and therefore society as a whole can be substantially improved.

The central argument in *The New Politics of Disablement* will remain the same, namely that it was the coming of capitalism that created disability as an individual problem and that it was not until the latter half of the twentieth century that this came to be challenged, largely by politicized disabled people. Where this edition will differ is in relation to our predictions about what was going to happen into the millennium and beyond where things have taken a more pessimistic turn than we had expected.

Organization of this Book

The structure of the new edition will stick as closely as possible to that of the first edition but will try to capture both the dynamism and the contested nature of the emergent disability studies. To this end we have divided this new edition into three sections each containing three chapters. The first looks at some of the key concepts of disability studies and discusses their origins. The second looks at the influences on the ways in which disability has been and is currently being represented. The final section attempts to capture the dynamics and the emerging field of study and considers the agendas and actions for those involved.

Chapter 1, *The Importance of Definitions in the Disability Debate*, is substantially the same as in the first edition, focusing initially on why definitions are important. We then go on to look at official definitions and the challenges they represent. This includes a discussion of recent attempts to bring together individual medical approaches as exemplified by the World Health Organization's (WHO) *International Classification of Impairments, Disabilities and Handicaps* (ICIDH) and the social model of disability into the *International Classification of Functioning and Health* (ICF). The narrative then turns to emerging emancipatory approaches to research based upon methodological individualism and investigatory foundationalism. We conclude by suggesting that we have to develop new ways of defining the world if we are ever to change it successfully.

The following chapter, *The Origins of Disability Studies*, discusses various anthropological contributions to our understandings of impairment and disability. We then go on to consider the work of sociologists within the field including contributions from functionalists, interactionists and deviance theorists and suggest that such work largely fails to challenge traditionalist assumptions about disability. Finally we consider the work of medical sociologists and policy analysts who have attempted to broaden their frameworks.

In Chapter 3, *The Rise of Disabling Capitalism*, we reassert the argument that it was the coming of capitalism that was responsible for creating and constructing disability in the ways we understand it today. We examine changes to the organization of work as well as our perceptions of and responses to disability. Finally we discuss the ways these changes have been explained.

The next two chapters, *Ideology and the Disabled Individual* (Chapter 4), and *Constructing Disabled Identities* (Chapter 5), consider the ways in which individualizing ideologies shape the experience of the disabled individual and the process of exclusion. This includes a focus on medicalization and how this influences understandings of disability. Chapter 4 concludes by linking these ideas to the 'normalizing society' and the rise and impact of the eugenics movement on contemporary thinking.

Chapter 5 focuses on how these ideas are reflected in western culture and the ways in which images of impairment and disability in the media influence the formation of what is widely regarded as a traditional, dependent 'disabled' identity.

We then turn to recent debates about the significance of this concept with reference to multiple and simultaneous oppression and their impact on identity formation generally.

In Chapter 6, *Creating the Disability Problem*, we turn our attention to the ways in which economic, political and social forces are mediated through social policy and so create dependency and disablement of people with impairments. This includes a discussion of the ways in which dependency is created by economic and social policies and professional ideologies and practices, as well as the responses of disabled people to all this. We also deal with what we call social constructionist and social creationist accounts of disablement and suggest that it is creationist accounts that are most useful.

Dealing with the Disabling Society is the subject of Chapter 7. It begins with reference to the recurring crises that have been a major characteristic of all capitalist societies. We then look at the various responses to these crises focusing on the market and disability and human rights. Finally we explore the globalization of capital, its implications for international organizations in general and for disabled people in particular.

The penultimate chapter, *Resisting the Disabling Society* (Chapter 8), focuses on how hitherto capitalist society incorporates and resists social change. We examine the potential of charity, the social model and independent living as well as the political possibilities of identity politics and groupings and social movements. We conclude with the assertion that ultimately only the transformation of capitalist society will ensure the full inclusion of disabled people and indeed all socially oppressed groups.

The final chapter, *Doing Disability Studies* (Chapter 9), discusses the emergence of and the issues facing those working in this academic field. While we recognize the contested nature of much of what is happening, we reassert our belief in and commitment to the transformative nature and emancipatory potential of disability studies as political action.

Disclaimers

The Introduction to the first edition began with a number of disclaimers which we need to reiterate here. We also include some new ones. We retain the term 'disabled people' in preference to 'people with disabilities' for the reasons originally outlined. In the first edition we rejected terminology based upon medical or social scientific constructions and divorced from the direct experience of people with impairments. Despite a plethora of attempts to clarify this terminology by policy makers, lawyers and social scientists, in this edition we stick to the term 'disabled people' and reassert the reasoning of the first edition.

All people with impairments experience disability as social restriction, whether those restrictions occur as a consequence of inaccessible built environments, questionable notions of intelligence and social competence, the inability of the general population to use sign language, the lack of reading material in Braille or hostile public attitudes to people with non-visible conditions and impairments. It's important to remember too that not all impairments have obvious functional limitations. Some conditions such as 'baldness' or 'skin blemishes' do not impede someone's ability to function 'normally' yet may have significant negative implications in particular social contexts. Therefore what is considered an impairment is both materially and culturally determined.

In sum, people who have impairments have 'disabilities' thrust upon them by an unjust and uncaring society. To accept the label 'people with disabilities' is to accept that disability is an individual rather than a social problem. As is argued in this book and its predecessor 'disability' is a social creation. Whilst impairment may be a human constant, disability is not and need not be.

We would also like to point out that in our discussions of disability politics we use the term 'disabled people's movement' to refer to what we originally called organizations of disabled people rather than the more recent term 'disability movement' which, in our view, refers to a ragbag collection of organizations and charities who are neither democratic nor a movement. In later chapters of this new edition we shall refer to this ragbag as 'disabling corporatism'.

The third disclaimer concerned the use of the term capitalist society in preference to industrial, modern or other such terminology. Over the last couple of decades the world has seen many changes and the capitalism/communism divide has all but disappeared with the demise of the Soviet Union. Capitalism itself is currently undergoing significant changes too, provoked by a succession of increasingly severe fiscal crises, the rise of radical fundamentalism, overpopulation and environmental degradation and diminishing resources. There are therefore many differences in the ways societies have developed and this has produced many varieties of social policies which have in turn had their effects on definitions and experiences of disability. However, despite these changes we will continue to assert that there is an underlying logic to the development of most societies which continues to create disability as an individual medical problem and that, in this respect at least, little has changed in the last twenty years.

We would also like to clarify our use of the term disablement. It refers to the economic and social processes that ultimately create both impairment and disability. It is of course mediated by personal experiences of impairment and influenced by the politics of disability as well as societal responses to the 'problem'. Critics of the first edition often accused us of ignoring impairment and personal experiences despite the fact that there were individual chapters on each. So while we reject these criticisms, we reiterate that this book is not about personal experiences or medical consequences of it. Nor is it about the social model, which again many of our critics seemed to think it was, despite the fact that our discussion of it was limited to three pages. Almost to the point of boredom, we have constantly stated that the social model is a tool to be used to produce changes in society and is not and was never intended to be a social theory.

One final disclaimer concerns the style of the book and the audience to which it is addressed. Our aim has been to produce a revised edition which will continue the process of encouraging academics to take disability more seriously as an analytical category, and to contribute to the continuing development of a theoretically informed understanding of disablement in society amongst disabled people. The dangers of such an approach are obvious: a book which is regarded as over-simplistic by academics or a book which is regarded as over-complex and mystifying by disabled people. All we can say is that in writing this book, we have fulfilled a personal need to make an ongoing contribution to attempts to develop a social theory of disablement, which began around the time the first edition was published. While the book addresses complex and contentious ideas and issues, we have tried to make it as accessible to as wide a variety of audiences as possible.

Part 1

Concepts and Origins

1

The Importance of Definitions in the Disability Debate

Introduction

In this opening chapter we suggest that despite the surge of interest in 'disability' in political and academic circles since the publication of the first edition of this book in 1990, the dominant meanings attached to 'disability' in most western industrial and post-industrial societies remain firmly rooted in personal tragedy theory. Although there has been a radical reappraisal of the meaning of disability by disabled activists and some academics across much of the developed world since the 1960s, disability is still widely regarded as primarily a health issue by politicians, practitioners and the general public. This is routinely reaffirmed by the activities of policy makers, professionals and mainstream scholars and researchers who in one way or another explain disability in terms of medical diagnoses of individual pathology, associated functional limitations and culturally determined deficits. These assertions are clearly reflected in official definitions of disability, such as the recent World Health Organization's (WHO) 'biophsyosocial' model of disability (WHO, 2001a), its predecessor, the *International Classification of Impairments, Disabilities and Handicaps* (ICIDH) (WHO, 1980) and subsequent academic debates that stress a 'relational' approach to understanding disability (Thomas,1999, 2007; Gustavsson, 2004; Shakespeare, 2006).

Crucially, such definitions and arguments become authoritative and are assumed to provide generalized explanations for the multiple deprivations associated with disablement and a justification for often routine and invasive interventions by health and social welfare professionals in disabled people's lives.

The challenge to these definitions and the dominant ideologies underpinning them began in the 1960s when disabled activists and writers in the UK, Scandinavia and North America started to ask questions as to why disabled people were treated in the ways they were in their own societies. Their aim was to shift public and policy attention away from established orthodoxy toward the role of 'disabling' economic, political and cultural barriers that prevented people with impairments and labelled 'disabled' from participating in mainstream society as equal citizens. These challenges found expression in the concept of independent living (De Jong, 1981), the social model of disability (Oliver, 1981) and the social oppression theory of disablement (Finkelstein, 1980; Abberley, 1987; Oliver, 1990). Yet the academic community was slow to attribute any significance to disabled people's political actions or social model inspired analyses of disability (Oliver, 1996; Linton, 1998).

We cannot exempt our own discipline of sociology from this criticism, which is surprising and disappointing given its structural focus. In response to this failure a growing literature including books, edited collections and journals produced by mainly disabled writers led to the development of a distinct field of interdisciplinary enquiry, 'Disability Studies', around the world which gradually awoke interest from across the social sciences, education, law, the humanities and sociology itself (see, for example, Albrecht, Seelman & Bury, 2001; Barnes, Oliver & Barton, 2002; Swain et al., 2004; Kristiansen, Velmas & Shakespeare, 2009; Davis, 2010).

In this chapter we explore one of the key issues and themes for developing a social theory of disability, that of how we define the world we are seeking to understand. We begin by asking why definitions are important. We then turn our attention to how this perspective is reflected in official definitions before turning to an alternative: the social barriers or social model perspective. We consider how recent attempts to reconcile the two are exemplified in the *International Classification of Functioning, Disability and Health* (ICF) and 'relational' analyses of disability that blur the distinction between the medical and social models. We conclude with the assertion that we urgently need to develop new ways of defining the world if we are ever to properly understand it and change it for the better.

Setting the Scene

In his exploration of the sociological imagination, C. Wright Mills (1970) stressed the importance of investigating the interplay between 'personal troubles' affecting individuals and their social relations with others and wider society, and how they are more appropriately understood as 'public issues' (p. 14). Mills was critical of sociologists for being either grand theorists or abstracted empiricists. The case for a methodological middle way has had a profound effect on sociologists' work ever since and there have been few areas, subjects or topics where theory and empiricism have not met. Hence the sociological interest in connections between people's experiences and wider historical and political circumstances, with the role of sociology being to identify

> the social in the individual, the general in the particular; this is precisely what sociologists can do for us. We would expect them to show how our individual biographies intertwine with the history we share with fellow human beings. (Bauman, 1990, p. 10)

To illustrate the point: a disabled person's inability to find paid work is widely attributed to their lack of ability to carry out the required tasks or capacity to undertake the necessary roles. However, such arguments ignore the fact that despite environmental and attitudinal barriers many disabled people compete successfully in the labour market and acquire a wide range of jobs. The problem is that the unemployment rate amongst disabled people is much higher than that of non-disabled peers and this suggests that a structural rather than a personal explanation is needed. We know, for example, that the disabled population generally experience exclusion from the workplace due to environmental and social barriers (UPIAS, 1976; Bowe, 1978; Barnes, 1991; Oliver & Barnes, 1998; Burchardt, 2000; Roulstone & Barnes, 2005; Berthoud, 2011; WHO, 2011). Thus we need an analysis which moves away from the individual to the social and the collective disadvantage of disabled people and which, most importantly, requires a different set of policy responses.

This example illustrates the value of a sociological re-assessment of common-sense thinking and behaviour. Apparently 'natural' attitudes, institutions, processes and structures are dependent on social factors and contexts, which are supported and transformed by human action. In the example cited above, our actions shift from socializing impaired individuals into a world of non-work and onto changing the operation of disabling labour markets and the attitudes of discriminatory employers. The point of this example is not to replace 'error' with 'truth' but rather to engage in critical reflection to improve our under-standing of the social world and our subsequent actions within it (Bauman, 1990).

The Importance of Definitions

The social world differs from the natural world in (at least) one fundamental respect: that is, human beings give meanings to objects in the social world and subsequently orientate their behaviour towards these objects in terms of the meanings given to them. Therefore if we define 'situations as real, they are real in their consequences' (Oliver, 1990, p. 2). As far as disability is concerned, if it is seen as a tragedy, then disabled people will be treated as if they are the victims of some tragic happening or circumstance. This treatment will occur not just in everyday interactions but will also be translated into social policies which will attempt to compensate these victims for the tragedies that have befallen them.

Alternatively, it logically follows that if disability is defined as social oppression, then disabled people will be seen as the collective victims of an uncaring or unknowing society rather than as individual victims of circumstance. Such a view will be translated into social policies geared towards alleviating oppression rather than compensating individuals. It almost goes without saying that despite recent initiatives at the national and international levels to address this problem, the individual and tragic view of disability continues to hold sway in almost all policy and social interactions. Indeed it remains true that society continues to respond to disability in predominantly individualistic ways. For example, although legislative initiatives have been introduced to eliminate discrimination on the grounds of impairment in many countries, the remedy remains largely dependent upon individual disabled people taking their cases to law (Doyle, 2008).

A second reason why definitions are important historically centres on the need to identify and classify the growing numbers of the urban poor in modern industrial societies. In this process of identification and classification, disability has always been an important category, in that it offers a legitimate social status to those who can be defined as unable to work as opposed to those who may be classified as unwilling to do so (Stone, 1984). Throughout the twentieth century this process has become ever more sophisticated, requiring access to expert knowledge, usually residing in the ever-burgeoning medical and para-medical professions. Hence the simple dichotomy of the nineteenth century has given way to a whole new range of definitions based upon clinical criteria or functional limitation. It is worth pointing out, however, that this attempt to distinguish between those unable and those unwilling to work remains prob-lematic for social policies as we move into the twenty-first century. In the last twenty years successive British governments have deliberately expanded and contracted the category 'incapacity to work' in order to address other particular political priorities prevailing at the time (Burchardt, 2000).

A third reason why definitions are important stems from what might be called 'the politics of minority groups'. From the 1950s onwards, though earlier in the case of people addicted to alcohol, there was a growing realization that if particular social problems were to be resolved, or at least ameliorated, then nothing more or less than a fundamental redefinition of the problem was necessary. Thus a number of groups, including women, black people and gay people, set about challenging the prevailing definitions of what constituted these problems by attacking the sexist, racist and heterosexist biases in the language used to underpin these dominant definitions. They did this by creating, substituting or taking over terminology to provide more positive imagery (e.g., gay is good, black is beautiful). Disabled people too have realized that dominant definitions of disability pose problems for individual and group identity and have begun to challenge the use of disablist language. Whether it be offensive (such as 'cripple', 'spastic' or 'mongol') or merely depersonalising ('the handicapped', 'the blind', 'the deaf', and so on), such terminology has been attacked, and organizations of disabled people have fostered a growing group consciousness and identity. This has led to attempts to build a disability culture in order to challenge the ideology of personal tragedy that continues to structure the dominant ways we continue to understand disability (Sutherland, 1981, 2006; Swain & French, 2000; Peters, Gabel & Symeonidou, 2009).

There is one final reason why this issue of definitions is important. From the late 1950s onwards there was a general upswing in the economic growth of many wealthy states and an increasing concern to provide more services for disabled people from their expanding national economies. But clearly no government (of whatever persuasion) was going to commit itself to a whole range of services without some idea of what the financial consequences of such a commitment might be. In the UK, for example, the data produced by two Office of Population, Census and Survey (OPCS) surveys (Martin, Meltzer & Elliot, 1988; Martin & White, 1988) during the 1980s proved inaccurate in their predictions about the numbers of disabled people entitled to disability benefits such as the Attendance Allowance and the Independent Living Fund respectively (Oliver & Barnes, 1998). In both cases, government found itself committed to far greater expenditure than it intended and as a consequence ended up in considerable political difficulties (Dwyer, 2000).

Official Definitions of Disability

Whilst there has been a consistent bias against people with assumed biological abnormalities and functional limitations throughout the recorded history of western culture, we would suggest that the gradual creation of the disabled individual occurred at a particular historical point, namely, the coming of industrial society. The collective labour of agrarian society gave way to the individualized wage labour of the factory, fundamentally changing all other social relationships as well. From this point on people with functional limitations become a problem for government because often they were not able to operate the new machinery on which industrial society was being built, nor were their families able to support them, being under severe pressure themselves. There followed the long process of constructing what was essentially a labour market issue into an individualized medical problem. We will return to this in later chapters, as our purpose here is to consider how disability has been described in official definitions and the implications this has had on both societal responses and personal experience.

Despite this long march of history, in the UK it was not until the emergence of the welfare state in the middle of the twentieth century that policy makers used the generic term 'disabled'. The 1948 National Assistance Act coined the word to encompass 'the blind, the partially sighted, the deaf, the hard of hearing, and the general classes of the physically handicapped' with reference to the need for specific eligibility criteria for access to welfare benefits and services. In the 1960s the British National Insurance Benefit Regulations stated that the loss of fingers and a leg removed below the knee constituted a 50 per cent 'disability'. The amputation of a foot or loss of an eye constituted only a 30 per cent rating (Sainsbury, 1973, pp. 26–7).

There were obvious limitations to this approach and there was a shift to a more explicit way of assessing an individual's ability to perform everyday tasks and activities. This found expression in the first national survey of disability conducted by the OPCS in the late 1960s (Harris et al., 1971). It used a three-fold distinction between

- impairment: 'lacking part or all of a limb, or having a defective limb, organ or mechanism of the body';
- disablement: 'the loss or reduction of functional ability'; and
- handicap: 'the disadvantage or restriction of activity caused by disability' (Harris et al., 1971, p. 2).

The degree of handicap was based on a series of questions about an individual's ability to undertake key personal activities such as using the toilet, eating and drinking, and doing up zips and buttons. Subsequently the definition of impairment, or 'disability', was extended to physical, sensory and psychological conditions said to impede routine daily functioning. This seemingly elegant construction prompted more confusion than it resolved and proved spectacularly unreliable for government planning and policy making; the search for more reliable measures remains ongoing (Meltzer et al., 2000).

In an effort to provide consistency and minimize confusion internationally, the World Health Organization (WHO) commissioned Dr Philip Wood at Manchester University to expand on the WHO's *International Classification of Disease* (WHO, 1976) to cover long-term or 'chronic illnesses'. The result, *The International Classification of Impairments, Disability and Handicap* (ICIDH) was published in 1980. Drawing heavily on the OPCS construct mentioned above, it uses a threefold typology of 'impairment', 'disability' and 'handicap'. Thus impairment refers to 'any loss or abnormality of psychological, physiological or anatomical structure or function'. Disability denotes 'any restriction or lack (resulting from an impairment) of ability to perform an activity in the manner or within the range considered normal for a human being'. Handicap is defined as 'a disadvantage for a given individual, resulting from an impairment or a disability that limits or prevents the fulfilment of a role that is normal (depending on age, sex, social and cultural factors) for that individual' (WHO, 1980, pp. 27–9).

Advocates maintain that the ICIDH represents a major departure from the previous classification, as the concept 'handicap' has been extended to take account of socio-economic disadvantage or 'economic self sufficiency' and therefore represents a 'socio medical model of disability' (Bury, 1996, 2000). It subsequently provided a basis for the second OPCS national study of disability conducted in Britain in the 1980s. Disability was measured in terms of ten levels of severity (Martin, Meltzer & Elliot, 1988). This resembles policy approaches in other western societies. For instance, the Americans with Disabilities Act of 1990 defines 'disability' as an 'impairment that substantially limits one or more of the major life activities', with 'normal' functioning as the main yardstick (Charlton, 1998).

Unlike its predecessor (Harris et al., 1971) which surveyed people with physical impairments only, the 1980s OPCS surveys included those with a 'mental illness and handicap' and those with 'less severe impairments'. Hence the estimated number of disabled adults in Britain (England, Scotland and Wales) doubled to 6.2 million, equivalent to 14.2 per cent of the total population. Both surveys concluded that a majority of the disabled population was over 60 years of age, and contained a higher proportion of women than men. Ageing was also linked to the 'severity of disability'. Moreover, almost a third of people sampled were deemed to be in the two 'least severe' categories.

More recent data from the *General Household Survey* based on the self-classifications of people with a 'limiting, long-standing' condition suggest an increase to nearly 12 million people, or around 19 per cent of the total population (ONS, 2005). The United States Census Bureau identified a similar proportion, 18.1 per cent, of the population in 2002 (Brault, 2008). Additionally, both national surveys related impairment to a wide range of social disadvantages, for example, in employment and transport. Clearly though, such data must be treated with the utmost caution when estimating and comparing the size of and trends within the disabled population. This is evident at both the national and international levels.

Internationally, the ICIDH has not been very successful at identifying who is and who is not disabled. It is based on a particularly narrow set of western values and assumptions of 'normality'. Davis (1995) maintains that the word 'normal' only enters the English language around 1840. This is around the time that the pressures of industrialization were forcing governments to define, classify and control populations (Oliver & Barnes, 1998). But perceptions of 'normality' change over time and place even within and across western cultures. For example, spectacles are a necessary aid for people with a visual impairment. Although their use was once considered out of the ordinary, they are now so widely used that few would now regard spectacle wearers as abnormal. Indeed, the apparently objective designation of someone as 'not normal' implies a value judgement on that person's social worth. This is most obvious with the application of labels such as 'mental illness' and 'mental handicap'.

Most importantly, by 'blindly' following orthodox medical definitions like those of the OPCS and ICIDH, 'impairment' is seen as the underlying cause of 'disability' and/or 'handicap'. Implicit in this assertion is that the human being is flexible and adaptable while physical and social environments are not. This flies in the face of reality since historically humans have moulded the environment to suit their needs rather than the other way round. It also downplays the role of legislation and policy reforms to address the various economic and social disadvantages encountered by the overwhelming majority of people with impairments and labelled 'disabled'.

The disabled person is expected to make the best of their diminished circumstances and focus on individual adjustment and coping strategies with appropriate professional direction (Finkelstein, 1993). Hence disabled people become objects to be treated, changed, improved and made 'normal' (Oliver & Barnes, 1998). Whilst medical and rehabilitative interventions may be appropriate to treat disease and illness, it is increasingly apparent that they are of little use for the treatment of disability:

> The problem ... is that medical people tend to see all difficulties solely from the perspective of proposed treatments for a 'patient', without recognising that the individual has to weigh up whether this treatment fits into the overall economy of their life. In the past especially, doctors have been too willing to suggest medical treatment and hospitalisation, even when this would not necessarily improve the quality of life for the person concerned. Indeed, questions about the quality of life have sometimes been portrayed as something of an intrusion upon the purely medical equation. (Brisenden, 1986, p. 176)

Further, the ICIDH implies that impairment, disability and handicap are essentially static states. Apart from the fact that this is clearly inaccurate, it creates artificial divisions between people with and without impairments where there should not and need not be any (Sutherland, 1981; Zola, 1982). Such a situation is especially ludicrous considering the range of conditions included in the WHO scheme. In terms of 'impairment', besides a whole host of illnesses and diseases, conditions such as 'baldness', 'pregnancy' and 'homosexuality' are listed. With reference to 'disability' items such as 'failure to get to work on time' or 'lack of interest in local or national events' are included. These so-called conditions might easily be questions of choice or environment rather than of organic or intellectual pathology. Yet the ICIDH 'has a classification for every feature of human physicality' (Shakespeare, 1994, p. 104). It is hardly surprising, then, that internationally interpretations of both impairment and disability vary considerably (see Chapter 2). Such considerations weaken, if not undermine altogether, the reliability of historical and international comparisons (Edie & Loeb, 2006).

In short, we would suggest that the central thrust of the individual model is to cast disability as a personal tragedy where the person with an impairment has a health or social problem that must be prevented, treated or cured: 'the assumption is, in health terms, that disability is a pathology and, in welfare terms, that disability is a social problem. To have a disability is to have "something wrong with you"' (Oliver, 1996, p. 30).

Challenging Official Definitions

Although disability activism in Britain and America has its roots in the nineteenth century (Campbell & Oliver, 1996; Longmore & Omansky, 2001), from the 1960s onwards disabled activists and their organizations became increasingly vocal in their condemnation of official definitions because they were based on the individual model of disability with its medicalization of personal experience and its welfare implications. Reflecting on their experiences of discrimination and disadvantage, they focused instead on the organization of society rather than their ascribed limitations or differences. Their conclusion was that contemporary society had failed to recognize or accommodate the reality of human diversity and impairment (UPIAS, 1976; Bowe, 1978; Finkelstein, 1980; Oliver, 1981, 1983; Zola, 1982).

In the UK, several groups of disabled people were formed to explore an alternative approach. These included the Liberation Network of People with Disabilities, which produced its own magazine, *In from the Cold*, containing political commentary and personal experiences of exclusion and discrimination (Sutherland, 2006). Another small group of disabled activists, including key figures in Britain's disabled people's movement Paul Hunt, Vic Finkelstein and Ken Davis, established the Union of the Physically Impaired Against Segregation (UPIAS) in 1974. Their 'manifesto', *Fundamental Principles of Disability* (UPIAS, 1976), criticized organizations controlled by non-disabled 'experts' for their failure to address the various barriers central to disabled people's exclusion from mainstream economic and social activity, and their lack of accountability to the disabled community. These assertions have exerted a major influence on the disabled people's movement and disability theorizing in the UK (Oliver, 1996) and elsewhere (Barnes & Mercer, 2005; Albert, 2006).

A crucial element in the UPIAS approach is their distinction between impairment and disability:

- impairment: 'lacking part or all of a limb, or having a defective limb, organ or mechanism of the body';
- disability: 'the disadvantage or restriction of activity caused by a contemporary social organisation which takes no or little account of people who have physical impairments and thus excludes them from participation in the mainstream of social activities'. (UPIAS, 1976, p. 14).

Subsequently, the restriction to 'physical impairments' was dropped to incorporate all impairments – physical, sensory and cognitive. This is simply because some conditions, both congenital and acquired, affect all bodily functions (WHO, 2011) and in a disablist society all impairments, to a greater or lesser degree, have negative psychological implications (see, for example, Goffman, 1968; Rieser, 1990; Thomas, 1999; Reeve, 2006). Furthermore, impairment-specific labels may have relevance when accessing appropriate medical and support needs, but otherwise they are usually imposed rather than chosen and therefore socially and politically divisive (Oliver & Barnes, 1998).

Moreover, the UPIAS reformulation led directly to the development of a radical reappraisal of the meaning of disability known as the 'social model of disability' (Oliver, 1981). This is that

[I]n the broadest sense, [disability] is about nothing more complicated than a clear focus on the economic, environmental and cultural barriers encountered by people who are viewed by others as having some form of impairment – whether physical, mental or intellectual. (Oliver, 2004, p. 21)

This social model breaks the causal link between impairment and disability. The reality of impairment is not denied but is not the cause of disabled people's economic and social disadvantage. Instead, the emphasis shifts to how far, and in what ways, society restricts their opportunities to participate in mainstream economic and social activities, rendering them more or less dependent. Therefore disability is redefined as 'the outcome of an oppressive relationship between people with impairments and the rest of society' (Finkelstein, 1980, p.47). The social model therefore shifts attention to disabled people's common experiences of oppression and exclusion and those areas that might be changed by collective political action and social change.

Nonetheless, since its inception the social model has been subject to various criticisms, largely because of its foundation on the distinction between impairment and disability. Disabled feminists called for the inclusion of impairment-related experiences when theorizing disability, as some conditions are accompanied by 'pain' and 'suffering' and most disabled people do not differentiate between impairment and disability. Replicating the feminist dictum that the 'personal is political', they drew attention to the need for a theory that addresses oppression in the private as well as the public sphere (Morris, 1991; Crow, 1996; Thomas, 1999). Others argue that the social model focus on barrier removal, implying that all activity restrictions encountered by disabled people can be eliminated by social change, is unrealistic as 'impairment effects' will continue to exclude some individuals from particular areas of social life (French, 1993; Wendell, 1996; Thomas, 1999, 2007).

Moreover, others have argued that both impairment and disability are social constructs and consequently the division upon which the social model is based is fallacious and no longer valid (Shakespeare & Watson, 2001; Tremain, 2002, 2005; Shakespeare, 2006). But to suggest that this distinction is anything other than a practical guide to action is false. Whilst such assertions may be of interest to philosophers and some social theorists, they have little, if any, practical value in terms of research, policy and practice. Besides helping to fuel further criticism of social model inspired writings by sociologists (Bury, 1997; Williams, G., 1998, 2001; Williams, S., 1999, 2003), they serve to reinforce within policy circles the traditional bias for 'changing the person rather than changing the world' (Bickenbach, 2009, p.110).

All of this sidesteps the fact that:

> The social model is not about showing that every dysfunction in our bodies can be compensated for by a gadget, or good design, so that everybody can work an 8-hour day and play badminton in the evenings. It's a way of demonstrating that everyone – even someone who has no movement, no sensory function and who is going to die tomorrow – has the right to a certain standard of living and to be treated with respect. (Vasey, 1992, p. 44)

The distinction between impairment and disability is a pragmatic one that does not deny that some impairments limit people's ability to function independently. Nor does it deny that disabled people have illnesses at various points in their lives and that appropriate medical interventions are sometimes necessary. But independence is a relative concept. Humans are social beings and no one, regardless of impairment, can function completely independently. Most people experience illness at various stages of the life course (Priestley, 2003). The important point is that individual medical explanations of disability under-pinned by 'personal tragedy theory' effectively 'individualize the problems of disability and hence [to] leave social and economic structures untouched' (Oliver, 1986, p.16). As a result, solutions to disabled people's assumed inadequa-cies are primarily medical ones determined by a veritable army of 'professionals allied to medicine' (Finkelstein, 1998).

The importance of the social model of disability is that it has provided disabled people with an alternative understanding of the experience and reality of disability. It has given disabled people a basis on which to organize them-selves collectively:

> Using the social model as a basis for explanation, disabled people have been drawing attention to the real problems of disability: the barriers they face; the patronizing attitude they have to deal with; the low expectations that are invested in them; and the limited options available to them. (Swain et al., 2003, p.24)

However, it is important to remember that the social model is a simplified repre-sentation of a complex social reality. Although it has been linked to various theories of disablement (Priestley, 1998a), it is not a social theory. Its strength lies in the fact that it offers a fundamental alternative to the individual model and poses a very different set of research questions, as we demonstrated in the first edition of this book. For this we were taken to task by Shakespeare (2006) who claims that our reformulation of the questions was unlikely to produce any useful data. Our point was, however, merely to show how different assumptions about the nature of disability lead to a different set of questions being asked. While Shakespeare failed to grasp this, the British government has subsequently taken it more seriously by commissioning research to standardize social model type questions in all future government surveys (Sykes & Groom, 2009).

In fact most debates on disability now routinely acknowledge the influence of social model thinking. What is particularly striking is its impact on current policies across a diverse range of organizations, including central and local governments, charities and voluntary agencies at both the national and international levels. The social model has also been embedded in the WHO's recent attempt to redefine disability as a 'biopsychosocial model of disability'.

Official Responses to this Challenge

The criticism of the ICIDH advanced particularly by disabled people, coupled with the emergence of the social model, prompted the WHO to commission the production of a revised definition of disability. The team responsible for the revision began their discussions in 1993, and ICIDH2, or the *International Classification of Functioning, Disability and Health* (ICF) (WHO, 2002), as it became known, was unveiled and finally endorsed by WHO member states in 2001. It was also incorporated into the United Nations Convention on the Rights of Persons with Disabilities in 2006 (UN, 2006).

The ICF represents a concerted attempt to bring together the traditional individual model of disability and the social model; partly as a result of the ICIDH's rejection by disabled people, their organizations and allies within and outside academia and partly because, although widely used, the ICIDH's usage has been subject to various interpretations (Coleridge, 1993; Ingstad, 2001). In short, it has proved unacceptable to many and has not provided the clarity of meaning that was originally intended. More importantly it has not yielded any consistently reliable data nor have any useful proposals for reform and change emerged from those who have used it.

In contrast to the ICIDH, the ICF is presented as a 'universal classification' of human functioning and as a move away from a classification system based upon individual pathology. Advocates claim it offers a complete picture of the 'functional aspects of the health experience'. Within this framework disability remains a health rather than a political concern. It is an outcome of the

> interactions between *health conditions* (diseases, disorders and injuries) and *contextual factors*.

> Among contextual factors are external *environmental factors* (for example, social attitudes, architectural characteristics, legal and social structures as well as climate, terrain and so forth), and internal *personal factors*. (WHO, 2002, p.10, original emphasis)

Yet in common with its predecessor it identifies three levels of human functioning: 'at the level of the body or body part, the whole person, and the whole person, in a social context.' The first level, impairment, as in the original, relates to 'body function and structure'. The second level, what was 'disability', is now referred to as 'activity', and the third: 'handicap' is termed 'participation'. Notwithstanding the fierce debate over the meaning of the word 'disability' within the English-speaking world, the term is retained to denote 'dysfunctioning at one or more of these levels' (WHO, 2002, p. 10). Hence, 'rather than simply a classification of persons with disabilities, or even of the problems that they may experience, the ICIDH2 is a classification of functionality at three levels, understood in neutral terms' (Ustun et al., 2001, pp. 6–7).

In acknowledging the importance of the social and physical environment as both cause and consequence of impairment and 'disability', the ICF can be seen as an improvement on its predecessor (Hurst, 2000). Nonetheless in our view it is unlikely to be any more successful than the ICIDH in generating a universal language of disability, because transforming cultural differences in conceptualizing impairment and disability is notoriously difficult to achieve (Miles, 2001). This is especially so given that although the ICF recognizes the cultural context of perceptions of 'disability', and by implication, 'normality', the actual classification system remains grounded firmly in 'western scientific concepts and formulations' (Finkelstein, 1998; Pfieffer, 2000; Baylies, 2002).

Furthermore, whilst the ICF asserts that individuals are but one element in the analysis of disability, the 'biopsychosocial' approach is not that far removed from its original formulation in that it retains the individual as the starting point for the analysis of 'bodily function and activity'. The concept of participation is included but underdeveloped in the ICF scheme and is still linked to individual circumstances or 'personal factors' rather than tied firmly to the social and political organization of society.

Impairment is presented as a 'significant variation from the statistical norm' (WHO, 2001a, p. 221) and therefore ignores the cultural and contextual basis upon which such judgements are made. An individual's capacities are assessed against that of someone without a similar health condition (disease, disorder or injury, etc.). The ICF identifies an extensive range of 'personal factors' that may impact on an individual, including:

> gender, race, age, other health conditions, fitness, lifestyle, habits, upbringing, coping styles, social background, education, profession, past and current experience (past life events and concurrent events), overall behaviour pattern and character style, individual psychological assets and other characteristics, all or any of which may play a role in disability at any level. (WHO, 2001a, p.17)

It also employs a much broader definition of disability that includes restrictions at the level of the body (impairment) as well as in social participation more generally. All of this raises serious doubts about how the ICF can be interpreted by policy makers, practitioners and researchers. Again, like its predecessor, little useful data has so far been yielded and no practical proposals for reform and action have emerged that were not previously available.

Further, whilst the significance of context is emphasized, within the ICF, strategies for its measurement are limited. Potential users are encouraged to classify environmental factors, but there are no effective tools with which to do so, nor, indeed, to assess the disabling tendencies of government policies and practices, physical environments and or cultural contexts (Baylies, 2002). Moreover, one of the principal architects of the ICF has recently cast doubt on its usefulness:

> So, how do we answer questions about who is disabled or the prevalence of disability in a country or region? As a multi-domain, multi-dimensional, inter-active and continuous phenomenon (as it is characterized in the ICF), we must specify which impairment domains qualify, to which degree of severity. Different prevalence rates flow from different decisions. If we are interested in any impairment domain, to any degree of severity, then prevalence is roughly universal – a conclusion of no use to policy makers whatsoever. If we restrict our scope to

specific domains and severity levels, then our prevalence levels will differ accordingly. *But these decisions cannot be made conceptually or scientifically, they are political. The scientific approach in a word, does not solve the problem the policy analyst needs to solve.* (Bickenbach, 2009, p.120, emphasis added)

When these internal doubts are added to the critiques by disabled people and the current attempts by the British government to produce yet another scheme to produce useful data on disability, it is pertinent to wonder how much time and money has been spent on these failed attempts to classify and categorize disabled people. We would go further and suggest that without a radical rethink future attempts will continue to be expensive failures. It is to this that we now turn.

Rethinking Disability Definitions

If we are ever to develop classification schemes to produce accurate and reliable data which is likely to lead to the successful development of policies and programmes, we need to go back to the basic tenets of both medical and social research. In common with almost all previous medical and social research the ICF is founded upon ideologies of 'methodological individualism' and 'investigative foundationalism'.

The former asserts that all attempts to explain social (or individual) phenomena are to be rejected unless they are couched wholly in terms of 'facts about individuals'. It is therefore an 'exclusivist, prescriptive doctrine about what explanations are to look like ... it excludes explanations which appeal to social forces, structural features of society, institutional factors and so on' (Lukes, 1973, p.122).

The latter is defined by Hammersley (2000) who uses the term foundationalism in his defence of objective social research undertaken by academia. He suggests (p.154), 'In its most extreme form, foundationalism presents research, when it is properly executed, as producing conclusions whose validity follows automatically from the 'givenness' of the data on which they are based.'

While many social researchers, including Hammersley, tend to distance themselves from this extreme position, it remains the case that most medical and social research continues to proceed on the assumption that there is a real world out there and that by using appropriate methods we can investigate it and therefore produce worthwhile and workable knowledge about that world. This is certainly the case with disability research which has led to it being criticized for its failure to capture and reflect the experience of disability from the perspective of disabled people themselves, to contribute to improving the material conditions under which disabled people live, and to acknowledge that disability is primarily a political rather than simply a welfare and or medical concern (Oliver, 1992, 2002). Unsurprisingly many disabled people have become alienated from both the process and product of social research, a situation common amongst other oppressed groups, such as women and minority ethnic communities in both rich and poor countries (WHO, 2001b; Barnes, Oliver & Barton, 2002).

We are not suggesting that there are any simple solutions to confronting these twin problems of methodological individualism and investigatory foundationalism. Indeed, some of those who have tried have been less than successful. For example, some researchers have tried to produce accurate accounts of the disability experience by identifying with their research subjects. Some have argued that shared experience is essential; in other words, only women can research women's experience, black people the black experience, disabled people the disability experience and so on. But as Denzin has pointed out:

> The standpoint theorist presumes a privileged but problematic place in her own textuality ... a romantic, utopian impulse organises this work: the belief that if lived experience is recovered, somehow something good will happen in the world. A politics of action or praxis is seldom offered. (Denzin, 1997, p.54)

As indicated elsewhere (Oliver, 1992, 1997; Barnes, 1992, 2008) we believe that the crucial issue in developing useful and less alienating research is control of the research process and its production. This does not deny the value of research which gives voice to those previously denied it, but to question whether this, by itself, is enough. If it were, then the world would be a far better place. Indeed, since the early 1900s social scientists from a variety of disciplines have drawn attention to the plight of poor people and other disadvantaged groups in both the developed and developing worlds, rendering faithful and accurate accounts. But the poor and disadvantaged remain with us.

For research to be truly useful, it must not only faithfully capture the experience of the group being researched but also be accessible to participants in their struggles for empowerment. This is nothing less than 'changing the social relations of research production' (Oliver, 1992). This does not mean that researchers give up doing social research, far from it, but rather that they put their knowledge and skills in the hands of potential research subjects. It also means the use of language that does not perpetuate the artificial distinction between 'researcher and researched' (Barnes, 2008). We are not suggesting the replacement of one naïve solution with another: let's do away with experiential research and give disabled people control of all research about them. Doing social research is far more complex than that as those of us who reflect on the relationship between our own politics and our own research practice are only too aware. With this in mind Silverman suggests that researchers can choose one of two roles in relation to their own work: the partisan or the scholar:

> The partisan is often condemned to ignore features of the world which do not fit his or her preconceived moral or political position. The scholar goes too far in the other direction, wrongly denying that research has any kind of involvement with existing forms of social organisation. Both positions are too extreme and thus fail to cope with the exigencies of the actual relationship between social researchers and society. (Silverman, 1998, p. 93)

But with a few notable exceptions researchers rarely have the opportunity to choose between a partisan or scholar position. This is simply because although research institutions and academia perpetuate 'the myth of the independent researcher' (Barnes, 1996) most researchers and the work that they produce is determined by the way research is funded and organized around the principles of methodological individualism and investigatory foundationalism (Oliver, 1997).

Nonetheless the legitimacy of this approach is now under attack from a variety of different standpoints. For us research has to be seen as a productive rather than an investigative exercise. As Denzin has noted, 'the worlds we study are created, in part, through the texts that we write and perform about them' (Denzin, 1997, p. xiii). Research is therefore a creative and a productive process in the world, not an investigation of that world from a viewpoint outside it (Oliver, 2002, 2009).

Therefore in our view an alternative epistemology for research praxis is necessary. This epistemology must reject discourses that sustain the myth of investigative research and replace them with arguments that recognize that research helps produce the world in which we live. This is not new, of course; Marx

(1904) argued that the class that owned the means of material production was also responsible for 'mental production' and Gramsci (1985) suggested that under certain conditions, ideas themselves could be material forces. Also, Foucault (1980) refused to separate knowledge and power, arguing that the structures that maintain one also sustain the other.

As researchers, then, we labour to produce ourselves and our worlds. We do not investigate something out there, we do not merely deconstruct and reconstruct discourses about our world. Research as production requires us to engage with the world, not distance ourselves from it, for ultimately we are responsible for the product of our labours and as such we must struggle to produce a world in which we can all live as truly human beings:

> Thus, the research act is not an attempt to change the world through investi-
> gation, but rather an attempt to change the world by producing ourselves and
> others in differing ways from those we have produced before, intentionally or
> not. (Oliver, 2002, p.14)

Moreover Abberley (1997) has suggested that an emancipatory disability research agenda based on the discourse of research as production, must also consider the ways in which oppressive structures are reproduced. In so doing researchers can avoid 'parasiting the experience of disabled people by focusing on the actions of oppressors'. This adds an important dimension to disability research and while it is unable to avoid the separation of researcher and researched because of the 'objective class privilege of the disability researcher' it nonetheless produces useful knowledge for disabled people and their organizations in the struggle against oppression.

This redefinition of research as production rather than investigation has impli-cations for social theory as well as research practice. As we move further into the twenty-first century it is increasingly apparent that the world faces unprecedented environmental, economic and political challenges that will almost certainly impact on the lives of disabled and non-disabled people in both rich and poor countries (Oliver & Barnes, 2006). Consequently our very survival may depend upon our ability to produce useful knowledge in the real world with which to address these issues. Engaging in just such a reconstructive project involves not just the reconstituting of social theory but a re-engagement with the real world through the practicalities of undertaking emancipatory research.

Conclusion

The purpose of this book, therefore, is to continue the process of developing a social theory of disability. This process will continue to locate it within the experience of disabled people themselves and their attempts not only to redefine disability but also to construct a political movement with the potential to contribute to the restructuring of a more equitable and just society fit for all, regardless of the nature and severity of impairment, age, gender, race or sexual preference. This process began with the redefinition of disability as social oppression by disabled people and their organizations. This chapter has focused on the ways that redefinition has influenced the ways disability is defined and understood in the context of research production.

Consequently in the rest of this book we will locate disability within the context of society and social organizations with particular emphasis on the working of the economy, politics and culture. Attention will centre on the ways in which both impairment and disability are 'produced' as individual and medical problems within capitalist society at both the national and international levels. The following chapter centres on anthropological analyses of social responses to impairment and disability across time and place and theoretical accounts of the production of the complex process of disablement.

2

The Origins of Disability Studies

Introduction

In the previous chapter we attempted to show that much of the work on defining disability has been underpinned by what we have called personal tragedy theory. Official definitions as represented by the WHO's *International Classification of Functioning, Disability and Health* (ICF), among others, have failed to move beyond the individualization and medicalization of disabled people's experiences even though they have begun to acknowledge that the environment plays a major part in the experience of impairment and disablement. We also suggested that this acknowledgement is largely due to the challenge of the disabled people's movement through its formulation of the social model of disability.

In this chapter we will explore studies of impairment by anthropologists in 'pre-modern' societies before going on to discuss the contributions made by sociologists in contemporary societies. We will suggest that although anthropological studies demonstrate that social responses to impairment and disability vary across time and place, these insights have as yet been largely ignored by medical and mainstream sociologists whose work we then consider. We will suggest that they have usually failed to take a critical approach to understanding disablement, instead remaining locked within personal tragedy theory. We also need to point out that within the works discussed there is little common agreement over the terms illness, impairment, handicap, disability and the like, making it difficult to interpret and abstract from them accurately.

Anthropology and Disability

There is a wealth of anthropologically inspired research which has explored

32

cross-cultural approaches that has included social responses to physical or cognitive abnormality and difference – from Durkheim to Douglas and Levi-Strauss (Ingstad & Whyte, 1995). Studies looking at a wide range of countries document the very diverse ways in which different cultures have responded to body-mind variations or what today would be referred to as impairments (Hanks & Hanks, 1948; Scheer & Groce, 1988; Miles, 1995, 2001; Ingstad & Whyte, 1995). This literature provides ample evidence of the considerable diversity in what is understood by impairment and disability, although most cultures have notions of a 'normal' or 'ideal' body-mind, and what constitute acceptable individual attributes, the specific character of those norms and the extent to which they are negotiable varies considerably across and within societies. Hence what is construed as an 'impairment' and what is regarded as an appropriate social response are far from universal features: 'The disfiguring scar in Dallas becomes an honorific mark in Dahomey' (Hanks & Hanks, 1948, p. 11). Moreover, the assumed 'defects' that mark individuals out as unacceptably different may include features that other cultures regard as benign, such as freckles, small or flabby buttocks, and protruding navels (Ingstad & Whyte, 1995, p. 6).

We would suggest that such variations do not occur randomly, but rather are influenced by a range of factors. In one path-breaking study of cross-cultural responses to 'physical disability' the authors ground this diversity in contrasting economic and material conditions. They argue that a primary consideration is the level of economic stability and viability of a society, the amount of surplus generated and how it is distributed. Social structure is also important, whether egalitarian or hierarchical, how achievement is defined, how it values age and sex. To these may be added the *Weltanschauung*, the position of the group in relation to its neighbours, its aesthetic values 'and many more functionally related factors' (Hanks & Hanks, 1948, p. 13).

Given these insights it is possible to identify at least three discrete theories of disability that underpin anthropological studies (Oliver, 1990). The first stems from the work of Evans-Pritchard (1937) and his study of *Witchcraft, Oracles and Magic among the Azande*, a people of the upper Nile. He suggests that in societies dominated by religious or magical ways of thinking, disability is likely to be perceived as punishment by the gods or that individual disabled people are the victims of sorcery. For example, the Wapogoro people of Tanzania are convinced that 'epilepsy is a tribal sickness, contagious, a punishment for sin or an incarnation of an evil spirit and the result of witchcraft'. As a consequence people with epilepsy were often treated with 'cruelty and neglect' by their families and the community (Aail-Jilek, 1965, pp. 63–4).

Indeed, religious teachings are often presented as the sole determinant of what is socially acceptable in non-western contexts (Coleridge, 1993). The problem with this explanation is that it presents religious or magical beliefs as autonomous and the only determining factor in both defining impairment and accounting for the ways people with perceived impairments are treated. In so doing it sidesteps other factors such as the workings of the economy, power relations and structural inequality.

Yet the role of material factors or other considerations upon which religious pronouncements on impairment may be based are rarely discussed in these studies. Notably, most anthropological research in poorer countries has reported responses to impairment in small-scale, rural-based groups. Here religious beliefs may have a far greater impact on people's thinking than they would in urban environments (Scheer &Groce,1988; Ingstad & Whyte, 1995).

Moreover there is no consensus among major religions such as Hinduism, Islam and Buddhism about the 'correct' way to regard impairment. In societies where these religions claim wide popular allegiance, perceived impairments are significant for people's life chances because they are widely regarded as 'misfortunes, sent by deity, fate, karma; often associated with parental sin' (Miles, 1995, p. 52). But these religions, like Christianity, also tend to emphasize ways of understanding and responding to misfortune through individual acceptance and spiritual salvation (Charlton, 1998).

The second discrete underpinning is based on the influential work of Douglas (1966) and Turner (1967) and develops the concept of 'liminality'. Following Claude Levi-Straus' (1958, 1983) assertion that all binary distinctions in human thought represent the separation of nature and culture, Douglas maintains that all cultures must come to terms with the anomalies that defy their assumptions. Objects that cannot be categorized neatly are conceived as threatening to social order and therefore dangerous and polluting. Physical and cognitive abnormalities that cannot be explained are considered symptomatic of a non-human status and the 'other'.

Cultures deal with these 'anomalies' by either attempting to control them in some way or by adopting them as ritual. An example is the Nuer practice of treating 'monstrous births as baby hippopotamuses, accidentally born to humans'. They respond by returning them to 'the river where they belong' (Douglas, 1966, p. 39). Scheper-Hughes adds further examples of 'crocodile infants', 'poor little critters' in Northeast Brazil, and Irish 'changelings', and concludes that 'The sickly, wasted, or congenitally deformed infant challenges the tentative and fragile symbolic boundaries between human and non-human, natural and supernatural, normal and abominable' (Scheper-Hughes, 1992, p. 375).

Murphy employed Turner's notion of 'liminality' to explain the social position of people with physical impairments in all societies:

> The long-term physically impaired are neither sick nor well, neither dead nor fully alive, neither out of society nor wholly in it. They are human beings but their bodies are warped or malfunctioning, leaving their full humanity in doubt. They are not ill, for illness is transitional to either death or recovery ... The sick person lives in a state of social suspension until he or she gets better. The disabled spend a lifetime in a similar suspended state. They are neither fish nor fowl; they exist in partial isolation from society as undefined, ambiguous people. (Murphy, 1987, p. 112)

There are two problems with this explanation. First, as indicated above, the exclusion of people with physical impairments from the mainstream of community life is not practised in all societies. Second, explaining the social position of such people in terms of binary opposites or the search for symbolic order is both simplistic and reductionist. It is a feature of 'a particular kind of descriptive anthropology' that presents societies as the embodiment of thought processes rather than economic and social relationships. It also serves to perpetuate the: 'idea of a metaphysical "otherness", whilst directing attention away from the real physical and social differences which disadvantage disabled people' (Abberley, 1988, p. 306).

Additionally such explanations lead to the absurd view that 'There are, however, no strong economic reasons for systematically excluding and abasing the physically handicapped, except for the minor fact that they are often supported and cared for at public expense' (Murphy, 1995, p.152).

There are, we would suggest, strong economic reasons for the systematic exclusion of people with impairments, whether physical, sensory or cognitive in nature, from mainstream society. And it is the embodiment of these economic and social relations which has led directly to the exclusion of disabled people within capitalist societies. This is a theme we will return to throughout this book.

The third theoretical foundation is the 'surplus population thesis', which argues that in societies where economic survival is a constant struggle, any weak or dependent members who threaten this survival will be dealt with. Consequently infants with obvious impairments may be killed at birth, disabled adults may be forced out of the community and disabled old people simply left to die. Rasmussen (1908) cites an example of an Eskimo man and one of his wives who were badly burned in an explosion. The wife was simply left to die, but the husband, if he recovered, might again make an economic contribution, and so was saved. Nevertheless he resolved the situation by flinging himself into the sea.

However we need to avoid simplistic approaches based upon economic determinism for

> One should not be misled by the simplicity of economic factors in this case. The Australians too had a slim margin of surplus, practised infanticide but seemed not to have disposed of the physically handicapped in this way. Certainly in Australia age was a mark of authority as to make this action difficult. The Paiute of the Great Basin of North America, had an almost equally precarious existence, and neither practised infanticide nor abandoned their disabled. (Hanks & Hanks, 1948, p. 15)

Moreover, in relation to studies of social responses to people labelled 'mentally retarded/handicapped', or more recently 'with learning difficulties', both Farber (1968) and Soder (1984) have attempted to go beyond economic determinism and pointed to the role of values and ideology in shaping social practices, in capitalist societies at least. This leads to the conclusion that historically 'the definitions of mental retardation have varied in direct correlation with the current social values and economic demands of the defining society (Manion & Bersani, 1987, p. 236).

In a similar vein Nicolaisen (1995) identifies the concepts of 'humanity' and 'personhood' to be considered in analyses of cultural responses to impairment and disability. There is ample evidence that perceptions of humanity diverge significantly across non-capitalist societies. Throughout recorded history different cultures have constructed elaborate hierarchies to locate individuals along a continuum of humanity and non-humanity. She shows that for the Punah Bah of Central Borneo, for example, only a narrow set of impairments, including epilepsy, 'madness' and severe birth defects, are regarded as evidence of a non-human status.

Personhood signifies a refinement of the notion of humanity that differentiates between specific roles or statuses. It focuses on expectations of what it means to be a child, adult, man or woman and therefore may change over the life course. Whereas in most western societies personhood is equated with earning an income from work, in China it has been more associated with marriage and producing a son to continue the family lineage (Stone, 1999). Hence perceived impairment does not necessarily lead to social exclusion. Another example is the Masai people of Kenya, where people with physical impairments may marry, become parents and participate in all communal activities 'to the best of their abilities' (Talle, 1995, p. 69).

These examples illustrate the diversity of cultural responses to people with impairments in pre-capitalist and 'developing societies' (Kisanji, 1995). The range of social statuses of people with impairments stretches from pariah, because the individual is deemed an economic or moral liability or threat, through limited participation, where the individual is granted selected social or other concessions, to *laissez-faire*, where some people enjoy opportunities to acquire prestige and wealth (Hanks & Hanks, 1948; Ingstad & Whyte, 1995).

Yet the spread of industrial capitalism has had a significant impact to traditional responses to impairment and disablement in many countries. Whilst the roots of a global capitalist economic system may be traced back to the expansion of markets and international trade in the fifteenth and sixteenth centuries (Wallerstein, 1990), it has intensified significantly over recent decades with the process of globalization. This represents the interconnection of individuals, groups and communities within international economic, political and cultural networks, as a consequence of the recent rapid development of communication and information technology. It has led to some of the world's largest transnational corporations, such as Coca-Cola, Exxon and Microsoft, becoming wealthier than many developing countries. Indeed, globalization has accelerated significantly the growth of a 'capitalist world order' (Held et al., 1990).

Moreover the concept of development is generally viewed positively and something that all nations should aspire to. It is widely associated with western economic, technological, cultural institutions and innovation. But terms such as 'developed' and 'developing' tend to sidestep the huge disparity of wealth and resources within and across nation states. They also obscure the extent to which rich nations and transnational organizations are actively engaged in the exploitation and 'underdevelopment' of poor countries by exercising their economic and political power (Charlton, 1998; Albert, 2006; Barnes and Sheldon, 2010). Notwithstanding that there may be significant differences in emphasis, there is general agreement that the industrialization, urbanization, liberal utilitarianism, and medicalization, along with cultural understandings of 'able bodied normalcy' (Coleridge, 1993) have had a profound influence upon understandings of impairment and the social creation of disability. Henceforth the disabling tendencies of western-style economic and cultural development are to varying degrees being reproduced throughout the world (Barnes & Mercer, 2003, p. 142).

Nicolaisen's (1995) study of the Punah Bah economy and culture of Central Borneo provides a fitting example. The arrival of wage labour has seriously undermined the local economy and conflicts with established interpretations of personhood and the status of people with impairments and older people no longer able to work. Also western-style family units unable to provide for disabled and older family members are replacing typical extended household that historically provided support. Moreover, traditional belief systems are giving way to 'capitalist Western values' and so 'imperceptibly permeate the Punah Bah view of themselves and the world' (p. 54).

Although all estimates of the disabled population within and across nation states should be treated with the utmost caution due to different understandings of impairment and disability and because data collection strategies are often diverse and unreliable, it is suggested that 'including children over a billion people (or about 15 per cent of the world's population) were estimated to be living with disability' (WHO, 2011, p. 29).

However, as we illustrate in the following section, these insights have not led sociologists to adopt a broader approach in the bulk of their writings on impairment and disability. Many have remained locked into personal tragedy theory with its medicalizing and individualizing tendencies.

Sociology and Disability

There is no doubt that the work of Parsons (1951) has dominated sociological work on disability in the twentieth century just as it has dominated sociological work generally. Employing an holistic functionalist approach, Parsons was the first sociologist to analyse illness-related behaviour and the role of the medical profession in modern society. He was also the first to focus on the medical profession as an example of professional power in sociological analysis. Although functionalism is no longer as dominant as it once was, Parsons' work still exerts a powerful influence on sociological approaches to impairment and disability. In this section we need to examine his work critically so that we can move beyond it in the rest of the book.

Parsons' account of social order presumes that the effective operation of the 'social system', or society, rests on individual performance of necessary social roles. Health is defined as a 'normal' and stable state that underpins optimum role capacity, whereas illness is disruptive insofar as it makes a person unproductive and dependent. For Parsons, the 'sick role' is a form of licensed deviance that has a kind of 'relative legitimacy' (Parsons, 1951, p.312). The individual is considered relatively blameless. This is true, however, only as long as the sick person tries to recover.

To describe the behaviour, Parsons associated the onset of illness with actions necessary to enable doctors to return the sick person back to health, devising a theoretical construct or 'ideal type'. This model suggests that at the onset of illness the 'sick' person adopts the sick role. Based on the assumption that illness and disease, regardless of cause or severity, impede both physiological and psychological abilities, the 'sick' individual is automatically relieved of all normal role expectations and responsibilities. They are not considered responsible for their condition, nor are they expected to recover through their own volition.

Consequently they are expected to seek help from professional medical experts, in order to regain their former status. Additionally 'sick' people are encouraged to view their new-found status as undesirable and 'abhorrent' (Parsons, 1951, pp. 312–3). In addition to identifying key elements of sickness-related behaviour, Parsons' account also clarifies the role of the medical profession in modern society. Their main function is to serve as agents of social control, to regulate and define illness, and to return 'sick' people to health – their 'normal' productive social status.

A central problem with this approach is that while acute and transitory illnesses may lend themselves to the sick role model, others which are permanent or 'chronic' in nature do not. Many conditions are congenital and/or irrevocable, such as some forms of deafness and amputated limbs. Hence a return to 'health' is impossible. Pointing to the distinction between 'acute' and 'chronic' illness, Kassebaum and Baumann (1965) maintain that people with 'chronic' conditions can only hope to regain limited 'functioning' within the 'sick role' model, and additionally, that this is often accompanied by a loss of income and resources which, in turn, makes eventual recovery even more difficult.

Not only does Parsons fail to separate acute and chronic illnesses, he also does not consider that impairment and illness may well be distinct conceptual categories as well as generating different forms of adaptive behaviour. Responses to chronic illness and impairment are rarely uniform among individuals or groups. They are influenced by various factors, including race, gender and social class, and the type and nature of medical interventions. For example Zola (1973) found that in America people from Irish, African and white Protestant backgrounds all responded differently to the onset of chronic illness. Verbrugge (1985) identified different responses by gender and age. Cole and Lejeune (1972) showed how economic factors influence the ways in which people deal with illness or impairment. This is especially important when access to medical services depends on the ability to pay.

Parsons also suggested that occupation of the sick role is only temporary. Nonetheless, as De Jong (1979a) points out, when applied to people with chronic conditions or long-term impairments recovery is unlikely. Thus impairment becomes part of the individual's identity and they begin to accept the dependence prescribed them under the sick role as normal. It therefore removes from the individual an obligation to take charge of their own affairs and sustains this on a more or less permanent basis.

Furthermore, as indicated above, illness and impairment are not the same thing. Many conditions do not impede 'normative' functioning and cannot be construed in medical terms but are culturally defined as 'abnormal' or simply different, as we discussed in some detail earlier. Thus it has become increasingly clear that the Parsonian framework cannot provide an adequate foundation for describing disability even within the social systems he was discussing.

Revisionist Sociology

Unsurprisingly, because of the limitations of the sick role several alternative but related models were developed. Examples include the 'impaired role' and the 'rehabilitation role'. The former was constructed by Gordon (1966) and the latter Safilios-Rothschild (1970). The 'impaired role' construct is applied to someone whose condition is unlikely to change and who is therefore unable to comply with the first prerequisite of the sick role, to try to 'recover' as quickly as possible. Sieglar and Osmond suggest that people who accept the 'impaired role' have abandoned all thoughts of 'rehabilitation' and largely accepted the notion of dependency as permanent. Thus,

> a person who fails to maintain the sick role may find himself [*sic*] in the impaired role, which, although easy to maintain is difficult to leave, for it is meant to be permanent. However, the impaired role also carries with it a loss of full human status. It is true that it does not require the exertions of co-operating with medical treatment and trying to regain one's health but the price for this is a second class citizenship. (Sieglar & Osmond, 1974, p.116)

De Jong (1981) maintains that the 'impaired role' is not a 'normal' role, but one that the individual is allowed to slip into as the passage of time weakens the assumptions of the sick role.

A further variation on this train of thought is the 'rehabilitation role' as articulated by Safilios-Rothschild (1970). She asserts that once the individual with the impairment becomes aware of their 'new' condition, they should accept it and learn to live with it. The major difference between the sick role and the rehabilitation role is that the person with a 'chronic' condition should take an active part in their 'rehabilitation'. This might be achieved through the development and maximization of their remaining abilities.

The disabled person is obliged to assume as many of their previous 'normal' roles as quickly as possible. They are therefore not exempt from social expectations and responsibilities, but expected to adapt accordingly. It is also assumed that not only will the person with the impairment co-operate with the medical and rehabilitative professionals, but that they will innovate and improve new methods of rehabilitation. Safilios-Rothschild's model of 'rehabilitation' was strongly endorsed by the American Independent Living Movement of the 1960s.

However, this approach fails to address the individualization of disability, leaving the responsibility for 'rehabilitation' with the individual with an impairment. It is they who must change, adapt, or learn how to cope. Their dependence on professional help is also endorsed and retained, as professionals are responsible for initiating the process of returning the individual back to 'normality' and helping the individual come to terms with their new 'disabled' identity. Clearly the concept of rehabilitation is laden with normative assumptions clustered around an able-bodied/mind ideal. And, despite its limitations in terms of returning people with acquired impairments such as spinal cord injury, for example, to their former status (Oliver et al., 1988), it has little or no relevance or meaning for people born with congenital conditions such as blindness or deafness other than to enforce their sense of inadequacy and difference (Barnes, 1990, 2003a).

Other sociologists also favoured this 'conventional' functionalist approach to explaining responses to impairment and disability. Haber and Smith (1971), for instance, focused on disablement as an extension of the sick role. They argued that rather than concentrate on 'specialised role repertoires' it is more useful to focus on the 'elaboration of behavioural alternatives' within existing role relationships. In this way disabled people's behaviour may be 'normalised' and may not constitute social deviance.

A further elaboration on role theory and disablement was elaborated by Anspach (1979). Following the work of Merton (1957) rather than Parsons, and clearly influenced by growing political activism amongst disabled Americans during the 1970s, Anspach produced a four-dimensional model which was intended to typify the ways people with impairments respond to negative societal attitudes. The first, termed the 'normaliser', relates to the situation in which the disabled person concurs with and accepts societal views of disablement and behaves accordingly by seeking acceptance at any price. The second is 'disassociation', where the individual accepts social responses to impairment, but is unwilling or unable to accept that it applies to them. As a consequence they have a lowered self-concept and avoid social interaction as it serves only to reinforce negative self-concepts. The third, 'retreatism' rejects negative views of impairment and has no self-esteem. Withdrawal from all social activity is the preferred pattern of behaviour. The fourth role is the 'political activist': 'Like the normaliser the activist seeks to attain a favourable conception of self, often asserting a claim to superiority over normals. But unlike the normaliser the activist seeks to relinquish any claim to an acceptance which s/he views as artificial' (Anspach, 1979, p. 770).

Moreover the idea of impairment as deviance found favour amongst many sociologists during the social and political upheavals of the 1960s. Studies of social reactions to people unwilling or unable to conform to social norms became a primary focus for sociologists working within the interpretive traditions of empirical sociology, in particular symbolic interactionsim, phenomenology and ethnomethodology, and it is to these we now turn.

Alternative Sociology and Disability

As the main alternative to functionalism during this and the following decade, symbolic interactionism has its roots in the work of Mead (1934), and the ethnography of the Chicago School of sociologists in the 1920s and 1930s (Bulmer, 1984). Symbolic interactionism rose to prominence in the 1960s, largely because of its emphasis on meaning, conflict and change – areas in which a functionalist perspective is generally considered inadequate (Blumer, 1969). At the forefront of the interactionist approach was the study of deviance and labelling.

Initially, attention centred on crime, prostitution and drug use. But following extensive field work theorists began to focus on the ways in which these and other forms of human activity were deemed socially unacceptable. Howard Becker summed up this particular perspective with the following statement:

> Deviance is not a quality of the act a person commits, but rather a consequence of the application by others of rules and sanctions to an 'offender'. The deviant is one to whom the label has successfully been applied. Deviant behaviour is behaviour that people so label. Deviance is not a quality that lies in the behaviour itself but in the interaction between the person who commits an act and those who respond to it. (Becker, 1963, p. 9)

Consequently what later became known as 'social reaction', 'labelling' or 'transactional' theory shifted its focus from the deviant – the problem for functionalists – toward the reaction of others and the process of definition, regulation and control: in other words, society. Hence, social control was the cause of deviant behaviour rather than the other way round.

The foundations for this approach were established by Lemert (1951). He makes the crucial distinction between 'primary' and 'secondary' deviance. The former refers to an act or attribute which has only marginal implications for the individual concerned. The latter denotes behaviour which results as a consequence of the social reaction to primary deviance: specifically, the ascription of a socially devalued status and identity. Secondary deviance becomes a central facet of existence or 'master status' for those so labelled, altering their self-concept, their status in the community, and their future actions.

In terms of the sociology of disability, Lemert (1951) is particularly important because he used the distinction between primary and secondary deviance with reference to people with ascribed impairments. However he endorsed the traditional view that disabled people, especially those with impairments, are different from other people in that they are 'defective' and unable to perform normal social roles. As an example he makes the disablist assertion that there is a higher instance of 'mental deficiency cases among the blind as a deviant class' (Lemert, 1951, p. 135).

Nonetheless, he does maintain that the extent to which the 'handicaps' physically limit the playing of social roles is 'culturally variable'. He also differentiates between impairments that affect function and those which affect conformity: 'Biological variations which do not impede bodily functions become a basic deviation only through interaction with cultural definitions and social perceptions' (Lemert, 1951, p. 29).

He developed these points further with an analysis of the relationship between societal reaction and speech impairment among North Pacific Coastal Indians. In contrast to other Native American communities, Lemert found evidence of 'stuttering' among one particular tribe living in the coastal area of British Columbia. Their culture placed a high priority on ceremony and tradition especially regarding public oratory. From an early age children were included in ceremonial life and the importance of public speaking and a faultless performance was expected. Those unable to meet these standards were ridiculed by peers and brought shame upon their parents. Lemert concluded that stuttering is produced by social reaction: the concern about, and the reaction to speech irregularities and impairments actually creates them. In other Native American communities where these concerns were absent stuttering was unknown.

Although Lemert's work is rooted in an orthodox personal tragedy view of disability, he takes a major step forward from previous sociological accounts by recognizing that social responses to impairment are culturally variable and that some impairments are socially constructed. These are important points which many sociologists and theorists working in the field of disability have subsequently forgotten.

Goffman (1968) used this insight to elaborate his work on the application of stigma to individuals and groups. According to him, the concept 'stigma' is derived from the ancient Greeks. It refers to a socially discrediting characteristic or attribute which denotes 'moral inferiority'. He maintains that stigmatized individuals, such as the 'dwarf, the blind man, the disfigured, the homosexual ... and the ex-mental patient' are viewed by society as not quite human. Therefore stigma is the outcome of situational considerations and social interactions between the 'abnormal' and the ''normal' or the 'deviant' and 'non-deviant' (Goffman, 1968). Building on Lemert's concept of a 'master status' he describes how stigmatized individuals manage a 'spoiled identity'. He illustrates in detail how people with impairments, prostitutes, criminals, members of racial and ethnic minorities and other socially unacceptable individuals interact with 'normals'.

Goffman distinguishes between people who are 'discredited' and those who are 'discreditable'. The former refers to people unable to conceal their stigmatizing feature, such as people with physical impairments, for example, who have to manage the 'tensions' arising from social encounters on a regular basis. The latter denotes those with less visible discrediting characteristics who are able to 'pass' as normal, namely, people with hidden impairments such as HIV. Such people often go to great lengths to appear 'normal' and conceal their difference (Taylor, 2001).

Indeed, in a disablist society 'pressures to pass as normal or to aspire to some approximation of normality, on non-disabled terms, are manifest for all disabled people' (Swain & Cameron, 1999, p. 69). It is even suggested that for stigmatized people the idea of 'normality' can take on an 'exaggerated importance' even though they may have 'no precise definition of normality except what they would be without their stigma' (Coleman, 1997, p. 225).

Goffman's analysis is based on the assumption that the same beliefs are shared by both stigmatized and non-stigmatized groups. He also suggests that disabled people have similar experiences to other groups such as women and racial and ethnic minorities, for example. Additionally, stigma is viewed as contagious.

Close friends and family of stigmatized people typically acquire a 'courtesy stigma'. Similarly, inanimate objects that are associated with stigmatized individuals, such as wheelchairs, for example, may also become stigmatized (Lonsdale,1990). Indeed, one study documenting support for people with visual impairments found that blind people are sometimes pressurized by their friends and family to try to walk without their white canes (Deshen & Deshen, 1989).

Nonetheless Goffman's work is overly descriptive and based entirely on secondary sources. Whilst he provides a description of one-to-one interaction, he fails to discuss the wider theoretical implications of the labelling process. As such, and in common with most interactionist accounts, important issues such as socio-economic power, inequality and the role of the state are ignored. Consequently he depoliticizes the oppression of disabled people (Charlton, 1998) and so obscures the true nature of disabled people's oppression (Finkelstein, 1980) in that he presents stigma in non-oppressive terms. Moreover, by adopting this perspective he asserts that the central feature of the stigmatized individual's existence is the eternal quest for 'acceptance'. In this way, disabled people are permanently placed in a dependency role, constantly seeking acceptance from the rest of society: 'those who are responsible for this dependence in the first place' (Finkelstein, 1980, p. 30).

In short, even though Goffman's work is concerned with interactions and processes, it is ultimately reductionist – there can be no stigmatizing process without a stigma or discrediting feature. In terms of impairment and disablement, the general approach is a reactionary one, and similar to that of Parsons. It confirms the inevitable: disability is a personal tragedy, there is no possibility for change, and it ignores the ways in which the experience of disability is historically, culturally and socially variable. It therefore neglects the ways in which stigma may be minimized or eradicated. However, the notion of stigma is still retained and widely used in many studies today: for example, stigma in relation to women's experience with 'chronic fatigue syndrome and fibromyalgia' (Åsbring & Närvänen, 2002), mental health systems users and survivors (Johnstone, 2001), people with epilepsy (Scambler, 1989, 2004), social exclusion in 'health care' (Mason et al., 2001) and people with HIV and AIDS (Taylor, 2001).

By way of contrast in a detailed empirical analysis based on acceptance not rejection, Taylor and Bogdan (1989) chronicle the long-term interactions between people with intellectual impairments and their non-disabled contemporaries in mid-western American communities. By focusing on four key areas – family, religious commitment, humanitarian sentiments, and feelings of friendship – they show how disabled people are accepted by non-disabled peers. They conclude that the sociology of deviance directs attention to what not to do rather than to what ought to be done.

Although prejudice and discrimination are pervasive in modern society, it does not necessarily follow that communities and 'typical' people will always reject disabled people, as we showed earlier in other societies. To assume that this is the case indicates a lack of understanding of how relationships between disabled and non-disabled people are formed and the role of professionals within the context of those relationships (Taylor & Bogdan, 1989, p. 33). This is an important corrective to most of the work cited above and an area to which we will return later in the book.

Certainly the notion of disability as social deviance and stigma was endorsed by sociologists favouring a phenomenological or ethnomethodological approach to explaining the social world. For theorists such as Schutz (1970) and Garfinkel (1967) society is made up of individually constructed life worlds and systems. Their aim therefore is to study empirically the deep-rooted meanings that people use and construct in their everyday routines and activities to inform social interaction. An example of this approach is provided by Dingwall (2003) who advances a 'social action' theoretical framework that reaffirms the notion of illness and disability as social deviance.

By providing a robust critique of 'positivist', 'absolutist', 'scientific' and 'interactionist' accounts he argues that 'illness' is a product of the systems of meaning and knowledge derived from people's, including patients' and doctors', life worlds. Scientific medicine' is therefore but one of a range of socially constructed 'folk' knowledge (p. 51). Moreover, the degree to which an ill or disabled person is considered culpable for their deviant condition is socially contingent. For researchers adopting this perspective the underlying cultural pattern or rule suggests that illness and disability are 'troubles' that should be avoided 'at all costs and if encountered remedied if at all possible' (Thomas, 2007, p. 28).

So while the work discussed above has attempted to adopt a sociological focus to the issue of understanding disability, by and large it has failed to move beyond traditional functionalist and interactionist accounts or to satisfactorily address the well known problems with them. In the final section of this chapter we need to move beyond these accounts to consider approaches which seek to develop a broader understanding of disability issues.

Developing a Social Theory of Disablement

During the 1970s some social scientists began to draw attention to the economic and social consequences of living with 'chronic illness' and disability. It was becoming increasingly obvious as countries like the United Kingdom and the United States recovered from the aftermath of World War Two and became increasingly affluent, that not all groups were sharing the rising living standards concomitant with this. Disabled people were one of those groups and this sparked growing disability activism and the introduction of legislative measures concerned with disability which included the Chronically Sick and Disabled Persons Act (1970) in the UK and America's Rehabilitation Act (1973).

Blaxter's (1976) year-long empirical study of the lives of people recently discharged from hospital with a long-term impairment in Glasgow illustrates how they are 'fettered and constrained not only by their social environment but also by the two major systems of society with which their lives were involved and structured: the system of medical care and the administrative system of welfare, employment and social security' (pp. 246–7). Townsend (1979) was involved with disabled people's organizations, including the Disablement Income Group and the Disability Alliance, and his national study of poverty in Britain highlighted the economic hardship encountered by disabled people and their families. This, he maintained, was due to their 'uneven or limited access to the principal resource systems of society – the labour market and wage system, national insurance and its associated schemes, and the wealth-accumulating systems, particularly home ownership, life insurance and occupational pension schemes' (p. 734).

The notion of a 'handicapping' environment is further highlighted in Locker's (1983) account of the experiences of people with rheumatoid arthritis. Dealing with environmental barriers is a drain on an individual's resources – energy, time and money – which often results in an 'enforced passivity' and reliance 'on the help of others' (p. 90). As noted in Chapter 1, the idea of a disabling or 'handicapping' society was a key feature of the writings of disabled people and their organizations during the 1960s and 1970s (Hunt,1966; UPIAS, 1976). In America Bowe's (1978) study *Handicapping America* provided a vivid description of the disabling social and environmental barriers encountered by disabled people. He identified six key areas of concern: public attitudes, the built environment, education, employment, the law and personal relations.

Zola was both a medical sociologist and disabled activist and one of the first to combine his professional and political activities. During the 1980s he wrote extensively about the social exclusion of disabled people within a mainly interactionist framework connecting personal experience to policy and politics. For instance, in one study he provides a sociologically informed personal account of life in Het Dorp, a village of some 65 acres in Holland, designed specifically for people with 'severe' physical impairments (1982).

Other sociologists continued to favour a more 'conventional' functionalist approach to explaining responses to impairment and disability, albeit in a broader sociological framework. This approach has had a particular appeal to medical sociologists concerned with the experience of 'chronic illness', especially in Britain. They have developed a growing literature on the mechanisms and processes by which people adapt to the onset of chronic illness and impairment. For example, Bury (1991) reflects on the changing nature of chronic illness, and suggests that our knowledge of how people react to it can only be understood in terms of a 'temporal framework' which takes into account a number of socioeconomic factors such as age, gender, ethnicity and social class.

For Bury, the experience of chronic illness is analogous to a 'biographical disruption' which transforms the individual's sense of self. It is an experience in which the 'structures of everyday life' and the perceptions which underpin them are fundamentally disrupted (Bury, 1982). His study provides an example of chronic illness as biological disruption. Bury maintains that people with chronic illness try to make sense of their condition by searching for meanings and answers, with questions such as 'why me?' or 'why now?' He maintains that people interpret their condition, incorporate it into a coherent biography, and adapt accordingly.

A host of others, some of whom have the condition themselves, have documented the ways in which people adapt to the onset of particular conditions. One important example is Kelly's (1992) analysis of coping with an ileostomy following the contraction of ulcerative colitis. A further example is found in Scambler and Hopkins' (1986) description of how people with epilepsy conceal their condition in order to deal with 'enacted stigma' or direct discrimination.

Indeed, the burgeoning interactionist 'sociology of chronic illness and disability' in Britain during the 1980s 'dampened down' (Thomas, 2007, p. 40) sociological interest in the wider social processes that create disability and as a result produced little in terms of theory and research (Barnes & Mercer, 1996, 2003, 2010; Oliver, 1996; Thomas, 2004, 2007). Subsequently the bulk of interpretive literature has become so absorbed by the 'failing body' and 'personal troubles' that it often disregards the social barriers to participation in everyday life. This has recently been acknowledged by some medical sociologists such as Williams, who writes: 'The oppressive quality of everyday life is indubitable, and the origins of much of this oppression lie in the hostile social environments and disabling barriers that society (politicians, architects, social workers, doctors and others) erects' (2001, p.135).

Moreover, Scambler (2004) provides a reappraisal of his earlier work on stigma in which he identifies a 'hidden distress model' of epilepsy. This earlier approach reflects Goffman's argument that the imposition of the label 'epilepsy' results in the acceptance by the individual so labelled and henceforth the fear of discrimination or 'enacted stigma'. He now maintains that this approach is at best '*partial* and at worst *deficient* in its failure to address sociologically a series of theoretical questions' (Scambler, 2004, p. 29, original emphasis).

Yet this critique does not reject or abandon the medically dominated perceptions of impairment as social deviance. Instead, the deviance perspective is to be strengthened with the development of a 'new' research agenda based on the assertion that 'Any appreciation of why and how epilepsy persists as a significant condition must be articulated against the background of the logics of capitalist accumulation (of the economy) and mode of regulation (of the state) and their respective relations of class and command' (Scambler, 2004, p. 42).

It is perhaps testament to the inward-looking practices of many medical sociologists, and academia generally (Barnes, Oliver & Barton, 2002), that Scambler chooses to ignore the wealth of material already produced by disabled people and their organizations and writers working from within a disability studies perspective in the UK and elsewhere that deal with these very issues. Indeed, as we shall see later, this is the work that provides the building blocks for the arguments presented in the following chapters of this book.

Conclusion

This chapter has focused on anthropological and sociological analyses of impairment and disablement. There is clear evidence from this brief overview of anthropological and sociological accounts that cultural responses to impairment are by no means universal. Yet this insight appears to have been lost or ignored in the work of many sociologists, particularly those working within a medical or sociology of health and illness perspective in the UK, who have opted, largely uncritically, for an 'illness' or social deviance perspective rooted in the work of Parsons and Goffman. As a consequence much attention has centred on interpersonal relations and the social consequences of 'chronic illness'. This in turn has served to reaffirm the orthodox personal tragedy view of disability within mainstream sociology and stifle the development of studies which focus on the structural forces, economic, political and cultural, that have created and continue to sustain disability.

It is notable too, that largely as a consequence of recent developments outside academia, some medical sociologists have begun to call for the development of a more nuanced broad-based approach that takes account of environmental and cultural factors (Thomas, 2007). But the traditional personal tragedy view of disability is still retained by many, and social model inspired accounts that have explained disability as a specific form of social oppression symptomatic of capitalist development are ignored or dismissed as overly simplistic or politically motivated (Williams, G.,1996; Williams, S., 1999; Bury, 1991, 2000).

As the rest of this book will demonstrate, there is nothing simplistic about such theorizing or research. It is of course politically motivated in that its aim is to generate social change. But then of course all social research is, or should be, politically motivated (Becker, 1963; Giddens, 1982). If it wasn't there would be no point in doing it (Barnes, Oliver & Barton, 2002). With this in mind the next chapter will explore the social creation of disability within capitalist society.

3

The Rise of Disabling Capitalism

Introduction

The previous chapters have suggested that the definitions, social responses to and experiences of disablement vary from society to society and depend on a whole range of material and social factors. However, as argued in the previous edition of this book, it is an inescapable fact that within modern, capitalist societies, disability is produced as an individual problem, underpinned by personal tragedy theory and shaped by the process of medicalization. While this thesis has been subjected to criticism on the grounds of historical accuracy and an overemphasis on the economic to the neglect of the cultural and personal aspects, no-one has seriously disputed the argument that changes to the 'mode of production', the organization of the economy, have played a crucial role in this process.

Since the 1980s there has been a growing interest in the history of disability, the economy and its links to the category 'disabled' within academia; examples include Finkelstein (1980), Stone (1984), Wolfensberger (1989), Oliver (1990), Barnes (1991; 1997), Albrecht (1992), Hevey (1992), Davis (1995), Garland (1995), Gleeson (1999), Stiker (1999) and Borsay, 2005). While much of this work has escaped the attention of mainstream sociologists, the rise of disability studies has begun to force disablement onto the sociological agenda. To further the development of a comprehensive sociological theory of disability, it is useful to begin where we began in the first edition with the work of the 'founding fathers' of the discipline, Comte, Marx and Weber, theorists whose main concern was the rise and progress of capitalism. While there have been various critiques of their evolutionary approaches to human history (Giddens,

2006), we will suggest that taken together, their work can, at least, provide an accessible framework within which to facilitate our understanding of the present situation of disabled people.

Therefore the key issue to be discussed in this and the following chapter is why the view of disability as an individual, medical problem and a 'personal tragedy' remains prevalent in capitalist societies. Consequently when considering questions such as 'How does disability arise?' or 'How does the phenomenon of 'the disabled' arise?', an understanding of history is essential. This is simply because 'there is no phenomenon that does not arise from history, and from social history' (Stiker, 1999, p.158).

However, to provide a comprehensive theoretical analysis of disablement that takes account of history, and in particular the role of capitalism, need not necessarily endorse a materialist perspective that focuses exclusively on how the economy shapes human development. Although all life is dependent upon material resources for survival and human history is nothing less than a protracted struggle for access to and control of those resources, 'it is not necessary to be a Marxist to recognise that economic conditions have a significant impact on social behaviour and on relationships between different groups of individuals in society' (Harbert, 1988, p.12).

Therefore we need to reiterate our position that we remain committed to a materialist view of human development. Indeed, as discussed in the last chapter, such an analysis is increasingly important given capitalism's recent domination of the world economy and its implications for disabled people in all nations. We begin with a discussion of a materialist interpretation of history and the creation of disability.

Creating Disability

It is notable that since the 1980s much, though not all, of the work produced on the history of disability, particularly in Britain, draws to varying degrees on the work of Marx and Engels and their materialist interpretation of history (1976). For them work (or productive labour) is the foundation of both individual and collective social life. All societies have to produce food, goods, shelter and so on, in order to reproduce both their individual members and their social system. The 'mode of production' refers to the ways in which the production process is organized and includes both the physical means and social relations of production.

This view of history has been accurately summarized as follows:

> In Marx's view, to understand the nature of human beings one must understand their relationship to the material environment and the historical nature of this relationship in creating and satisfying human needs. This material environment may, in the first instance, be the constraints of the physical environment. However, as societies develop and become more complicated, the environment itself will become more complicated and comprise more socio-cultural constraints. (Forder et al., 1984, p. 89)

These socio-cultural constraints may include the nature of the work environment, the living conditions of people in rural or urban environments and the relationships between institutions, groups and individuals, all of which are related to the socio-economic structure of society at particular points in history. It is important to realize, however, that this approach, sometimes referred to as 'historical materialism' (Giddens, 2006), is an analytical framework and not an empirical social theory. Rather, the materialist framework outlines a 'set of basic epistemological and ontological principles to guide the study of societies as historically contingent and structurally conditioned' (Gleeson, 1999, p. 26).

But a materialist interpretation of history is not just about placing social relationships within a historical setting. It also attempts to provide an evolutionary perspective on the whole of human history. Of particular relevance here are the transitions from 'feudal' through capitalist to socialist society. One of the first attempts to employ this approach specifically in respect of disabled people was produced by Finkelstein (1980), a disabled activist and writer. His model includes three phases of historical development. Phase 1 corresponds to Britain before the industrial revolution, generally known as feudal society. Phase 2 relates to the transition to industrial capitalism when the focus of work shifted from the home to the factory. Phase 3 refers to the kind of society to which we are currently moving. Notably he does not link Phase 3 to the shift to socialism as in Marx and Engels' materialist account of history.

In Phase 1, the pre-industrial period, economic activity was agrarian or cottage-based. This mode of production and the social relations associated with it did not preclude people with impairments from economic activity (Gleeson, 1999).They were nevertheless often at the foot of the social hierarchy along with 'the poor and unemployed' (Ryan & Thomas, 1987; Barnes, 1991, 1997; Stiker, 1999; Borsay, 2005).

Phase 2 relates to the onset of industrial capitalism in the eighteenth and nineteenth centuries across Western Europe and North America. People with impairments were increasingly excluded from paid work in Phase 2 on the grounds that they were unable to keep pace with the 'disciplinary power' of the new mechanized, factory-based production system. This exclusion justified the segregation of many individuals with impairments who were often segregated within families, various residential institutions which began to emerge or simply left to beg on the streets. We will consider this in more detail later in the book.

As capitalism developed, the process of exclusion from the workforce continued for all kinds of people:

> By the 1890s, the population of Britain was increasingly urban and the employment of the majority was industrial, rather than rural. The blind and the deaf growing up in slowly changing scattered rural communities had more easily been absorbed into the work and life of those societies without the need for special provision. Deafness, while working alone at agricultural tasks that all children learned by observation with little formal schooling, did not limit the capacity for employment too severely. Blindness was less of a hazard in uncongested familiar rural surroundings, and routine tasks involving repetitive tactile skills could be learned and practised by many of the blind without special training. The environment of an industrial society was however different. (Topliss, 1979, p. 11)

Changes in the organization of work from a rural-based, co-operative system where individuals contributed what they could to the production process, to an urban, factory-based system, one organized around the individual waged labourer, had profound consequences. 'The operation of the labour market in the nineteenth century effectively depressed handicapped people of all kinds to the bottom of the market' (Morris, 1969, p. 9). As a result these people came to be regarded as a social and educational problem, and increasing numbers were segregated into institutions of all kinds. These included workhouses, asylums, impairment-specific colonies and special schools and out of the mainstream of economic and social life.

However, Finkelstein points out that disability is a relationship involving the state of the individual (their impairment) and the state of society (the social restrictions imposed on individuals). By adopting a three-stage evolutionary perspective, this relationship emerges in Phase 2. In Phase 1 individuals with impairments formed part of a larger 'underclass' (Mann, 1992), but in Phase 2 they were separated from their class origins and became a special, segregated group and disability came to be regarded both as individual impairment and social restriction.

Phase 3, which Finkelstein argued began in the latter half of the twentieth century, would see the end of the paradox whereby disability would be viewed as exclusively the result of social restriction. In turn this would herald the struggle for the reintegration of disabled people into the mainstream of society. It corresponds with the emergence of 'post-industrial' society and the liberation of disabled people from society's segregative practices. It would be facilitated by the widespread utilization of new technologies and the working together of disabled people and professionals towards 'common goals' (Finkelstein, 1980, p.11).

We have considered Finkelstein's account in considerable detail, because like a materialist account of history, it has explanatory power, particularly in helping us to understand what happened in Phase 2 with the emergence of industrial capitalism. However, it does tend to oversimplify what was happening prior to the industrialization of the economy. It may be interpreted as suggesting that in Phase 1 some kind of idealized community existed and that disabled people, amongst other minority groups, were treated more benignly.

While it is certainly true that the vast majority of disabled people were integrated into the community prior to the industrial revolution, there is also growing evidence that oppression and prejudice was widespread within the context of western cultures, particularly toward people born with visible and intellectual impairments. This took many forms and has its roots in the ancient world of Greece and Rome (Ryan & Thomas, 1987; Barnes, 1991, 1997; Hevey, 1992; Garland, 1995; Stiker, 1999).

Unfortunately Finkelstein's hopes for Phase 3 now also seem a long way off as capitalism has been able to survive the collapse of state socialism, the radicalization of Islam and the recent series of global fiscal crises (Harvey, 2010). Nor has the rise of technology liberated disabled people in the ways he envisioned. And finally his hopes of the emergence of a radical alliance between disabled people and professionals has yet to materialize (Roulstone, 1998; Sheldon, 2004a).

Despite these criticisms Finkelstein's pioneering work has exerted a considerable influence not just on us but others as well (for example, Sokolowska et al.,

1981). His work remains of considerable value in highlighting the importance of the mode of production in influencing perceptions and experiences of disability. It is also important to point out that some critiques of his work have often gone too far and ignored both the relational and interactive nature of it. Finkelstein has always insisted that 'disability was a relationship' long before those critics of a materialist view of disability launched their attacks with claims that this view failed to understand that disablement was an interaction between impairment and disability (Shakespeare & Watson, 2001; Shakespeare 2006; Tremaine, 2002; Goodley, 2011).

Given that materialist accounts of disability recognize the interactive and relational aspects of disability, we now need to turn to what some have called the mode of thought and others have called culture in order to better understand how this comes about. We call this the construction of disability.

Constructing Disability

In *The Positive Philosophy* Comte provided an evolutionary model aimed at providing an understanding of the development of human history. He suggested that the human intellectual process could be understood in terms of three phases of development: the theological, the metaphysical and the positivistic stage. This approach suggests that there has been a shift from a religious interpretation of reality to a more naturalistic one and finally to a scientific way of understanding both the natural and social worlds:

> Each branch of our understanding passes through three different stages: the theological or fictitious stage; the metaphysical or abstract stage; and the scientific or positive stage. In other words, the human mind, by its very nature, employs successively in each of its fields of investigation three methods of philosophising whose character is essentially different and even radically opposed: first, the theological method, next the metaphysical method, and finally the positive method. This gives rise to three kinds of philosophy or of general conceptual systems about all phenomena which are mutually exclusive. (Comte, 1987, p. 2)

This evolutionary analysis has proved useful in developing an understanding of changing historical perceptions of deviance of all kinds (Kittrie, 1971). These changing perceptions include drug addiction, homosexuality, alcoholism and 'mental illness', each being regarded first as moral, then legal and now medical problems. As a consequence people defined as deviant were subjected to moral, then legal and now medical mechanisms of social control. Similarly, a review of the medicalization of deviance suggests that three major paradigms may be identified that have held reign over deviance designations in various historical periods: deviance as sin, deviance as crime and deviance as sickness (see, for example, Conrad & Schneider, 1992). This has led to what has been termed the 'therapeutic state' where a vast area of personal and social problems are subsumed under the category of 'illness' and subject to 'treatment'. This is viewed as 'apolitical and value free and nothing more than the application of technical expertise' (Ingleby, 1985, p. 141).

Surprisingly there have been relatively few attempts to utilize this evolution-ary approach to develop an understanding of changing historical perceptions of disability. However, an analysis of the ideology of 'care' underpinning the devel-opment of services for people with 'mental illness' employs a similar approach (Soder, 1984). This analysis suggests that initially the limited services available were based on a philosophy of compassion linked to religious and philanthropic perspectives. These were followed by support founded on the philosophy of protection, both for the disabled individuals and society. Finally 'care' was provided on the basis of optimism, linked to the development of new scientific and pedagogic approaches to the 'problem' of mental illness and emotional distress.

The Comtean influence is also evident in Pasternak's (1981) account of the changing patterns of prejudice encountered by people with epilepsy:

> Increasing rationalisation did not ameliorate social prejudice against epileptics
> – it merely caused one form of prejudice to be substituted for another. He was
> no longer isolated as unclean, as a ritually untouchable person, but instead he
> was isolated as insane, and placed in institutions where he was subjected to
> extremely substandard conditions of life. However later evidence suggests that
> further rationalisation and increasing knowledge of the causation of epilepsy,
> separating it from insanity, may lead to improvements in social conditions for
> epileptics – as the culture catches up with findings of the scientific community.
> (Pasternak, 1981, p. 227)

This optimism mirrors optimism found in the work of Comte and in Soder's analysis of mental illness, but whether this is justified in respect of the medicalization of disablement generally will be returned to in later chapters. For now it is necessary that we consider two important criticisms of this evolutionary approach and its application, one internal and the other external.

The internal criticism of evolutionary analyses of human thought processes maintains that the 'phenomena' of different discourses of reality are not, as Comte implies, 'mutually exclusive'. Whilst one perception may dominate at a particular point in history, it does not do so at the expense of the others. There is a wealth of evidence that despite the advent of modernity, theological and naturalistic explanations for reality take many forms and continue to coexist alongside scientific accounts in both industrial and post-industrial societies (Giddens, 2006).

For instance, people with epilepsy may still be perceived by some as possessed by demons, still subject to legal regulation with regard to marriage, work or accessing a driving licence, for example, and yet be the recipients of sophisticated medical treatments of one kind or another (Oliver, 1979; Scambler, 1989). Similarly, the explanation for the birth of a disabled child will clearly be a medical or scientific one, but that does not mean that some parents may believe that it is a punishment for some previous sin. The co-existence of different epistemologies or 'truths' are especially prevalent in the poorer nations of the world (Miles, 1995, 2001, 2006; Coleridge, 1993; Ingstad and Whyte, 1995; Ingstad, 1999, 2001; Stone, 1999). Consequently whilst an evolutionary analysis may aid an understanding of changing perceptions of deviance and disablement, it cannot and does not explain them, in causal terms.

The external criticism of evolutionary accounts concerns the issue of causality, and takes us back to Marx and Weber's work concerning the main drivers of human development as capitalism progressed. It was the economy according to Marx, and ideas and values according to Weber (Giddens, 2006, p. 18). It is clear that changing perceptions of impairments such as epilepsy, for example, cannot be accounted for solely in terms of one or the other:

> The drift to the town and the growing complexity of industrial machinery at the time meant the development of a class of industrial rejects for whom it was clear that special provision would have to be made ... The problem of severe epileptics in a city such as Bradford, where the wool trade meant fast moving machinery, and crowded workshops, must have been particularly acute. (Jones & Tillotson, 1965, pp. 5–6)

Therefore, the process of disablement can only be understood by utilizing an analysis that takes account of both changes in the mode of production and the mode of thought, and the relationship between the two. What we now need to consider in this relationship is the ways in which the economic surplus is redistributed through social policies which both meet the needs of the changing mode of production and are commensurate with current social perceptions about what are, and what are not, appropriate ways of dealing with the 'problem of disability'.

The State and Disability

The ascendance of capitalism led to unprecedented changes to the organization of work and social relations and attitudes. The transition from an agricultural economy based on feudal relations to an industrial one based on capitalist wage labour generated massive social upheavals. Mass migration from the countryside to cities resulted in loss of traditional craft skills, community ties and cultures, widespread poverty and social unrest (Hobsbawm, 1995). All of this posed new problems for social order and with the breakdown of traditional social relations, new problems of classification and control.

The coming of capitalism spawned major changes throughout the eighteenth century. There was an intensification of the commercialization of land and agriculture, and a marked rise in industrialization and urbanization. These had significant consequences for communities and families who had hitherto provided the main means of support for those who experience economic or social dislocation or disruption. Often these traditional support mechanisms were unable to cope and this meant large numbers of individuals were left to cope as best they could.

The main solution to this problem was the institution, namely 'any long term provision of a highly organised kind on a residential basis with the expressed aims of "care", "treatment" or "custody"' (Jones & Fowles, 1984, p. 207, original emphasis). But whilst institutions existed in pre-industrial times (Stiker, 1999), it was with the rise of capitalism that they became the major mechanism of social control (Rothman, 1971).

As far as disabled people were concerned:

the speed of factory work, the enforced discipline, the time keeping and the production norms – all these were a highly unfavourable change from the slower, more self determined and flexible methods of work into which many handicapped people had been integrated. (Ryan &Thomas, 1987, p. 101)

Consequently what might be ignored or tolerated in the slower and more flexible pattern of agricultural or domestic labour became a source of friction and lost income, if not a threat to survival, within the new industrial system. The coming of individual wage labour with industrialization precluded co-operation amongst the labour force as workers competed with each other to keep up with fast moving machinery.

In Britain, amidst concerns that the 'poor laws', which date back to the fourteenth century (Stone, 1984, p. 34), were not coping with the increased demands for assistance and the rising numbers of people left to beg on the streets of the new industrial towns. Local authorities and communities coped as best they could and this resulted in considerable local variation in provision. To counter this, the new Poor Law of 1834 emphasized national standards, denial of relief outside an institution, and setting support at particularly low levels to deter claimants. A variety of institutional 'solutions' were promoted to contain the rising number of 'casualties' of the 'far-reaching changes in work and family life' (Ryan & Thomas, 1987, p. 101), aided and abetted by a rapidly expanding medical profession which we will discuss in the next chapter.

Defining and Dealing with Disability

Following these legislative changes there was an increased categorization of the problem population into a variety of different groupings. The 'aged and infirm' comprised one of the main categories in the new workhouse population. There was also an upward trend in incarcerating people defined as 'defectives', including people with visual, hearing or communication impairments and epilepsy. As yet, there was no distinct social group identified as 'disabled' people, just as there were competing explanations for the causes and possible remedies for disease, illness and impairment (Jewson, 1976). One of the most high-profile attempts to confine problem groups underscored the growth of asylums for those diagnosed as 'mad'. Yet there was little agreement amongst professionals about what madness actually was or what caused it. The incarcerated population rose substantially from three to 30 per 10,000 through the nineteenth century (Scull, 1978). The inmate population in 'mental handicap' institutions also expanded significantly into the twentieth century (Ryan & Thomas, 1987; Potts & Fido, 1991). .

The rise of social darwinism and the eugenics movement offered fresh scientific justification for 'intellectual' divisions and hierarchies based on the 'survival of the fittest'. Those categorized as 'subnormal' inspired fears of moral collapse, with resumptions of close links to sexual and criminal deviance. Additionally, the introduction of diagnostic labels such as 'mongol' suggested that 'mental deficiency' constituted a potential racial threat to civilized society (Barnes & Mercer, 2003). Thus, to use the terminology we have used earlier, changes in the mode of production were mirrored in changes in the mode of thought in emerging capitalism.

The institution proved to be a remarkably successful vehicle in dealing with the problem of imposing order and it was in accord with changing social values consequent upon the 'civilising process' (Elias, 1978) and the switch from 'punishment of the body to punishment of the mind' (Foucault, 1977). The institution was successful because it embodied both repressive and ideological mechanisms of control (Althusser, 1971).

The possibilities of locating ideas and practices towards disability within broader socio-historical trends are illustrated by Elias' (1978) detailed analysis of the 'civilising process' in which people learn to revise their perceptions of repugnance and shame and restraint in social relationships. His comparison of medieval and eighteenth-century European court societies illustrates how public manners and body control became targets for 'improvement', ranging from eating and drinking, farting, spitting, blowing one's nose, urinating and defecating in public.

Historically, the increasing emphasis was on 'external' surveillance' which helped to transform self-control into a mark of social esteem. Yet, conversely, unruly bodies became a sign of animality, and a rationale for the spatial segregation of increasing numbers of disabled people. This encompassed a general individualization of the body as a self-contained and controlled entity (Shilling, 1993).

As we have already suggested, the institution was especially effective for maintaining capitalist social relations as it combined a 'repressive' and 'ideological state apparatus' (Althusser, 1971). It was repressive in that it offered the possibility of forced removal from the community for anyone who refused to conform to the new order. It was ideological too as it acted as a visible monument, replacing the public spectacle of the stocks, the pillory and the gallows, to the fate of those who would not or could not conform. Further, it represented a 'symbolic system of reform' in which the 'rehabilitation' of the deviant

> was held to reveal the triumph of good over evil, conscience over desire, in all men and women. If there was a social message in the ideal of reform through institutional discipline, it was that the institutional salvation of the deviant acted out the salvation of all men and women, rich and poor alike. (Ignatieff, 1985, p. 92)

However it was not just the prisons and asylums which operated as a mechanisms of social control; the workhouse was also significant, and its ideological function was always more important than its repressive one:

> The workhouse represented the ultimate sanction. The fact that comparatively few people came to be admitted did not detract from the power of its negative image, an image that was sustained by the accounts that circulated about the harsh treatment and separation of families that admission entailed. The success of 'less eligibility' in deterring the able bodied and others from seeking relief relied heavily on the currency of such images. Newspapers, songs and gossip, as well as orchestrated campaigns for the abolition or reform of the system, all lent support to the deliberate attempts that were made to ensure that entry to a workhouse was widely regarded as an awful fate. (Parker, 1988, p. 9)

In the institution, the state found a successful method of dealing with the problem of order, and in the workhouse, a successful method of imposing discipline on the potential workforce. But it still faced the age-old problem of separating out those who would not from those who could not conform. Hence, throughout the eighteenth and nineteenth centuries institutions became ever more specific in their purposes, and selective in their 'client' group. This distinction between the deserving and the undeserving poor which has shaped the development of welfare policies throughout history, has never been satisfactorily resolved.

These developments, then, facilitated the segregation of people designated as 'disabled', initially in workhouses and asylums, but gradually in more specialist establishments of one kind or another:

> The rise of specialist asylums signified an important shift in the way in which
> the poor, dependent and deviant were contained ... Public workhouses, as
> opposed to domestic relief, were increasingly used for all those who could not
> or would not support themselves economically. In these, idiots, lunatics, the
> chronic sick, the old and vagrants were mixed up with allegedly able-bodied
> unemployed. (Ryan & Thomas, 1987, p.100)

Yet it soon became apparent that workhouses could not simply function as residual dumping grounds for such disparate groups of people. Effective discipline
and deterrence required that these groups should be separated from each other.
But further separation and specialization was necessary within those few people
unable to work in order to successfully manage and control them in ways that
were socially acceptable at the time.

The Poor Law Amendment Act (1834) played an important role in the
process of increasing specialization. In the regulations of the Poor Law administration and thus in the eyes of the Poor Law administrators, five categories
were important in defining the internal universe of paupers; children, the sick,
the insane, 'defectives', and the 'aged and infirm'. Of these, all but the first are
part of today's concept of disability. The five groups were the means of defining
who was able-bodied; if a person didn't fall into one of them, he was able-
bodied by default. This strategy of definition by default remains at the core of
current disability programs. None provides positive definition of 'able-bodied';
instead, 'able to work' is a residual category whose meaning can be known only
after the 'unable to work' categories have been precisely defined (Stone, 1984,
p. 40).

It would be a mistake to assume that the coming of the institution meant that
all or even a majority of people with impairments ended up in one. In pre-
industrial times the family and the community were the places in which such
people existed (Barnes, 1990; Gleeson, 1999; Borsay, 2005). With the rise of
capitalism the family remained the setting where the majority of people with
impairments lived out their lives. What did change, however, partly as a consequence
of the ideological climate created by institutions setting people apart from the
rest of society, was that impairment became a thing of shame. The process of
stigmatization caught the deserving as well as the undeserving because 'the poor
law system of welfare reform maintained the shackles of stigma and penury around
those unable to find, or carry out, paid labour' (O'Brien & Penna, 1998, p. 46).

Consequently not all families could cope with the financial and social consequences of supporting stigmatized and impaired individuals unable to work. This was a particular problem for working class families already under extreme pressure in the new capitalist social order. Hence people with impairments became segregated from their communities and wider societies, and only when the families were unwilling or unable to cope did they become possible candidates for the institution. 'Nobody wanted to go into an institution but not every relative found it possible to keep their dependent kin, especially so it seems, the mentally disordered and the aged' (Parker, 1988, p. 23).

Both the family and the institution, therefore, became places of segregation. But, as far as the balance between institutional and family provision for disabled people is concerned:

> We know next to nothing about this, but it is reasonable to suppose, for example, that the undoubted decline in domestic production in the outwork industries, the artisanal sector and the cottage economy of the agricultural labourer made it more difficult for poor families, particularly women, to provide domestic care for the aged and insane. (Ignatieff, 1983, p. 172)

Thus, as a consequence of the increasing separation between work and home, the boundaries of family obligations towards people with impairments were redrawn. So the new asylums and workhouses met a need among poor families struggling to cope with burdens which for the first time may have been felt to be 'unbearable' (Ignatieff, 1983, p.173).

Disability in the Twentieth Century

This distinction between segregation in the family and in the institution remained well into the twentieth century as the state became more interventionist and the foundations of the welfare state as we know it today developed. As one commentator puts it, 'The provision of personal care and practical assistance to disabled people falls into two main divisions, that of residential care and that of support and assistance to disabled people in their own homes' (Topliss, 1982, p. 77).

In the first half of the twentieth century, the growth of segregated, residential institutions continued apace across the UK and much of Europe and America. The live-in solution was particularly significant for the high number of children with impairments, with many common childhood diseases carrying a significant risk of impairment, if not death. In the UK in a period of minimal social welfare provision, poorer families found it very difficult to meet the high medical costs and support required by a disabled child (Humphries & Gordon, 1992).

There was also a widening impact of the medical profession's authority on policies towards disabled people regarding an individual's claim to sickness and impairment. However, how far this translated into social and welfare benefits remained a contested area, and in general, a low priority for governments and public alike. The result was an uneasy trade-off between economic and human- itarian factors (Blaxter, 1976; Borsay, 1986, 2005).

What changed in the latter part of the twentieth century was the balance between institutional and family support. There has been a significant 'decarceration' movement in many countries, including the UK and America, over recent decades (Scull, 1984) and undoubtedly many people previously living in institutions have been returned to the community. But although the closure, initially of the workhouses and colonies and later the long-stay hospitals, has put many thousands of those previously incarcerated people back into the community, two points need to be made about this development.

First, whilst the process of incarceration for different groups of people defined in various ways as 'sick', 'insane', 'defectives' and the 'aged and infirm' differed for each group, so too did the rates of discharge back into the community. Second, notwithstanding that the numbers of people may vary significantly, the ideological shift from institutional to 'community care' has been much more significant. Indeed,

> To the politician 'community care' is a useful piece of rhetoric; to the sociologist it is stick to beat institutional care with; to the civil servant it is a cheap alternative to institutional care, which can be passed to the local authorities for action – or inaction; to the visionary, it is the dream of a new society in which people really do care; to social service departments, it is a nightmare of height- ened public expectations and inadequate resources to meet them. (Jones et al., 1978, p. 14)

For many disabled people the concept 'care' is both patronising and oppressive. Broadly speaking the verb 'care' means to look after or protect 'with a definite implication of dependence in the person cared for' (Rae, 1989; Barnes, 1990; Morris 1993). Consequently what is implied by the term 'community care' is community dependence or, to be more precise, 'dependence on the community'

(Barnes, 1991, p. 124). As we will indicate in following chapters, as far as people with impairments and considered disabled are concerned, the majority have always lived in the community, albeit to varying degrees segregated within it, and so perhaps the shift has been more apparent than real.

A similar point was made in an analysis of the historical development of social control with the rise of capitalism:

> There have been two transformations, one transparent, the other opaque, one real, the other eventually illusory, in the master patterns and strategies for controlling deviance in Western industrial societies. The first, which took place between the end of the eighteenth and nineteenth centuries, laid the foundations of all deviancy control systems. The second, which is supposed to be happening now, is thought by some to represent a questioning, even a radical reversal of that earlier transformation, by others merely to signify a continuation and intensification of its patterns. (Cohen, 1985, p. 13)

It is important to note too that whilst this pattern of social policy responses to people with impairments appears evident in several rich nations across the world, incarceration is not uncommon for particular groups in many poor states. Children and older people with impairments, and people labelled with 'learning difficulties' and 'mental illness' are especially vulnerable (see, for example, Priestley, 2003; Clements & Read 2008; Fiala & Lewis, 2008; Saupe, 2008).

However, rather than consider here whether these transformations actually mean a loosening of the structures of social control or not in today's societies, what we now need to consider is why these changes took place.

Explaining Disability Responses

In seeking to explain, rather than merely describe, what happened to people with impairments within the context of a capitalist society, we wish to point out that neither the movement to institutional care nor the movement away from it represent a radical shift in state responses. They are simply part of the same process as capitalism has developed, adapted and changed over time. In so doing we need to consider the attempts of others to do the same thing.

The first explanation draws heavily on the Comtean evolutionary framework mentioned earlier. Thus what happened to people considered sick or dependent upon others can be seen as the progressive evolution of reason and humanity. Hence the move from community to institution and back again, reflects changing ideas about social progress. This view is what Abrams (1982) calls 'the enlightenment theory of social welfare' and incorporates the establishment of segregated institutions in liberal philanthropic or Benthamite terms as improvements on previous forms of provision. It also incorporates variants of the anti-institution movement of the late twentieth century, sparked off by the work of Goffman (1961) and a number of damning public enquiries about the conditions in long-stay hospitals (Jones & Fowles, 1984), suggesting that the move back to community care reflects our changing ideas about the appropriateness of institutional provision in contemporary society.

What it fails to explain, however, is that many of those confined to institutions experienced this as punishment rather than treatment (Scull, 1978, 1984; Potts and Fido, 1991) and that as several studies have made clear (Humphries & Gordon, 1992; Bartlett & Wright, 1999; Borsay, 2005), the return to the community can also often be an extremely punitive experience. Changing ideas about the nature of the institution and of community incorporated in the enlightenment theory are thus

> too one-dimensional to be altogether satisfactory. It recognises, one might say, that men make their own history but not the equally important fact that they do not make it just as they please. Of course men act on the basis of ideas but the ideas they have at any particular time and still more the influence of these ideas is not just an intellectual matter. Many good ideas never get a hearing; many bad ideas flourish for generations. (Abrams, 1982, pp.11–12)

The success or failure of these ideas is dependent upon a whole range of other factors such as the economic and social conditions under which they develop and the support or resistance they encounter from people in powerful political positions and institutions.

The second explanation draws on the Marxist framework and suggests that changes in policy and provision for people with impairments were determined by changes in the mode of production:

> The asylums of the nineteenth century were ... as much the result of far-reaching changes in work and family life, and corresponding methods of containing the poor, as they were the inspiration of philanthropists and scientists. With other similar institutions of the period, they have remained the main alternative to the family ever since. (Ryan & Thomas, 1987, p.101)

Similarly, the change back to community care was not simply the product of anti-institution ideas, which had been around in the nineteenth as well as the twentieth centuries, but also because 'segregative modes of social control became … far more costly and difficult to justify' (Scull, 1984, p.135).

This explanation is what Abrams (1982) calls 'the necessity theory of social welfare' and incorporates not just the economic rationality underpinning much social provision, but also the need to impose and maintain order in the changing industrial world. While this theory

> forces us to pay attention to the ways in which social facts and conditions constrain and impel men to act in certain ways … it corrects the bland tendency of enlightenment theory to detach ideas from their social context. But at the same time it tends to deny the equally important fact that what men do in the face of even the most constraining social conditions is indeed something they choose to do. (Abrams, 1982, pp.12–13)

But neither the institution nor community care can be explained solely in terms of humanitarianism or necessity. The 'action theory of welfare' is also important and Parker (1988), in his historical review of residential care, suggests two factors of relevance. First, he suggests that the willingness, or otherwise, of families to care for their dependents was important and he cites historians like Ignatieff (1983) who have claimed that the working-class family has played an active rather than a passive part in the history of institutional development. Therefore he suggests that

> the level of demand for institutional care seems to have been a function of (a) the acceptability of that care as perceived by relatives; (b) the costs which they consider they and their families bear in continuing to look after the dependent or disruptive member; and (c) the number of dependent people without close relatives. (Parker, 1988, p. 24)

Some families have also played an active role in seeking to have relatives removed from long-stay hospitals, special schools and children's homes, though as the defects in community care become more and more apparent, other families are actively campaigning for institutions to remain.

Parker also suggests that institutions have been important historically because of the role they played in campaigns of rescue, notably of children in the latter half of the nineteenth century. This rescue mission was also an important factor in the development of residential care for disabled people after the Second World War, when the Cheshire Foundation 'rescued' many disabled adults from isolation in families, from long-stay hospitals, from geriatric wards and other unsuitable provision (Clark, 2003). That history may subsequently reinterpret such action as incarceration rather than rescue does not invalidate the actions of particular individuals at particular historical points.

Consequently although the 'action theory of welfare' may not explain the forms that provision may take when extracted from historical context, it is useful in developing an understanding of the precise nature and form of that provision, consequent upon the influence of individuals, families and groups at a particular point in time. However, what the action theory does not explain, according to Abrams (1982), is that some groups 'prove persistently more influential than others', necessitating the development of a 'power theory of welfare'.

Undoubtedly the group that has been most persistently influential in the context of disablement has been the medical and related professions and this will be discussed more fully in the following chapter. Before that, there is one further explanation which needs to be discussed and this draws upon Weberian notions of rationality, though it does also incorporate elements of the necessity theory.

Rationalizing Disability

We cannot leave these explanations without discussing the work of Stone (1984). It is different from that discussed previously in this chapter in that it takes the concept 'disability' itself seriously as a theoretical category and grounds its theorizing in a discussion of the development of welfare policies for 'disabled people' in Britain, the USA and Germany. While making no reference to the work of Weber (1994), the argument she presents can be located in his notion of capitalist development being accompanied by an increasing 'rationalisation' of the world. Weber's approach can be summarized as follows:

> By 'rationalisation' Weber meant the process by which explicit, abstract, calculable rules and procedures are increasingly substituted for sentiment, tradition and rule of thumb in all spheres of activity. Rationalisation leads to the displacement of religion by specialised science as a major source of intellectual authority; the substitution of the trained expert for the cultivated man of letters; the ousting of the skilled hand worker by machine technology; the replacement of traditional

judicial wisdom by abstract, systematic statutory codes. Rationalisation demystifies and instrumentalises life. (Wrong, 1970, p. 26)

In respect of provision to meet the changing needs of people considered disabled within the development of capitalism, this was done through the elaboration of ever more detailed systems of bureaucratic organization and administration.

Stone's (1984) basic argument is that all societies function through the 'distributive principle', in that goods and services produced have to be allocated amongst the population as a whole. The major mechanism of distribution, and production, is work, but not everyone is able or willing to work. This will be accompanied by a distributive system based on need and a 'distributive dilemma' that centres on how to allocate goods and services based on the very different principles of work and need. With the rise of capitalism 'disability' becomes an important boundary category through which people are allocated either to the work-based or needs-based system of distribution. The increasing specialization of both categorization and provision is therefore a function of the increasing rationalization of the world.

This explanation incorporates elements of necessity theory, both in the need to redistribute goods and services and in relation to labour supply. 'The disability concept was essential to the development of a workforce in early capitalism and remains indispensable as an instrument of the state in controlling labour supply' (Stone, 1984, p.179).

However, it fails to acknowledge the contradictory aspects of rationalization noted by Weber in the distinction he makes between formal rationality and substantive rationality (Weber, 1994) and the way the latter may contradict the former. Like Stone it is possible to argue that the formal rationality underpinning the disability category makes it the ascription of privilege, in that it offers legitimate social status to those classified as unable to work. But the substantive rationality enshrined in the experience of disablement is much more concerned with the processes of stigmatization and oppression.

Stone acknowledges the contradictions inherent in the development of capitalism discussed both by Marx and Weber and discusses what she calls 'economic and political versions of contradiction theory'. In the economic version, the state experiences a fiscal crisis because it must constantly expand its expenditures while its revenues cannot grow fast enough to meet these expenditures. The political version stresses 'legal rights to social aid' which engenders political support from some sections of society but opposition from others. Both versions predict eventual system breakdown because of either economic crises or the erosion of political support. However, by concentrating on the boundaries between various parts of the capitalist system, rather than on its internal logic she concludes that: 'The interpretation of disability as a concept that mediates the boundary between two conflicting distributive principles offers a very different answer to the question of co-existence' (Stone, 1984, p. 20). The answer, at least in the short term, therefore, is that the disability category, because it is socially constructed and flexible, can resolve any systemic contradictions that may occur.

By the late twentieth century, however, Stone notes that the disability category has become less flexible as the standards for eligibility get more and more detailed: once certain groups are accepted into the category they cannot be ejected from it. People become socialized into their role as disabled and disability categorization is legitimated by the medical and welfare bureaucracies. This has provoked a crisis in disability programmes which may not be subject to categorical resolution, for 'keepers of the category will have to elaborate ever more situations in which people are legitimately needy, until the categories became so large as to engulf the whole' (Stone, 1984, p. 192).

If such a situation were to occur, where the distributive dilemma was resolved solely on the basis of need, then that would surely mark the transition from capitalism to socialism as predicted by Marx. But that is to go too far, too fast, and we need to resume the consideration of what disability under capitalism is actually like rather than consider what it might be like under socialism. However, it is worth noting that since 1990 successive governments in Britain and elsewhere have sought and failed to resolve the problem of who can and who cannot work, amid moral panics about the spiralling costs of various sickness and incapacity benefits. They have had little success so far even though the 'disability category' becomes increasingly contested with every economic crisis that occurs. Needless to say we shall return to these issues later.

Conclusion

This chapter has discussed the process of disablement in relation to the development of capitalism in Britain and other industrial and post-industrial societies. It was suggested that the changing economy, industrialization, urbanization, the changing nature of ideas, and the need to maintain order have all influenced social responses to the process of and experience of disablement. The rise of the institution as a mechanism of both social provision and social control has played a major role in structuring a physical and cultural environment that facilitated the systematic exclusion of people with all manner of impairments from the mainstream of economic and social life.

It is also evident that ideological forces of liberalism, scientific rationality and the medicalization of social deviance, were at least as important as the institution, and it is precisely this ideological dimension which is now being challenged with the development of community care. What needs to be considered next is the way the individualization of life under capitalism has contributed to the individualization of disability and the role of powerful groups, notably the medical profession, in this process. It is to this that we shall turn in the next chapter.

Part II

Representation and Discourses

4

Ideology and the Disabled Individual

Introduction

Since the introduction of 'liberal democratic' forms of government and the modern welfare state, the role of ideology in formulating economic and social affairs has become a hotly contested issue amongst theorists, politicians and policy makers. Therefore no attempt to develop a social theory of disablement can ignore the role of ideology, for there is a clear relationship between prevalent social structures, dominant ideologies and policies and practices for those considered 'disabled' (Oliver, 1990; Oliver & Barnes, 1998). But part of the problem for social theorists is that there is no generally agreed definition of ideology. This is largely because its influence is not always clear as it passes from theorist to politician to policy maker and practitioner and, finally, to disabled individuals.

A host of other economic and social factors often intervene in the process. Hence the role of ideology and its link to policy and practice is often obscured (George & Wilding, 1994; O'Brien & Penna, 1998). In order to demonstrate how ideology has influenced the social construction of the disabled individual in capitalist societies, this chapter will explore the relationship between ideology and individualism, the medicalization of impairment and disability and the concepts 'normality' and 'eugenics'.

Ideology and the Individual

The term 'ideology' was first used by de Tracy in 1797 immediately after the French Revolution to refer to a 'science of ideas: a rational new way of gathering information to inform government decisions for the betterment of society'

(George & Wilding, 1994, p. 2). The aim was to counter traditional forms of government founded on superstition and religion. This positive view of ideology is reflected in the work of several American sociologists such as Parsons (1951) during the 1950s and 1960s who viewed ideology as a system of values and beliefs that increases social cohesion in society for the benefit of all.

For Marx, on the other hand, ideology was also important but it was not people's ideas and beliefs that influenced social development as suggested by de Tracy and Parsons, but rather the conflict over material resources that shapes human history and people's ideas and beliefs. Hence, 'the mode of production of material life conditions the social, political and intellectual life process in general. It is not the consciousness of men (sic) that determines their being, but on the contrary their social being that determines their consciousness' (Marx, 1904 [1859], pp.11–12).

According to Marx, in all societies the dominant ideas, values and beliefs are those of the most powerful groups or classes. Consequently ideology was to be defined as values and beliefs which help secure the position of more powerful groups at the expense of less powerful ones. Thus, according to Giddens (2006, p. 110), 'power, ideology and conflict are always closely connected'.

Both Parsons and Marx present ideology as essential for the stability and continuity of a given society, albeit the former perceives it as beneficial to all and the latter a privileged minority only. We would argue, however, that both approaches are over-simplistic, historically bound and that in the 'post-modern' globalized world of the twenty-first century neither is particularly useful. Therefore we suggest that a more appropriate use of the concept 'ideology' relates to 'a set of values and beliefs held by individuals, groups and societies that influence their conduct' (George & Wilding, 1994, p. 5).

But that in itself is not enough, for, by leaving it there, social consciousness can be reduced to a pluralist vision of sets of competing ideologies. This essentially relativist approach fits well with pluralist views of the capitalist world with its liberal notions of democracy. But it sidesteps the uncomfortable fact that all liberal capitalist democracies are structured by power and run for the benefit of particular groups. Therefore it is necessary to turn to the work of Gramsci (1985) who explored the links between social structures and ideologies by distinguishing between what he called 'organic' and 'arbitrary' ideologies. He particularly addressed the issue of power in capitalist society and focused on ways in which the dominant group's world view becomes accepted by subordinate groups even when it may not be in their best interests. He explained this situation with reference to the notion of 'hegemony', a concept more all-embracing than ideology. Thus hegemony often becomes a taken-for-granted reality and can clearly be seen in the way capitalist societies have come to view both impairment and disability as a personal tragedy. Our confrontation with this hegemony was, in our view, a major reason for the impact of the first edition of this book.

According to Gramsci, ideological hegemony is achieved by the creation and support of networks of political alliances and institutions; notable examples include the Church, schools, media and welfare systems. They disseminate in various forms particular ideologies and at the same time are represented as necessary to the maintenance of order, prosperity, social well-being and so on. In so doing a particular set of values and beliefs become naturalized and regarded as 'common-sense'. In these respects, Gramsci emphasized the 'importance of cultural – as well as political and economic – forces in sustaining the capitalist system' (O'Brien & Penna, 1998, p. 60).

The hegemony that defines disability in capitalist societies, we would argue, is constituted by the organic ideology of individualism, the arbitrary ideologies of medicalization, normality and eugenics. All of these ideologies underpin and support contemporary notions of 'able-bodiedness' and 'able-mindedness' which reify and endorse both personal tragedy theory and much of social policy in the developed wealthy nations of the north and the developing poorer nations of the south. We begin with an exploration of the relationship between individualism and disability.

Individualism and Disability

The ways in which the rise of industrial capitalism excluded disabled people from the process of work and its consequent social relations was described in previous chapters. But it also changed the way people thought about themselves and about others. In short, 'Capitalism, whether free market or welfare, encourages us to view people ... as a commodity for sale in the labour market' (Burton, 1983, p. 67). The requirements of the capitalist economy were and remain for individuals to sell their labour in a free market and this necessitated a break from collectivist notions of work as the product of family and group involvement.

The difficulties encountered by people with impairments in the wage labour economy of the eighteenth and nineteenth centuries were exacerbated by 'the ascendant egocentric philosophies of the period, which stressed the rights and privileges of the individual over and above those of the group and the state; in relation to property rights, politics and culture' (Barnes, 1991, p. 18).

Thus individualism is seen as being the ideological foundation upon which the 'transition to industrial capitalism was based' (Dalley, 1988, p. 32). That this ideological construction of the individual was rooted in history, Marx had no doubt:

> The further back we go into history, the more the individual, and, therefore, the producing individual seems to depend on and constitute a part of a larger whole: at first it is, quite naturally, the family and the clan, which is but an enlarged family; later on, it is the community growing up in its different forms out of the clash and the amalgamation of clans. (Marx, 1904, p. 267)

Hence, individuals always existed but only as part of larger social groupings, whether they be families, clans or communities. It was only with the rise of the industrial revolution that the isolated, private individual appeared on the historical stage:

> It is but in the eighteenth century, in 'bourgeois society', that the different forms of social union confront the individual as a mere means to his private ends, as an outward necessity. But the period in which this view of the isolated individual becomes prevalent, is the very one in which the interrelations of society (general from this point of view) have reached the highest state of development. Man [*sic*] is in the most literal sense of the word ... not only a social animal, but an animal, which can develop into an individual only in society. (Marx, 1904, pp. 267–8)

This highest state of development (that is, the rise of industrial capitalism) did not simply bring with it new problems for social order and social control. It also required new ways of seeing or constructing these problems arising out of the need for order and control, particularly in the new industrial towns

> Within this set of problems, the 'body' – the body of individuals and the body of populations appears as the bearer of new variables, not merely between the scarce and the numerous, the submissive and the restive, rich and poor, healthy and sick, strong and weak, but also between the more or less utilizable, more

or less amenable to profitable investment, those with greater or lesser prospects of survival, death and illness, and with more or less capacity for being usefully trained. (Foucault, 1980, p. 172)

This, then, is the ideological underpinning for the separation and specialization processes which took place with the rise and development of the institution and which we described in the previous chapter. Further, this ideological construction of, or way of seeing, the individual not only legitimates one particular view but makes all others appear as incorrect, misguided, utopian or simply wrong:

> every way of seeing is also a way of not seeing; and in this case a view of man as essentially property-owning or self-interested or 'rational' or concerned to maximise his utility amounts to the ideological legitimation of a particular view of society and social relations – and the implicit delegitimation of others. (Lukes, 1973, pp.149–50)

In relating this discussion to disability, it is not the ideological construction of property-owning, self-interested or rational individuals that is important. Rather it is the construction of 'able-bodied/minded' individuals that is significant. In essence, the value of the non-disabled individual was essential as part of a capable and compliant workforce within the context of an emergent industrialized work environment and an intensifying culture of competitive individualism.

This particular ideological construction can best be understood within Gramsci's distinction between 'organic' and 'arbitrary' ideologies:

> One must distinguish between historically organic ideologies, those, that is, which are necessary to a given structure, and ideologies that are arbitrary, rationalistic, or 'willed'. To the extent that ideologies are historically necessary they have a validity which is 'psychological'; they 'organise' human masses, and create the terrain on which men [*sic*] move, acquire consciousness of their position, struggle, etc. To the extent that they are arbitrary they only create individual 'movements', polemics and so on. (Gramsci, 1985, p. 377)

These organic and arbitrary ideologies, would better be called 'core' and 'peripheral', simply because they are interrelated and interdependent. In this particular case we would suggest that the core (organic) ideology of individualism gave rise to the ideological construction of the 'disabled' individual as the antithesis of able-bodiedness and able-mindedness, and the medicalization of disability became the acceptable response to a specific political and social problem. We will discuss precisely how this occurred in the next section.

The Ideological Exclusion of Disabled Individuals

How disability came to be conceived within the core ideology of individualism as an individual problem can be understood with reference to the work of Foucault (1967) in general and, particularly, his work on mental illness, emotional distress or 'madness'. His views have been summarized as follows:

> The very idea that 'madness' is individual pathology, a negative phenomenon, a defect to be remedied, is the object of his investigation. This concept of madness is not the achievement of psychiatric rationality. Rather it is a complex and non-intentional social product, which formed the basis for psychiatry. (Hirst & Woolley, 1982, p. 165)

Therefore for Foucault, psychiatry as organized professional activity only becomes possible when (i) madness has been transformed from a diverse set of social valuations to a uniform category of pathology, and (ii) when people defined as 'mad' have been excluded from normal social life and isolated in a specialist domain or institution. At the core of this argument is the claim that there can be no such thing as 'madness' without the idea of 'unmadness' or, to be more precise, 'reason' without 'unreason'.

A similar argument is applicable to the notion of disability. The idea of disability as individual pathology only becomes possible when we have an idea of individual 'able-bodiedness/mindedness', even if such an idea becomes part of taken-for-granted reality and is rarely questioned. The contemporary concept of disability is clearly linked to the rise of industrial capitalism and the development of wage labour requiring a specific kind of individual, namely, one able to operate dangerous machinery in competition with his peers.

Prior to this, as we have already suggested, individuals, whether with impairments or otherwise, had worked co-operatively within the family, the community and the 'clan' or band. Although ignorance and prejudice were not uncommon and differences in individual contributions noted and often sanctions applied, individuals were rarely segregated from everyday life as a result of difference in performance (Barnes, 1991, 1997; Gleeson, 1999; Stiker, 1999; Borsay, 2005).

Under industrial capitalism that is precisely what happened, and disability became individual pathology; people with impairments could not meet the demands of wage labour and so became controlled through exclusion. Families dependent solely on the wages of 'able-bodied' individuals could not provide for relatives unable to find work in the new factory system, so large groups of dependent people were created by the process of industrialization. Also, the Elizabethan system of domestic relief for those unable to support themselves, dating back to the Poor Law of 1601, was directly at odds with the ascending free market economy. Waged labour made the distinction between the 'able and less able' poor crucially important, since parochial 'outdoor' relief to the 'able-bodied' poor interfered with labour mobility.

Segregating poor people into institutions, on the other hand, had several advantages over domestic relief; 'it was efficient, it acted as a major deterrent to the "able bodied malingerer", and it could instill good work habits into inmates' (Barnes, 1991, pp. 15–16). And as Foucault has pointed out, once this separation between individuals has occurred through segregation, it becomes necessary for a specifically designated group to legitimate it. In the case of the disabled individual this became the medical profession.

The Medicalization of Disability

The process of exclusion was facilitated by the focus on 'the body', of both individuals and populations. The main group to centre their gaze on 'the body' were doctors, and this medicalization process gradually gave rise to a number of associated professions – what Finkelstein (1999) termed 'PAMs': professionals allied to medicine.

Consequently thereafter disability was connected to the medical profession and the 'biomedical model of health'. People with impairments, or 'chronic ill health', were subject to control and exclusion by this newly emerging group of professionals who readily seized the opportunity to increase their power and influence by classifying people in relation to the labour market and by facilitating their segregation.

The concept of 'public health' emerged as a consequence of the state's attempt to eradicate pathologies from the general population or 'social body'. This newly emergent profession were quick to develop the 'scientific' biomedical model of health and the germ theory of illness and disease. Germ theory suggests that there is a specific identifiable component responsible for every illness and disease, and this enabled a 'scientific' foundation for the development of medicine as a profession equipped with a politically expedient 'objective' knowledge base (Bynum, 2008).

The biomedical model of health 'approached the problem of disease through the 'gaze' of germ theory and involved a highly interventionist and specific form of medical practice' (Turner, 1987, p.217). It suggested that illness and disease represented a breakdown within the human body and therefore was distinct from the 'normal' state of being. The mind and body could be treated separately. The emphasis was on the 'sickness' or 'pathology' rather then the whole person. Doctors were required to adopt a medical gaze and were considered the only experts in the treatment of disease and ill health. Their expertise was presented as neutral and value-free with the result that 'patients' could be manipulated, investigated and treated in isolation and irrespective of other factors (Gerhardt, 1989; Lupton, 1994).

Thus since then there has been an escalating medicalization of almost every aspect of everyday life and not just in the lives of disabled individuals as has been our focus here. Medicine as an institutional complex has acquired the right to define and treat a whole range of conditions and problems that previously would have been regarded as moral or social in origin. Consequently people perhaps previously categorized as 'bad' or 'weak' are deemed 'ill' and targets for medical intervention (Conrad & Schneider, 1992). This professional takeover of moral/social issues is evident across the life cycle, from pregnancy and childbirth (Oakley, 1980), behavioural problems in children (Conrad, 1975), ageing (Zola, 1991), through to dying (Clark & Seymour, 1999).

Inevitably impairment and disability have become widely perceived as a health problem within the domain of medicine. Doctors are centrally involved in the lives of people with impairments and those labelled disabled, from the determination of whether an unborn child is deemed 'handicapped' or not through to the deaths of older people from a variety of 'disabling' conditions. Some of these interventions may be entirely appropriate, as in the diagnosis of impairment, the stabilization of a particular condition following trauma, the treatment of illness occurring independently of impairment and the provision of appropriate rehabilitation services (Oliver, 1996, 2009). Other interventions may be more problematic but that is not our argument here. Our position on this issue has often been misunderstood and we have been accused of being 'anti-medicine'. This is not the case. Rather we are anti-medical imperialism, that is, the intervention of doctors into areas of our lives where it is not appropriate for them to be.

There have, of course been some very real gains from medical interventions where they are appropriate. Survival rates have increased and life expectancy has been prolonged for people with particular impairments such as spinal cord injury, for example (Oliver et al., 1988). Also some conditions have been erad-icated or substantially reduced, usually through prevention programmes and vaccinations (Lupton, 1994). Finally, some medical interventions have been successful; for example, some cancers have been reduced through surgery and drug therapy (Allen, 2009), while laser treatment and cataract surgery has reduced the incidence of particular types of blindness (Rabiu, 2001). It is important to remember, though, that access to such treatments is by no means universal across and within nation states for both rich and poor (Bartley, 2004). As we shall see in the next chapter, the overwhelming majority of the world's disabled population do not have regular access to either medical treatments or disability-related support.

But the issue for the globalized world of the twenty-first century is not one of life expectancy but expectation of life and it is here that the negative and partial view prompted by medicalization is most open to criticism:

> The medical model of disability is one rooted in an undue emphasis on clinical diagnosis, the very nature of which is destined to lead to a partial and inhibit-ing view of the disabled individual ... In order to understand disability as an experience, as a lived thing, we need much more than the medical 'facts', however necessary these are in determining medication. The problem comes when they determine not only the form of treatment (if treatment is appropri-ate), but also the form of life for the person who happens to be disabled. (Brisenden, 1986, p.173)

The medicalization of everyday life and of society is thus a fact for the current population whether labelled disabled or otherwise. How this general phenomenon came about now needs to be considered in some depth along with specific explanations of how the process occurred with respect to impairment and disability, particularly with reference to developments over the last fifty years. We begin with the medicalization of everyday living and then turn our attention to peripheral ideologies: those of normality and eugenics.

The Medicalization of Everyday Life

The enlightenment theory of medicalization suggests that it is an inevitable consequence of both the pre-eminence attached to scientific as opposed to other forms of knowledge, and the progress of humanitarian ideas in the nineteenth century. Within this explanation, medicine is seen as largely beneficial and progressive, providing treatment to sick and ill people rather than physical punishment for sinners or deprivation of liberty for the criminal. While this may be viewed positively, treatment may not always be experienced in this light and the consequences of medical and impairment-specific labels are all too frequently negative and profound.

An alternative approach suggests that medicalization is a key element in the reproduction of capitalist society that advances private, corporate interests, and an emergent 'medical-industrial complex' (Navarro, 1976). Medicine's involvement in eligibility criteria for compensation, resources or support services is compatible with capitalist interests as it depoliticizes and individualizes social problems. Medicine helps to 'pacify the individual with the rewards and benefits of the sick role' and 'ameliorates or makes palatable those diswelfares generated by the economic system' (Navarro, 1978, p. 214).

It encourages an ideology of 'victim blaming'. At the same time, the economic context of dangerous working conditions, contaminated environments and toxic waste products are seen as personal troubles. These troubles encourage anti-social behaviours such as excessive tobacco and alcohol consumption, crime and public disorder. External pressures are then downplayed, along with other causes of ill health resulting from the pressures of living and working in an alienating society. Drug companies and manufacturers of medical technology are happy to step into this emerging market with ever more sophisticated therapeutic solutions to the problems of social control. In this the media becomes an ally in its enthusiastic pursuit of stories about health risks, new diseases and 'miracle cures' (Karpf, 1988: Barnes, 1992; Meekosha & Dowse, 1997; Ross, 1997; Cumberbatch & Negrine, 1992; Sancho, 2003; Cumberbatch & Gauntlett, 2006).

We can perhaps best illustrate this by discussing what has been called the 'psychiatrization of everyday life'. It includes the development of other institutions besides the asylum or hospital, the growing use of 'social therapies', increasing public awareness of the importance of 'healthy minds' and the growth of voluntary use of various psychological experts on 'everyday worries' (Pilgrim & Rogers, 1993, p. 91). All of this is evident with the extensive prescribing of minor tranquillisers, principally by general practitioners (GPs) for all manner of social ills such as broken relationships, insomnia, nerves and employment problems.

This corresponds with the proliferation of a 'psy-complex' and new occupational groups engaged in 'mental health work' (Ramon, 1996). For example, clinical psychologists have colonized some of the territory traditionally held by psychiatry. This includes the profession's establishing its expertise through state registration and willing involvement in welfare bureaucracies. Examples include the regulation and control of child behaviour and treating people labelled with 'mental illness' and 'learning difficulties' (Pilgrim & Treacher,1992).

This exemplifies arguments that current societies embrace a 'therapeutic culture of the self' (Rose, 1989) in which self-development and emotion management are promoted as ongoing personal projects (Giddens, 1991; Shilling, 2003). Thus people are much more likely to seek solutions to personal difficulties in terms set by professionals. Such trends indicate the 'medicalisation of underperformance' (Conrad & Potter, 2000) and 'the public's decreased tolerance for mild symptoms and benign problems' (Conrad, 2005, p. 9). The reported rise in social phobias and anxiety disorders since the 1980s which have attracted fears of a 'cultural epidemic' (Henderson & Zimbardo, 2005) are a prime example of this phenomenon. Indeed, research shows how the psychiatric and pharmaceutical industries are working to export and promote western understandings of 'mental illness' to the rest of the world (see, for example, Davis, 2010; Watters, 2011).

It is not only the medical profession and its therapeutic allies that have contributed to the medicalization of everyday life. There is also evidence of the impact of other important interests including the state, private-corporate and voluntary sectors as well as lay self-help groups. Many years ago Conrad (1975) traced the medicalization of childhood 'behavioural difficulties' to the therapeutic alliance described above who were willingly supported by teachers and parents' groups who desperately needed a non-stigmatizing label for problem behaviour. Since then the label may have changed to attention deficit hyperactivity disorder (ADHD) and been applied to a wider population, but the underlying process remains the same (Barnes & Mercer, 2010).

Furthermore, aggressive marketing by corporate interests and professional groups, using various media including the internet are all implicated in the emergence of hitherto unknown health problems. These include post-traumatic stress disorder (Scott, 1990), Alzheimer's disease, Asperger's syndrome, repetitive strain injury and chronic fatigue syndrome among others. Increasingly, the whole body is being medicalized 'piece by piece' (Conrad, 2005, p. 8).

More recently, the potential of genomic medicine has seen germ theory replaced by 'gene theory' (Conrad, 2005; Conrad & Leiter, 2005). Advocates now argue that all aspects of the human condition, including health, longevity and behaviour, are subject to genetic manipulation. Certainly since the 1990s the drive towards the medicalization of ever more areas of life has intensified and is 'now driven more by commercial and market interests than by professional claims-makers' (Conrad, 2005, p. 10).

This systematic and intensifying medicalization of everyday life is but one example of the social creation of impairment, dependence and disability which implicitly, if not explicitly, serves to shift attention away from an increasingly unequal and alienating global society. The emphasis on the importance of the able-bodied/minded individual is further reinforced by the peripheral ideologies of 'normality' and 'eugenics' which followed in the wake of the rise of industrial capitalism. All this has given rise to what we shall call the normalizing society.

The Normalizing Society

A key feature of medicalization and the personal tragedy theory of disability is the assertion that 'able-bodied/mindedness' is 'normal'. The social construction of the concept 'normality' became a major concern for advocates of post-modernist or poststructuralist perspectives during the 1990s. As we noted in Chapter 1, these approaches require a move away from an emphasis on the primacy of material factors in the creation of disability toward a more nuanced focus on culture, language and discourse.

Whilst the importance of language in the disablement process has been a major concern for disability activists and writers since the 1970s (Rae, 1989; Oliver, 1990; Rieser & Mason, 1990; Barnes 1992; Hevey, 1992; Linton, 1998; Clark & Marsh, 2002; Swain et al., 2003; Haller et al., 2003), it has focused on the use of particular words or 'hate speech' as it is sometimes called.

More recently there has been an expanding literature on lay and scientific terminology used to define and categorize people with impairments from writers influenced by the writings of social theorists like Derrida and Foucault.

Derrida (1990), for example, is concerned with ways of thinking that formulate and establish the meanings surrounding 'identity' and 'difference'. For him meanings are organized through a continuous and dynamic process of interaction that can only be understood through the systematic deconstruction of orthodox assumptions and discourses. Consequentially a key feature of postmodernist writings is the rejection of assumed Cartesian dualisms that proliferate within Enlightenment-inspired theorizing and culturally dominant discourses associated with 'modernist' society. Examples include: mind/body, individual/society, normal/abnormal distinctions.

There have been attempts to apply this argument to disability. Hence

> A Derridean perspective on disability would argue that although they are antagonistic, 'normativism' needs disability for its own definition: a person without an impairment can define him/herself as 'normal' only in opposition to that which s/he is not – a person with an impairment. (Corker & Shakespeare, 2002, p. 7)

A deconstruction of the concept of normality or 'normalcy' and its discursive impact on societal responses to impairment is provided by Davis, (1995. 2006). His analysis of changing cultural responses to impairment provides a useful addition to materialist accounts of the emergence of the disability category discussed earlier. He argues that 'the social processes of disabling arrived with industrialisation' (p. 24) as a new set of discourses and practices. In earlier epochs, perceptions of the human body and mind were visualized against the 'ideal' as represented in art, mythology or imagination. Hence all human beings were thought to be imperfect at this time. Thus, prior to the political and cultural upheavals of the Enlightenment, people with impairments were not distinguishable as a group and marked out by specific discursive practices.

According to Davis the construction of the 'disabled' individual and group was an inevitable outcome of the displacement of the 'ideal' by the 'normal/abnormal' divide. Consequently the dominant discourses around notions of the 'grotesque' and the ideal body in the Middle Ages were completely overturned by the 'normalizing gaze' of modern science.

Notably, the connection between the body and industry is tellingly revealed in the fact that the leading members of the first British statistical societies formed in the 1830s and 1840s were industrialists or men who had close ties to industry. This established a hierarchical standard for pronouncing some bodies and minds as abnormal and inferior – in terms of appearance and performance. Standards of physical health, mental balance and moral soundness became closely linked, so that defective bodies and minds were associated with 'degeneracy' (Young, 1990; Davis, 1995, 2006).

Clearly these accounts provide a useful insight into the genesis of and continued ideological hegemony of able-bodied/minded normality in late capitalist society. However the emphasis on discourses alone cannot account for the economic and social deprivations encountered by people considered 'not normal'. These analyses fail to address in any depth the very real material forces that under-pinned and precipitated their development which we discussed in the previous chapter.

In particular, we would argue that it was the transition to industrial capitalism and the ensuing inhuman treatment meted out to those unable or unwilling to compete for work in an increasingly alienating political and cultural environ-ment that was a major factor in this discursive separation. As Abberley pointed out several years ago:

> Our abnormality results from the failure of society to meet our 'normal' needs as impaired people, which are different from some, but by no means all, of our fellow citizens. Our abnormality consists in us having, compared to the general population, a particular and larger set of needs un-provided for, or met in inappropriate and disempowering ways. (Abberley, 1993, p.111)

Perceptions of disabled people's assumed abnormality are compounded by the normalizing practices of service providers which are often underpinned by the principle of 'normalization'. Originating in a rights-based ethos in Scandinavia in the late 1960s, the idea of 'normalization' was pioneered by Bank-Mikkelson in Denmark and Nijre in Sweden as 'making available to the "mentally retarded" patterns and conditions of everyday life which are as close as possible to the norms and patterns of the mainstream of society' (Nijre, 1969, p. 181).

It was in North America, however, that normalization was elaborated into a more scientific and theoretical discourse and practice. Wolfensberger (1972) drew on deviance and labelling theory, discussed in Chapter 2, to explain the ways in which disabled people, and particularly those labelled 'retarded' or with learning difficulties, were devalued in society. He later downgraded use of the term normalization in favour of 'social role valorisation' (SRV) and argued that the main function of 'human service industries' was to reverse the process of devaluation by enhancing the social image and competence of service users. This was achievable by assisting individuals into 'socially valued life conditions and socially valued roles' (Wolfensberger & Thomas, 1983, p.24).

This represents a significant shift away from the early Scandinavian emphasis on people's rights (Perrin & Nirje, 1989), although Wolfensberger refused to rule out the application of SRV to persons. In other words the application of SRV techniques inevitably required disabled people to change their appearance, attitudes and behaviour in order to become 'more normal' and fit in, although the normalizers would probably not put it in quite those terms (Oliver, 2009, Chapter 6).

Inevitably the emphasis on changing the appearance and behaviour of people with impairments, whether physical, sensory or cognitive in nature, generated extensive criticism. First, normalization theory largely ignores differences in terms of gender, age, class and race within and across marginalized groups. Second, the emphasis on changing the behaviour and attitudes of marginalized individuals so that they became more like 'normal' people does not question prevailing notions of 'normality'. Further, the principle of normalization does little to diminish the impact of professional authority over the lives of disabled people. The emphasis is on consensus and shared values rather than power relations between professional and service users. Therefore normalization requires individuals to adapt to the norms of society, to 'compete in the world of the able-bodied and the able-minded' (Walmsley, 1991, p. 227), as if 'the values and norms of behaviour and appearance in society are worth striving for' (Hattersley, 1991, p. 3).

A key feature of personal tragedy theory is that people with impairments should strive to be as 'normal' as possible whatever the cost to themselves or their families. The medical and rehabilitation professions have rarely confronted this, instead promoting a range of disabling practices commensurate with the normal/disabled dichotomy. As a consequence deaf children were prevented from using sign language (Corker, 1998), people with mobility-related impairments were encouraged to walk with artificial aids such as callipers and crutches rather than use wheelchairs (Finkelstein, 1998), and people with missing limbs coerced into using artificial ones.

For example, Lapper (2005) recalls how she was pressured into using artificial limbs at the residential home and school she attended:

> Staff were very keen that we all became proficient in the use of our artificial limbs. The added limbs were considered a fundamental aspect of our being able to function properly and fulfil the ultimate aim of the home .... They had great faith in those artificial limbs and thought that if we would only practice and use them regularly we would soon be picking up the most delicate items without breaking or damaging them. But we all instinctively knew those sorry little bits of metal were never going to fulfil their hoped for potential. (Lapper, 2005, cited in French & Swain, 2008, p.10)

The ideology of normality has also been influential not just in current medical interventions and rehabilitation practices but also in developing areas of medical knowledge such as the emergence and growing influence of eugenics in the nineteenth, twentieth and twenty-first centuries. It is to this that we now turn.

Normality and Eugenics

The normalizing tendencies of the nineteenth century were boosted by the increasing use of statistics to monitor and control the activities of the general population and the 'science of eugenics'. The word eugenics was first coined in the nineteenth century by Francis Galton, a cousin of Charles Darwin, in 1892 to refer to the 'science of improvement of the human germ plasm through better breeding' (Kerr & Shakespeare, 2002, p.4). Galton distinguished a positive and negative approach to eugenics. Positive eugenics referred to policies and practices that were designed to encourage 'so called good stock to breed'. By way of contrast, negative eugenics applied to policies and actions designed to prevent 'the mentally and morally unfit from breeding' (p. 8).

Scientific legitimacy for such ideas was provided by post-Enlightenment thinkers such as Malthus, Spencer and Darwin. In 1798 Malthus first noted that the population across Europe was growing rapidly and that if unchecked this would outstrip natural resources and the food supply. The inevitable outcome, he believed, would be famine, disease and war unless people exercised 'moral restraint' and had fewer children (Wrigley & Souden, 1986). Spencer claimed that over time there was a tendency towards 'the survival of the fittest'. He maintained that if left to compete amongst themselves, the most intelligent, ambitious and productive people would win out. He endorsed a fiercely competitive world of free market economics in the belief that as the fittest survived society would undergo steady improvement (Andreski, 1975).

These ideas, coupled with Darwin's (1996; first published in 1859) theory of natural selection as evolutionary progress gave authority to a common belief that the capacity for rational judgment, moral behaviour and business acumen and enterprise was not equally distributed throughout the human population. Prominent figures in late nineteenth-century social science detailed their conviction that certain groups in society including criminals, non-white 'races' and even women had limited intelligence and therefore a reduced capacity for rational thought and moral conduct (Dickens, 2000). Such views provided the foundations for an ideology that

> allayed the qualms of the rich about not helping the poor by telling them that the latter's sufferings were the inevitable price of progress which could only occur through the struggle for existence ending in the survival of the fittest and the elimination of the unfit. (Andreski, 1975, p.26)

Social darwinists classified disabled people with 'severe' impairments as 'mutants' (Radford, 1994). The spectre of 'race degeneration' was fostered by Langdon Down's (1866), cited in Gould (1980), classification of the 'mongolian idiot' as a throwback to a non-Caucasian type (Gould, 1980). Defective bodies and minds were perceived as 'dangerous' and 'threatening' to the rest of society. Eugenicists further highlighted links between intellectual and physical deficiency and a range of social evils including crime, vagrancy, alcoholism, prostitution and unemployment (Kevles, 1985). Hence all forms of physical and sensory impairment were identified as a threat to social progress:

> We civilised men, on the other hand, do our utmost to check the process of elimination; we build asylums for the imbecile, the maimed, and the sick; we institute poor-laws; and our medical men exert their utmost to save the life of everyone to the last moment ... Thus the weak members of society propagate their kind. No one who has attended to the breeding of domestic animals will doubt that this must be highly injurious to the race of man. (Darwin, 1922, p. 136)

Several eminent statisticians, including Galton, Pearson and Fisher, promoted eugenic applications for 'improving the human race'. Initially, the merger between statistics and biology promised a science of the average effects of the laws of heredity (Abrams,1968, p. 89). The notion of 'normality' gave way to ranking with those deviating from the norm located on a hierarchy from higher to lower scores. This is illustrated in the case of intelligence quotient (IQ) test and scores. They quickly acquired a moral judgement of superior and inferior 'intellectual' functioning. Statistical theories such as these reinforced a deterministic account of intelligence, 'race' and human evolution (Davis, 2006).

Eugenic policies espousing 'social hygiene' quickly gained ground across Europe and North America. These ranged from segregation in institutions to state and medically sponsored schemes for sterilization and selective abortion. Such practices had a particular appeal in America due to the unprecedented levels of immigration from Europe and other parts of the world in the first decades of the twentieth century. The American eugenic movement had widespread support including prominent politicians, doctors and public figures and promoted a diverse range of activities.

These included advanced statistical analyses of human pedigrees, and 'better baby contests' modelled on rural livestock shows. Compulsory sterilization of criminals and 'the retarded' and selective ethnic restrictions on immigration was also promoted. These were all aimed at 'improving human heredity' (Pernick 1997, pp. 89–90).

These ideas were spread much more widely into the twentieth century, most notably in Germany. The German Society for Race Hygiene won support from all political parties including the Social Democrats. But policy revolved mainly around positive eugenics until the early 1920s and the radicalization of German politics in the aftermath of Germany's defeat in the First World War (Burleigh, 1994). In 1920 a lawyer, Karl Binding, and a psychiatrist, Alfred Hoche, published the book *Permission for the Destruction of Life Unworthy of Life*. In it they challenged values such as the 'sanctity of life' and recourse to irrational emotions like pity as responses to impairment and disability. Instead they focused on the economic burden posed by impairment and the logic of 'mercy killing' for disabled people.

Three groups of people were singled out for such treatment. First, terminally ill or 'mortally wounded' individuals who expressed the desire to die. Second, 'incurable idiots' regardless of whether the 'idiocy' was congenital or acquired. They were considered 'a terrible heavy burden upon their relatives and society as a whole' and 'a travesty of real human beings, occasioning disgust in everyone who encounters them'. The third group included 'mentally healthy people' who had been rendered unconscious through accident or illness and would be 'appalled' at their condition in the event of their regaining consciousness. Others were encouraged to anticipate their wishes on their behalf (Burleigh, 1994, pp. 17–18).

Binding and Hoche proposed several ways of conducting euthanasia including legislative protection for doctors against the possible objection of relatives and the additional benefits that the killing of defectives might offer medical research. They proposed various procedures in order to implement 'mercy killing' for 'defectives', such as 'permitting committees' composed of lawyers and physicians who would be obliged to keep records. These arguments were welcomed by many doctors, half of whom joined the Nazi party (Gallagher, 1995).

Throughout the 1920s and 1930s the Nazi propaganda machine promoted eugenic imagery representing disabled people as 'useless eaters' and 'life unworthy of life' in the media, and Germany introduced the Law for the Prevention of Genetically Diseased Progeny (1933). Between then and 1 September 1939, German doctors sterilized approximately 375,000 people to prevent the birth of children with a range of hereditary conditions. Hitler secretly ordered the adult euthanasia programme to begin in September 1939. It was never a formal law or government order because 'mercy killing' was technically against the law at that time. There was also concern that such a policy may generate opposition. This led to the murder of over 270,000 disabled people regarded as 'travesties of human form and spirit' (Burleigh, 1995, p. 194).

Although Nazi Germany is undoubtedly the most extreme example of eugenic practices, it is notable that for much of the twentieth century eugenic or 'population policies' were practised in several other European countries and the USA against people regarded as biologically inferior (Kevles, 1985). By 1938, thirty-three American states had a law allowing the forced sterilization of women with intellectual impairments who were labelled as 'feeble minded'. Racism led to black women being grossly over-represented among the 60,000 people forcibly sterilized in American states between 1907 and 1960.

In Scandinavian countries such as Denmark, Finland, Norway and Sweden politicians and policy makers introduced compulsory sterilization laws because they were concerned that the emerging welfare state would encourage the 'unfit' to reproduce and reduce the quality of the 'national stock'. In Sweden alone 63,000 people, 90 per cent of them women, were sterilized between 1934 and 1975. Norway, a much smaller country, sterilized 48,000 people in the same period (Giddens, 2006, p. 263). British and Dutch policy makers adopted 'voluntary' rather than compulsory sterilization. Nonetheless in the post-1945 period sterilization for women termed 'handicapped' or 'mentally subnormal and sexually vulnerable' was common and supported by politicians and public alike. Between April 1968 and 1969 '10,545 women were sterilised during abortions in the UK' (Kerr & Shakespeare, 2002, p. 73).

Largely as a consequence of these policies, the concepts of eugenics and social Darwinism became widely discredited amongst politicians and policy makers (Dickens, 2000). Yet despite substantial evidence to the contrary (Gallagher, 1995), 'modern day eugenicists' (Goble, 2003, p. 48) argue that it was not scientists and doctors but politicians and policy makers that were responsible for the oppressive policies and practices of the past. Such arguments enabled scientists and doctors to utilize eugenic arguments in the rhetoric surrounding recent developments in bio-technology and bio-medicine (Kerr & Shakespeare, 2002; Goble, 2003).

Prenatal screening for and the abortion of unborn children deemed 'handicapped' is now practised in many countries across the world, including the UK. Similarly there is now widespread and growing support for mercy killing or 'assisted suicide' for people with 'degenerative illnesses' such as multiple sclerosis and motor neurone diseases (Mclean, 2007). All of this has significant implications for both disabled and non-disabled people as we move ever further into the twenty-first century.

Conclusion

Clearly the idea of the disabled individual is an ideological construction related to the core ideology of individualism and the peripheral ideologies of medicalization, able-bodied/minded normality and eugenics. Therefore the individual experience of disability is influenced to varying degrees by the discursive constructions and professional practices which have stemmed from these ideologies. This ideological construction of the individual within capitalism has produced considerable gains for the overwhelming majority of the general population and is clearly evident in the breaking down of traditional hierarchies and privileges and the establishment of legal frameworks with which to secure the civil, political and human rights of individuals.

Yet access to these frameworks is not available to everyone within and across both rich and poor nations. Consequently oppression and inequality are common features in all societies and, as we shall see later, are in some contexts increasing. Therefore, as Lukes pointed out several decades ago:

> if we are to take equality and liberty seriously, they must be transcended. And that this can only be achieved on the basis of a view of un-abstracted individuals in their concrete, social specificity, who in virtue of being persons all require to be treated and to live in a social order which treats them as possessing dignity, as capable of exercising and increasing their autonomy, of engaging in valid activities within a private space, and of developing their several potentialities. (Lukes, 1973, p. 153)

Before considering the implications of this view of un-abstracted individuals for disability policy, it is necessary to consider the disabled individual who is located within this ideological construction and that will be discussed in the following chapter.

5

Constructing Disabled Identities

Introduction

In previous chapters we argued that the impact of the unprecedented structural changes to the organization of work and the newly emergent ideology of individualism that accompanied industrial capitalism in the nineteenth century was primarily responsible for the social creation of 'disability' as an individual medical and social problem. This creation has remained dominant throughout the nineteenth and twentieth centuries despite some challenges by disabled people and their organizations, and remains with us today in both wealthy and poor societies.

The personal responses of disabled individuals to their impairments cannot be understood simply as a reaction to 'trauma' or 'tragedy', but have to be located within a contextual framework that takes account of both history and ideology. Consequently, a materialist understanding of the individual must centre upon two aspects of the ensemble of social relations of which the person is constituted: the performance of labour and the incorporation of ideology' (Leonard, 1984, p.180).

There is no doubt that the historical process has a significant influence on identity formation in general, for

> there is a considerable consensus, about the extent to which the process must be seen as a matter of a specifically historical entry into some specific historical figuration – an interweaving of personal and collective histories. In this double sense identity formation en masse is seen as a historically located historical sequence. (Abrams, 1982, p. 241)

This 'historically located historical sequence' implies that there is a cultural context to identity formation. Here culture 'consists of the values the members of a given group hold, the norms they follow, and the material goods they create' (Giddens, 1989, p. 31). Although values may be 'abstract ideals', 'norms' connote the rules and guidelines for social interaction. Therefore to become a member of a given social group or society, it is necessary to learn, or be socialized into, its cultural values and rules. Cultures therefore establish both the criteria for what is considered 'normal' and typical, and also what is viewed as 'abnormal', different and unacceptable (Barnes & Mercer, 2010, p.186).

As noted in the previous chapter, a materialist analysis emphasizes the role of culture in the production and consumption of capitalist values and norms in such areas as education, the law, the media, literature and art. So the cultural images stemming from them support the ideology of individualism upon which capitalism depends, presenting the disabled individual as more or less than human. Following Gramsci (1985), these institutions are the arenas which shape individual identities and have played key roles in producing disabled individuals as victims, villains or superheroes (Barnes, 1992; Hevey, 1992).

However, such cultural production has also seen the emergence and role of 'sub', 'counter', or 'oppositional' cultures as sources of resistance (Hall et al.,1980) to dominant capitalist imagery in culture generally and disability culture in particular. An exploration of the origins and development of this cultural opposition will be discussed in later chapters; here we limit our discussion to analyses of mainstream cultural representations of impairment and disability.

In this chapter we turn our attention to how these forces influence the formation of what is widely regarded as a conventional apolitical 'disabled identity'. We begin with an analysis of cultural representations of impairment and disability. This is followed by a discussion of the consequences of this for those with impairments and considered disabled. The discussion then turns to the relationship between the experience of disablism within other oppressed groups.

Before doing so, however, we need to reiterate that frequently materialist-inspired accounts are largely overshadowed by poststructuralist/modernist writings (Foucault, 1967, 1972; Derrida, 1990). While these analyses of 'changing linguistic-discursive practices' or 'ways of knowing' have added a different dimension to disability theory, the 'deconstruction' of particular discourses around impairment and disability has been generally inaccessible to a non-academic audience and also politically benign (see, for example, Corker & Shakespeare, 2002, Chapter 1).

Culture, Impairment and Disability

As indicated earlier, there is substantial evidence that social responses to impairments and disablement vary across time and place and different cultures respond to different impairments in different ways. Consequently it is fair to say that impairment is a human constant (Scheer & Groce, 1988, p. 23) and has existed in all known human societies since at least the Neanderthal period. There is also substantial evidence that people with impairments were to varying degrees included rather than excluded from the mainstream of community life in many societies, including western Europe prior to the dawn of industrial capitalism (Gleeson, 1999).

It is also evident that their exclusion as a consequence of the rise of capitalism had an important influence on 'popular' cultural contexts (Fielder, 1981; Oliver, 1990; Davis, 1995, 2006; Mitchell & Snyder, 1997; Oliver & Barnes, 1998). But this should not distract attention from the fact that there has been a discernable cultural bias against people with any form of perceived impairment or abnormality since at least the ancient world of Greece and Rome (Shearer, 1981; Thomas, 1982; Barnes, 1991, 1997; Hevey, 1992; Garland, 1995; Mitchell & Snyder, 1997; Stiker, 1999).

It is widely acknowledged that the foundations of western culture were laid by the ancient Greeks and Romans. Their achievements in philosophy, the arts and architecture have had a profound effect on the cultures of the entire western world. But the Greek and Roman economies were dependent upon slavery and military conquest. In these societies physical and intellectual fitness was a necessary prerequisite for inclusion and citizenship. There was little room for people with any form of flaw or imperfection.

The Greek obsession with bodily perfection, which can be traced back to 700–675 BC (Dutton, 1996), found expression in prescribed infanticide for children with perceived imperfections, in education, the gymnasium, and in competitive sports. Greek practice of infanticide is evident in the writings a Greek physician, Soranos, in the second century AD. The child

> should be perfect in all its parts, limbs and senses, and have passages that are not obstructed, including the ears, nose, throat urethra and anus. Its natural movements be neither slow nor feeble, its limbs bend and stretch, its size and shape should be appropriate, and it should respond to natural stimuli. (Cited in Garland, 1995, p. 14.)

These preoccupations were reflected in Greek philosophy and culture. The Greek gods and goddesses were perceived not as divine beings in anthropomorphic form but rather as 'idealised representations of perfected humanity' (Dutton, 1996, p. 25), an ideal that all Greeks sought to achieve. It is significant that there was only one physically flawed God, Hephaestes, the son of Zeus and Hera. Indeed, Zeus practises a sort of infanticide by banishing his son from heaven. Later Aphrodite, the goddess of love, takes pity on Hephaestes and marries him. Yet the marriage does not last as she takes an able-bodied lover, Ares, because her husband is a 'cripple' (Graves, 1960).

Following their conquest of Greece, the Romans absorbed and passed on the Greek legacy to the rest of the known world as their empire expanded. Even so the Greeks and the Romans developed various 'scientific' medical treatments, but these were only available to the rich and powerful. Consequently impairment was common amongst the lower classes. But survival for those in poverty and without familial or other supports was almost certainly short-lived, as 'there were very few poor in the ancient world; for the simple reason that destitution was the first step on a fast track to death' (Beard, 2008, p.105).

Although they were opposed to infanticide, these disabling characteristics are clearly evident in Judeo-Christian religions. The Jewish culture of the ancient world viewed impairment as ungodly and the consequences of wrongdoing. Leviticus chronicles a catalogue of bodily imperfections that preclude the bearer from religious practices and events. The Old and New Testaments are replete with references to impairment as the consequences of sin. Here both perceived impairments and sin, however they are defined and in whatever form they take, represent nothing less than a threat to the material and social well being of Judeo-Christian communities (Barnes, 1997).

Following the fall of Rome in the fifth century AD the Christian Church became a formidable force in English and European culture. Besides offering forgiveness and a democratic afterlife in a frequently hostile world where for many life could be 'solitary, poor, nasty, brutish and short' (Hobbes, 1660, unpaged), the Christian Church asserted and retained its authority by propagating and perpetuating fear – fear of the Devil and of his influence. The biblical link between impairment, impurity and sin was central to this process. St Augustine, the man credited with bringing Christianity to mainland Britain at the end of the sixth century AD, claimed that impairment was 'a punishment for the fall of Adam and other sins' (Ryan & Thomas, 1987, p. 87).

For centuries afterwards disabled people were seen as providing living proof of Satan's existence and of his power over humans. Thus, visibly impaired infants were seen as 'changelings' – the Devil's substitutes for human children. The *Malleus Maleficarum* of 1487 declared that such children were the product of the mother's involvement with sorcery and witchcraft. The religious leader and scholar credited with the formation of the Protestant Reformation, Martin Luther (1485–1546) proclaimed he saw the Devil in disabled children and recommended killing them (Ryan & Thomas, 1987, p. 88).

These beliefs were also reflected in medieval literature and art. Probably the most famous example is Shakespeare's Richard III. Although Richard had no physical impairments (Rieser & Mason, 1990), Shakespeare portrays him as twisted in both body and mind. People with impairments were also primary targets for ridicule during the Middle Ages (Thomas, K., 1977; Ryan & Thomas, 1987) in common with foreigners, women and the clergy. Images and practices such as these not only shaped culture at the time but have had a pervasive influence ever since.

Disabling Imagery in Recent History

These myths and prejudices were given additional scientific and ideological legitimacy by the material and social forces that shaped European cultures in the eighteenth and nineteenth centuries. The unprecedented upsurge of 'sentimentality' and voyeuristic preoccupation with assumed biological and social deviance amongst the wealthy and literate classes during the Victorian years led to the production of a plethora of novels, short stories, journal and newspaper articles which included stereotypical portrayals of people with impairments. According to one commentator:

> Not until the rise of sentimentalism and the obsession with the excluded and the marginal, which climaxes in the reign of Victoria, did the blind, the deaf and the halt become major characters in large numbers of books written by authors and intended for readers who, thinking of themselves as non-handicapped, are able to regard the handicapped as essentially alien, absolute others. In such a context, fellow human beings with drastically impaired perception, manipulation and ambulation tend, of course, to be stereotyped, either negatively or positively; but in any case rendered as something more or less than human. (Fielder, 1981, pp. 5–6)

These ranged from either overtly negative to superhuman portrayals but always something less or more than simply human.

Subsequently 'clichéd, stereotyped and archetypical' representations of impairment have proliferated throughout the media over the last two centuries. This has been dominated by 'imagery where disability is understood to be the impairment almost devoid of political significance of social construction. Impairment imagery abounds on all channels and in all media forms: television, film, radio and in print. If anything, impairment imagery is on the increase' (Darke, 2004, p.100).

Undoubtedly the most extreme form of such imagery was that produced by advocates of 'mercy killing' for people with impairments in the first half of the twentieth century. For instance, between 1915 and 1918 Dr Harry Haiselden, a Chicago surgeon, publicized his efforts to eliminate those he considered 'unfit'. He displayed dying infants he defined as 'defective' to journalists and wrote a book-length series about them for the Hearst newspapers. His campaign was front-page news for several weeks. He also wrote and starred in a film that fictionalized an account of his cases entitled The Black Stork. In the debates that followed, a majority of those quoted in the press supported Haiselden's views and actions (Pernick, 1997, p. 89).

As noted in the previous chapter, the Nazi media were enthusiastic exponents of eugenic propaganda. One notable example is the film *I Accuse*, directed by Wolfgang Liebeneiner, which tells the story of how two doctors love a woman. She marries one but falls ill after contracting multiple sclerosis. She then asks her husband to put her out of her misery by killing her. He refuses so she appeals to her former lover who sympathizes with her request and kills her. A trial follows but the case is dismissed on compassionate grounds (Burleigh, 1994, p. 210). The film was immensely popular at the time and was eventually seen by more than 15 million people across Europe.

During the twentieth century, whether in the novel, newspaper stories or television and films, disabled people continued to be portrayed as more than or less than human, rarely as ordinary people doing ordinary things. Without a full analysis of images of disability it is not possible to do other than present examples of these images. Sir Clifford, in *Lady Chatterley's Lover*, is an obvious example of the presentation of disabled people as less than human. The story of Sir Douglas Bader as portrayed in the film *Reach for the Sky* is an example of a disabled person being portrayed as more than human. These portrayals see disabled people either as pathetic victims of some appalling tragedy or as superheroes struggling to overcome a tremendous burden.

The image of disabled people as more than human is not always positive either, for as an analysis of children's fiction has shown:

> the disabled adult has often been portrayed as an embittered and menacing character who, like Long John Silver, seeks to manipulate children for his own ends, or as a man bearing a grudge against society, who uses his distorted body or artificial limbs in a sinister and aggressive fashion, e.g. Captain Hook. (Quicke, 1985, p.122)

Regrettably these images continue to permeate children's literature and are commonly available to pupils in English primary schools (Beckett et al., 2010). Even so it may be argued that the turn of the twenty-first century has witnessed something of a sea change in cultural representations of people with impairments.

Resisting Disabling Imagery

In recent years there has been a growing recognition of the fact that these dominant cultural images not only violate the actual experience of disability, but are also positively unhelpful in providing role models for disabled people and in breaking down prejudice amongst the rest of the population. Yet there is still a long way to go. At present, the best that can be said is that dominant images are being challenged but they are far from being replaced by more authentic ones.

The disability arts movement is increasingly becoming the focus of the mounting of these challenges but it has, itself, had to struggle to free itself from the domination of able-bodied professionals who tended to stress arts as therapy (Lord, 1981) rather than arts as cultural imagery. That, too, is changing, as disabled people struggle to take control over their own lives,

One of the first people to focus on the overtly negative coverage of impairment in the media was the disabled writer Battye. In his 1966 analysis of D. H. Lawrence's novel *Lady Chatterley's Lover* he shows how Lawrence perpetuates the age-old myth that impairment equals impotency. Subsequently, as disabled people and others became more active and more vocal, a number of studies looked at stereotypical representations of people with impairments in the media including literature, television, film, newspapers and the advertising industry.

Many of these studies called for the development of more positive depictions of disabled people (Biklen & Bogdana, 1977; Gartner & Joe, 1987; Karpf, 1988; Rieser & Mason, 1990; Barnes, 1992; Cumberbatch & Negrine, 1992; Hevey, 1992; Norden, 1994). This triggered something of a media shift in emphasis in the 1980s and 1990s toward a more socio-political response to disability in the UK and elsewhere. Several minority programmes began to appear on television and the radio. British examples include the British Broadcasting Corporation's *One in Four*, ITV's *Link*, Channel 4's *Same Difference* and BBC Radio 4's *Does He Take Sugar?* (Barnes, 1992; Sweeney & Riddell, 2003).

Over recent years, however, these programmes have largely disappeared and given way to the mainstreaming or 'normalizing' of the more media-friendly aspects of impairment and health-related issues into regular programming, more in keeping with traditional individualistic medical approaches. The overall result of this is that politicized, or rather politically aware, programmes have tended to disappear and it is 'impairment almost devoid of political significance or social construction' (Darke, 2004, p.100) that now finds its way into mainstream programming.

Several studies have highlighted the continued prevalence of negative representations of impairment in both fictional and factual broadcasting and the communications media (Riddell & Watson, 2003; Cumberbatch & Gauntlett, 2006; Chivers & Markotic, 2010) alongside these de-politicized images of impairment. For example, it is no longer uncommon to see impaired individuals appearing on chat shows, quiz programmes, dramas and soap operas. Thus there have been a few attempts, particularly by some in the mass media, to break down some of these images through the development of specialist programmes, drama and documentaries. One notable example was *Cast Offs*, a series shown by Britain's Channel 4 in 2009 with the aim of challenging 'tedious old stereotypes' by featuring all disabled people playing disabled characters. A spoof survival show set on a British island portraying the complex relationships between disabled people with different impairments over six hour-long episodes. Moreover, its 'mockumentary' style allowed the cast to ridicule reality TV formats, conventional stereotypes of disabled people and non-disabled people. But whilst the show challenged in many ways conventional stereotypical assumptions about the experience of people with sensory and physical impairments, it may be criticized for its neglect of issues relating to cognitive impairments, learning difficulties and 'mental health', and the link between disability, ethnicity and race, as 'the central characters were all white'. Nonetheless it represents a major step forward as it puts 'disabled people centre stage as actors and writers as creators and subjects of culture' (Wilde, 2009, unpaged).

The advent of popular 'reality TV' shows such as *Big Brother*, *Beyond Boundaries*, and *Britain's Missing Top Model* may also be viewed as a significant advance in media representations of disability as they often include individuals with impairments. For instance, 'The visibility of people with disabilities in entertainment media helps subtly educate diverse audiences about the disability experience in America' (Holler, 2009, unpaged). But they don't tell us much about the reality of living with impairment in a disabling society. These attempts to normalize what might be regarded as media-friendly impairments and mainstream particular impairment-related issues only serve to reinforce negative imagery.

Further, by presenting the acceptable face of impairment rather than the reality of disablement, such programming, whatever its intentions, can only prove divisive amongst the disabled population and so undermine and obscure the ongoing struggle for meaningful change (Barnes, 1992; Darke, 2004). As we have already argued, any notion of 'normality' is both ideologically and culturally contentious. Moreover the increasing media representation of disabled people represents:

> a shifting focus of governance, one which aims to hold individuals more accountable by making them increasingly attentive to their own behaviour. Programmes directing public gaze at people with impairments are part of a myriad of new formats depicting the irregularities and incivilities of everyday life, enabling us to pass judgement on our everyday lives ... Seeing squabbling disabled people on reality TV programmes such as *Beyond Boundaries* and *Britain's Missing Top Model* seems less to do with valuing diversity than with a combination of sentimentality with what Richard Hoggart has called 'Ooh-ah' appeal, 'a mixture of fear, cruelty and collective self-righteouness'. (Cameron, 2010, unpaged).

Indeed, as the importance of the media has escalated over the last century, both nationally and internationally, so too have arguments about its role in shaping public attitudes. Until recently the prevalent view was that media messages have a potent if not direct influence on audiences. This is reflected in much of the literature on disability representation cited above. Conversely it is claimed that people are not cultural dupes, but rather interpret media messages according to their needs and interests (McQuail, 1971). Consequently assertions that media messages are always able to generate consent tend to be sidestepped with the recognition that the media may be read in different ways, so that audiences sometimes revise or reject these messages (Hall et al., 1980, 1997).

These debates are reflected in analyses of audience responses to media representations of impairment and disablement. For example, a study sponsored by the BBC found a 'high degree of acceptance of the principles for increased inclusion, and positive attitudes towards increased representation of disabled people on television in a wider variety of roles' (Sancho, 2003, p. 8).

But some opposition to disabled people's involvement came from those who felt uncomfortable when watching individuals with an impairment. This point was reiterated by media personnel who suggested that the continued marginal-ization of disabled people on television is due to a combination of commercial constraints, the structure of the industry and audience prejudices, more so than for women or minority ethnic groups. In other words the under-representation of disabled people in the media is more a reflection of what the public wants rather than a problem of disabling culture and disablist institutions and practices.

We should point out, however, that material factors have a pivotal role in construction of disabling imagery and it is to this that we now turn.

Poverty, Inequality and Identity

Although historically all social inequality has been justified on assumptions of biological inferiority, for one disabled sociologist (Abberley, 1987) the crucial difference between the oppression experienced by disabled people and that of other oppressed groups, such as women, minority ethnic communities and lesbians and gay men, in late capitalist society is the presence of impairment. Therefore analysis of the acquisition of a disabled identity must begin with an exploration of the social origins of impairment.

Of course the connection between impairment and inequality are well estab-lished within the social sciences. As far back as the middle of the nineteenth century Engels (1969) provided a detailed account of the social creation of 'deformities and mutilations' amongst the working class arising from the 'injurious working practices' that accompanied industrial capitalism, based on official government reports and personal experience. Subsequent studies have confirmed this and although long-term illnesses and impairments are evident in all social classes and groups there is a general consensus that particular sections of the population are far more vulnerable than others (Townsend, 1979; Bartley, 2004).

There is, for example, a well established link between poverty, ill health and impairment. However it is defined there is growing evidence that people with impairments are generally 'the poorest of the poor' in rich and poor countries alike (Coleridge, 1993; Charlton, 1998; Stone, 1999; Hurst & Albert, 2006; Yeo, 2006). Successive studies have shown that poor health, impairment and mortality rates are significantly higher amongst those at the foot of the social hierarchy in all societies (Bartley, 2004)

In the UK, for instance, a government-sponsored study produced in 2010 found that during a period of increased spending on the National Health Service (NHS) and rising prosperity generally: 'Not only is life expectancy linked to social standing, but so is the time spent in good health: the average difference in "disability-free life expectancy" is now 17 years between those at the top and those at the bottom of the economic ladder' (Ramesh, 2010, p.1).

The incidence of impairment is also higher among other socially disadvantaged groups such as women and members of minority ethnic communities. For example, women and members of minority ethnic communities are far more likely to be diagnosed as 'mentally ill' than the rest of the population (Barnes & Mercer, 2010). Similarly poverty is the main cause of chronic diseases and long term impairments in poor and developing countries (WHO, 2001b; 2011). Overall international data suggest that around one-half of the world's impairment is linked directly to poverty (DFID, 2000, 2011).

In both wealthy and poor countries poverty is the inevitable outcome of skewed economic development. Even so, whilst the disparity between rich and poor people has increased over recent years in wealthy states such as the UK and USA, it is even more pronounced at the international level. It has been estimated that in 1820 the gap between the world's richest and poorest nations was approximately three to one. By 1992 it had risen to a staggering seventy-two to one (Giddens, 2001, p. 70).

Currently over a billion people are forced to exist on less than one US dollar a day (UNDP, 2005). But poverty is not the only cause of impairment. Other social and preventable causes across all societies include poor sanitation, dangerous cultural and working practices, environmental pollution, violence and war, and inappropriate and/or inadequate medical treatments and support.

The situation is especially acute in developing countries where over three-quarters of the world's people considered 'disabled' now live (DFID, 2000; WHO, 2001b; Swain, 2004). Disabled women and children are particularly vulnerable (Miles, 1995). In India, for example, disabled women and girls experience particularly high levels of poverty, leading to chronic malnutrition and difficulty in resisting debilitating sickness; and disabled girls in many countries have fewer opportunities than disabled boys to access basic medical services, rehabilitation and education (Ghai, 2001). This leads to the unavoidable conclusion that 'as far as the majority of the world's disabled people are concerned, impairment is very clearly, primarily the consequence of social and political factors, not an unavoidable "fact of nature"' (Abberley, 1987, p. 11).

There is little doubt that within the context of an increasingly globalized world in which western cultures are pre-eminent, to have an impairment, whether present at birth or acquired in later life, is considered abnormal and something to be avoided at all costs. Men and women with any hint of congenital impairment are encouraged to take steps to avoid having a child with a similar condition. Pregnant women at risk of giving birth to a 'handicapped fetus', the medical euphemism for an unborn disabled child (Oliver & Barnes, 1998, p. 66), are often encouraged to have abortions (Ettorre, 2000; Rogers, 2006). As indicated above, living with impairment is generally associated with poverty, social isolation and stigmatization (Goffman, 1968) and 'second class citizenship' (Sieglar & Osmond, 1974).

This is the material base for disabled identity formation. To be born with an impairment is to be assigned a negative identity at the point of detection and diagnosis. To become 'disabled' is to be consigned to membership of a different tribe or species (Murphy, 1987). Both involve a social learning process in which the nuances and meanings of this identity have to be internalized and addressed.

Disabling Culture and Identity Formation

We learn the social norms, cultural expectations and shared standards of behaviour of society through the process of socialization. Through interaction with significant and generalized others we learn the roles we are expected to play in society. Our perceptions of ourselves are therefore derived through the continuous process of interaction with other people and societal institutions. Our sense of identity is constructed on the basis of other people's definitions of and responses to us, but it is also dependent upon the cultural and material context in which this construction takes place.

As noted in Chapter 2, Goffman (1968) provided an early account of how this identity construction takes place in social interaction. Whilst he may be criticized for his failure to locate social interactions within a material and cultural context, his work does provide valuable insights into the complexity of the psychological consequences of the complexity of disablement. He notes, for example, that congenital impairments have different implications for the process of identity formation from those acquired later during the life course. The timing of this can be very important as it can influence an individual's ability to respond to their ascribed or acquired status as a 'disabled person' (Oliver & Barnes, 1998, p. 67; see also Priestley, 2003).

People who are born with an impairment learn the standards against which they are judged and society's responses to their devalued and disadvantaged status throughout their lives. Growing up with an impairment can often be an isolating and lonely experience. In households and communities where there are few other people with impairments, children's perceptions of themselves are shaped by their treatment by others they interact with, all of whose perceptions are shaped by the things we have discussed in this chapter.

Consequently, unlike other groups such as women and members of minority ethnic communities, for instance, the overwhelming majority of disabled children do not have strong supportive role models with which to identify. A number of factors including the actions of well-meaning but often ill-informed parents, protracted professional interventions, sometimes lengthy periods in hospital, segregated schools and colleges, and a largely inaccessible built environment combine to ensure that many children with impairments grow up accepting the various economic and social deprivations that accompany a conventional 'disabled identity' (Barnes, 1990; Oliver & Barnes, 1998, p. 67).

This often results in an extreme form of self-depreciation or 'internalized oppression', the consequences of which are very difficult to overcome. Internal oppression is similar to what Scambler (1989, 2004) refers to as 'felt stigma', or what Thomas (1999, p. 46) defines as the 'psycho emotional dimensions of disablism'. This, she attests, is distinct from 'impairment effects', that is, the functional limitations imposed by impairments such as limited vision or inability to walk. Mason, a disabled mother and activist, summarizes the situation well:

> Once oppression has been internalised, little force is needed to keep us submissive. We harbour inside ourselves the pain and the memories, the fears and the confusion, the negative and the low expectations, turning them into weapons with which to injure ourselves every day of our lives. (Mason, 1990, p. 27)

People with acquired impairments obviously have different experiences from those with congenital ones. 'People who acquire impairment later in life have already been immersed in the personal tragedy viewpoint and it is not therefore surprising that many of these individuals find it difficult to respond in any other way' (Oliver, 2004, p. 21).

Much of the professional literature, at least until the advent of disability studies, suggests that such people are said to 'grieve' and 'mourn' for their lost abilities (for a critique of this view, see Sapey, 2004; Oliver and Sapey, 2006). This is often caused by the realization that becoming disabled usually means the exclusion from previously taken-for-granted every day activities, and 'in many ways it encapsulates the perspective of all disabled people struggling to retain a sense of self-worth in a culture increasingly geared to the myth of non-disabled normality' (Oliver & Barnes, 1998, p. 68).

Inevitably, then, many disabled people identify with the non-disabled world and deny, disregard or minimize the reality of their impairment during the course of their daily lives. This may involve various strategies such as passing, covering, withdrawal, or seeking acceptance by 'cheerfully' making the best of things (Goffman, 1968). Notwithstanding that these and other strategies demonstrate the human capacity for 'adaptation' (Parsons, 1951), they each contain an element of denial and failure, and an acceptance of external disempowering cultural environments. Further, they each represent a compromise solution which is 'ultimately fragile' and brings with it considerable risks in terms of 'psychological stability and social wellbeing' (Oliver & Barnes, 1998, p. 69).

In an increasingly disabling world the adoption of a conventional disabled identity is often the only option available to many disabled people. This is especially so for those at the foot of the class structure and already subject to multiple deprivations. Indeed, in the absence of other socially sanctioned activities, the 'professional cripple role' enables individuals with impairments to interact with professionals and offers the promise of 'sympathy and concern' from non-disabled peers. In short, the combination of necessity, acceptance and assimilation 'take precedence over self realisation' (Oliver & Barnes, 1998, p. 69).

Taken together, then, these strategies are the inevitable outcome of what Marx termed false consciousness and alienation. Here, false consciousness refers to explanations of social problems grounded in the assumed shortcomings of individuals rather than the flaws in society. Alienation denotes the feelings of self-estrangement, social isolation and powerlessness that disabled people encounter as a result of their systematic exclusion from the mainstream of economic and social activity in industrial and post-industrial capitalist societies.

Most people with impairments and labelled 'disabled' come to believe in one way or another that they are somehow 'abnormal' and less capable than non-disabled peers. Furthermore, false consciousness and alienation obscure the real sources of disabled people's oppression. Hence

> They cannot recognise that their self perceived pitiful lives are simply a perverse mirroring of a pitiful world order. In this regard people with disabilities have much in common with others who have also internalised their own oppression. (Charlton, 1998, p. 26)

With this in mind, in the final section we will explore recent debates about divisions and hierarchies within the disabled population and the links between the experience of disablism and other forms of social oppression within disabling capitalism. Before we do, however, we would wish to re-iterate the point that we regard the acquisition of disabled identities as being largely but not solely externally imposed, as there are clearly psychological dimensions to impairment, however it is acquired.

Social Divisions and Identity

The assumed homogeneity of disabled people's experiences has come under increasing scrutiny in recent years (Vernon & Swain, 2002). This has led to calls for accounts that incorporate the complexity of divisions and hierarchies within the disabled population. These include impairment-specific groups such as people labelled with 'learning difficulties', 'mental health' systems users and survivors, and disabled women, disabled members of minority ethnic communities, disabled lesbians, gay men, transsexuals, and disabled older people.

Part of the reason for this assumed homogeneity has been the success of the social model. Both supporters and critics often commonly associate the social model with the experiences of people with physical impairments, but we would argue strongly that it is applicable to all sections of the disabled population. As we have already indicated, experiences of disablement are generated by a combination of material and cultural forces. Impairment-specific labels are generally imposed rather than chosen. They are historically, culturally and situationally variable and have little value beyond impairment-related needs and support. They are also socially and politically divisive.

For instance, people who are born deaf have consistently argued that they are not disabled but a cultural minority due to their use of sign rather than spoken language. Yet throughout recorded history deaf people have encountered oppression similar to that of other sections of the disabled population and as a consequence been coerced into denying or making invisible their deafness (Harris, 1997). Moreover, although sign language is now officially recognized as a minority language in many countries including the UK (*Disabled World*, undated) deaf people may still experience institutional discrimination due to the fact that in most societies few people use it.

Whilst deafness may not be considered an impairment by those who are born deaf and identify with a separatist 'deaf culture', this is not generally the view of the majority of people with acquired hearing loss (Corker, 1998). Similarly, Sayce (2000) and Beresford (2002) both maintain that although the social model is applicable for mental health systems users and survivors, tensions arise due to the fact that many people diagnosed as 'mentally ill' would not consider their 'emotional distress' an 'impairment'. Few would dispute, however, that emotional distress is generally triggered by material and social forces that can only be addressed by political rather than medical interventions. Similar arguments are applicable to people labelled with 'learning difficulties', who may not consider themselves disabled in the conventional sense, but experience considerable discrimination and prejudice on the basis of assumed intellectual inferiority (Ryan &Thomas, 1987; Walmsley, 1997; Goodley, 2000, 2001).

But divisions along impairment-specific lines are difficult to sustain as they overlap with other social divisions like gender, ethnicity, age and class, or indeed any combination of contributing factors. Even so some of the earliest attempts to address the experience of impairment and disablement were developed by disabled women. Many years ago Campling (1979, 1981) gave voice to disabled women, enabling them to draw attention to the problems faced in such key areas as personal relationships, sexuality, motherhood, education, employment, and media stereotypes. Another early study argued that women with impairments are 'doubly oppressed' because they are excluded from the 'male' productive role and the 'female' nurturing one (Fine & Asch, 1988, p. 13).

Empirical evidence from America and Britain confirms the extent of social exclusion encountered by disabled women in the labour market (Fine & Asch, 1988; Lonsdale, 1990). Women with impairments are often discouraged from becoming mothers on various grounds such as perceived threats to their own health, passing on an impairment to their children, or their capacity to be a 'good mother' (Finger, 1991; Thomas, 1997, 1999; Wates & Jade, 1999). Thus disabled women experience disadvantages that set them apart from both disabled men and non-disabled women – economically, socially and psychologically. Therefore they are either ignored or portrayed as passive victims in feminist analyses (Fine & Asch, 1988; Morris, 1991; Begum, 1992).

Furthermore, there has been a tendency in recent disabled women's writings to eschew the 'malestream' focus on environmental and social barriers as they pay scant attention to the everyday realities of the personal experience of impairment and its consequences (Morris, 1991; French, 1993; Crow, 1996; Fawcett, 2000). But as Sheldon (1999, 2004) has pointed out, whilst experience is important, the feminist maxim of 'the personal is political' is limited and can be counter-productive as an analytical tool with which to confront social injustice.

For Sheldon the slogan 'the personal is political'

> has become a means of encouraging women to think that the experience of discrimination, exploitation or oppression automatically corresponds with an understanding of the ideological and institutional apparatus shaping one's social status ... When women internalised the idea that describing their own woe was synonymous with developing a political consciousness, the progress of the feminist movement was stalled. (hooks, 1984, pp. 24–5, cited in Sheldon, 2004, pp. 72–3)

In common with the views of Finkelstein (1996, 2002), she argues that those who demand a bigger place for including the personal experience of both impairment and disability are hampering the further development of the disabled people's movement and the struggle for meaningful equality.

Similarly the various deprivations encountered by people with impairments from minority ethnic communities point to major barriers at all levels of society. Two studies of the families of Asian people with 'learning difficulties' (ADAPT, 1993; Azmi et al., 1996), for example, provide evidence of high levels of poverty with 69 per cent of families having no full-time wage earner, and half of the families being on income support. There is also a lack of understanding among the general population of the 'life style, social customs and religious practices of people from ethnic minority groups' (French & Vernon, 1997, p. 62).

Additionally there is evidence to suggest that discrimination within services is endemic but denied and rationalized with reference to generalized assumptions that families from minority ethnic communities 'look after their own' (Baxter, 1995; Vernon & Swain, 2002). Moreover,

> the fact that major surveys of the experience of disability persist in hardly mentioning the experience of black disabled people should not deter us from appreciating the messages that emerge from existing work. Racism, sexism and disablism intermingle to amplify the need for supportive social care. However, these same factors sometimes mean that black disabled people and their carers get a less than adequate service. (Butt & Mizra, 1996, p. 94)

For the Confederation of Indian Organisations (1987), therefore, a 'black disabled identity' can only be understood within the context of the deeply embedded social exclusion of black people that is 'institutional racism'. The extent of this oppression means that 'Black' disabled people form 'a discrete minority within a minority' and often face exclusion and marginalisation even within disabled communities and the disability movement (Hill, 1994, p. 74). Indeed, much research on the interaction of different social divisions and processes suggests a picture of 'double' or 'multiple' oppression (Baxter et al., 1990).

Yet Stuart (1993) argues that 'being a black disabled person is not a double' experience but a single one grounded in British racism'. He contends that

> racism is not so much located in 'colour' but widened to cultural and religious

differences so that 'black' disabled people are distanced from both antiracists and the disabled people's movement. This is evident in the absence of 'black' people and members of minority ethnic groups in disabled people's organisations, and suggests the need to build a distinct and separate black disabled identity. (Stuart, 1993, p. 94)

But black disabled people are also marginalized within the black community because of their exclusion from employment and leisure activities, and assumed inability to attain accepted roles within black communities (Vernon & Swain, 2002). Therefore we would suggest that divisions along impairment, gender, age and/or sexual orientation lines within the 'black' disabled population will engender further 'unique' forms of simultaneous oppression. For Begum (1994) this results in complex survival strategies and alliances between black disabled people and other oppressed groups. Specific aspects will be prioritized according to the context. Sometimes black disabled people form alliances with other disabled people to challenge disability, while on other occasions they may unite with other black people to fight racism. Hence

the very nature of simultaneous oppression means that as black disabled men and women, and black disabled lesbians and gay men we cannot identify a single source of oppression to reflect the reality of our lives ... It is not possible to simply prioritise one aspect of our oppression to the exclusion of others. (Begum, 1994, p. 35)

Yet the notion of 'multiple oppression' can be misleading because it separates the many different dimensions to inequality, as if these can be compartmentalized in everyday experience, and then added together in an overall balance sheet.

Comparable analyses of the experiences of the interaction of other social divisions such as impairment and age, childhood, gay or lesbian, transsexual and working-class, all show that there are parallels similar to those discussed above. For instance, research documenting the experiences and views of disabled lesbians and bisexual women indicate that they felt marginalized by mainstream lesbian and gay groups: 'many disabled lesbian and bisexual women have experienced alienation rather than nurturing and support from the lesbian and gay community' (Gillespie-Sells, Hill & Robbins, 1998, p. 57).

It is important to remember that the experience of oppression, however complex and whatever forms it takes, is almost always influenced by social class. As Hill-Collins (1990) points out in her discussion of 'privilege and penalty', social class is an important determinant of many critical factors. Consequently as class privilege increases, the impact of disablism, racism, sexism, heterosexism and ageism may decrease. The situation will almost certainly be reversed for those at the foot of the class structure. Thus, although the potential for discrimination is greatly increased for people with multiple identities, because the ideologies of oppression do not operate independently of one another, their effects cannot always be assumed to be experienced simultaneously (Vernon & Swain, 2002).

The focus on the interrelationship or 'intersectionality' (Soder, 2009) of different (simultaneous) lines of oppression exposes the internal fault lines but still leaves open how exclusionary processes operate across social contexts. As Fawcett (2000) argues, a middle-class, white disabled man challenging a restaurant's lack of accessibility may appear very powerful to a black, non-disabled waitress. Conversely, the same waitress may demand that a white man with learning difficulties leaves the restaurant because his table manners are upsetting non-disabled customers. 'The challenge then becomes to recognise and challenge oppression, whilst fully acknowledging complexity and inter-relational elements' (Fawcett, 2000, p. 53).

What is clearly evident is that oppression within capitalist societies creates, sustains and exacerbates social divisions and hierarchies within and across communities and in so doing casts one group against another. Therefore it is inevitable that

> the politics of disablement is about far more than disabled people, it is about challenging oppression in all its forms … Like racism, sexism, heterosexism and all other forms of social oppression, it is a human creation. It is impossible, therefore, to confront one type of oppression without confronting them all and, of course, the cultural values that created and sustain them. (Barnes, 1996, p. ix)

And that

> Political economy is crucial in constructing a theory of disability oppression because poverty and powerlessness are cornerstones of the dependency people with disabilities experience. (Charlton, 1998, p. 23)

Conclusion

In this chapter we have argued that the process of identity formation in respect of people with impairments cannot be properly understood without reference to the history of human development and its influence on cultural representations of impairment and disability. This has resulted in the portrayal of people designated as 'disabled' as either 'less than or more than human' (Oliver, 1990) and in one way or another, a threat to the wellbeing of both individuals and society. To varying degrees and in various forms these representations continue to be reproduced in all social institutions within and across all capitalist societies.

The end result is that at the general level impairment and disability are still perceived as a personal tragedy and something to be avoided at all costs. This has important negative implications for anyone coming to terms with the ascription of a 'disabled' identity which are exacerbated by the experience of overlapping membership of other socially devalued groups. But whilst recognition of the significance of multiple identities is important, it must not obscure or distract attention away from a critical analysis of the material and cultural forces that generate and sustain the inequality and dependence encountered by people with impairments whatever the nature of their condition, gender, social background or sexual orientation.

Nor indeed must it obscure or distract attention from the growing resistance and challenges to these forces that have emerged over the last couple of decades by disabled people, their organizations and allies. These will be returned to later. Before then we need to consider the ways in which these forces and experiences have contributed to the social construction of the 'problem of disability' in general and the social construction of dependence in particular, with which we deal in the following chapter.

6

Creating the Disability Problem

Introduction

So far we have suggested that the ideological construction of the concept of disability has been determined by the core ideology of capitalism – individualism – and peripheral ideologies associated with medicalization. Underpinned by personal tragedy theory, these ideas have generated and perpetuated a particular view of the 'disabled' individual. But this is only part of the story, as the category 'disability' has also been presented as a particular kind of social problem. Hence

> We contend that disability definitions are not rationally determined but socially constructed. Despite the objective reality, what becomes a disability is determined by the social meanings individuals attach to particular physical and mental impairments. Certain disabilities become defined as social problems through the successful efforts of powerful groups to market their own self interests. Consequently the so-called 'objective' criteria of disability reflects the biases, self-interests, and moral evaluations of those in a position to influence policy. (Albrecht and Levy, 1981, p.14)

In this chapter we turn our attention to the ways in which economic, political and social forces are mediated through social policy and so create dependency and the disablement of people with impairments. We will deal with what we call social constructionist and social creationist accounts of disablement and argue that it is the latter which provides the most convincing and useful arguments.

We also look at the ways in which dependency is created by economic and social policies and professional ideologies and practices, as well as the responses of disabled people to all this.

119

Defining the Disability Problem

The process of definition is not reliant solely on individual meanings or the activities of powerful groups and vested interests, for the category disability is itself produced in part by policy responses to it. Thus, to take an extreme position,

> Fundamentally, disability is defined by public policy. In other words, disability is whatever policy says it is. This observation embodies an authoritative recognition that a disability implies a problem or a disadvantage that requires compensatory or ameliorative action. The concept does not seek to specify whether the problem is located in the individual or in the environment. Nor does it attempt to identify the rationale for measures that are taken in reaction to the perceived disadvantage. Nonetheless, such policies represent an official belief that a disability constitutes a disadvantageous circumstance that obliges a public or a private agency to offer some type of response. (Hahn, 1985, p. 294)

While we would not deny that policy definitions play an important role in the defining of disability, it is clear that these definitions are themselves shaped by other things. The core and peripheral ideologies discussed earlier have influenced these definitions to the point where disability has become a problem of personal disadvantage to be remedied through the development of appropriate social policies (Borsay, 1986, 2005; Oliver, 1986,1990; Barnes, 1991; Finkelstein, 1991; Albrecht 1992; Oliver & Barnes, 1998; Drake, 1999).

Before the mid-twentieth century people with impairments were labelled according to their impairment – examples include 'the blind', 'the deaf', 'the insane', 'defectives' and 'epileptics' – and from the eighteenth century onwards they were increasingly hidden from public view. State policies such as the 1834 Poor Law, for instance, were introduced specifically to remove such people along with other 'undesirables' from the mainstream of community life into various forms of 'institutional care'. As we noted earlier, such policies gathered considerable momentum in the 1890s and the first half of the last century due to the influence of eugenics in policy circles across much of the industrialized world.

However, following the Second World War, the coming of the welfare state and political activism amongst disabled people and their allies in the 1960s and 1970s, many western countries began to introduce measures specifically designed for people viewed as 'disabled'. Early examples include the UK's 1970 Chronically Sick and Disabled Persons Act and the American Rehabilitation Act of 1973 which for the first time (in Section 504) provided limited protection for disabled people against discrimination in federally funded programmes.

Since the 1990s, of course, there has been a huge expansion of such measures aimed at the disability problem specifically including various anti-discrimination and human rights laws at both the national and international levels. But whilst there have been some improvements in the quality of life for some sections of the now specifically identified disabled population, disablism and social exclusion are still common experiences for the overwhelming majority of people with impairments in rich and poor countries alike (Clements & Read, 2003; Albert, 2006; Katsui, 2006; Miller, Gillinson & Huber, 2006; Sheldon, 2005; Barnes & Sheldon, 2010).

Hence given that social policy is generally defined as 'government interventions that are designed to effect individual behaviour or command over resources, or are designed to influence the economic system so as to shape society in some way (Drake, 1999, p. 22), there is a need to identify the hidden assumptions and ideologies that lie behind these initiatives in order to explain why their impact has been only marginally effective.

Disabling Social Policies

Part of the problem, we would suggest, is that the negative assumptions and ideologies surrounding impairment are so deeply embedded within social consciousness that they have become naturalized as social 'facts'. Thus 'everyone knows that disability is a personal tragedy for individuals so "afflicted"; hence ideology becomes common sense' (Oliver, 1990, p. 80). And this common-sense view is reinforced both by 'aesthetic' and 'existential' anxiety:

> …widespread aversion toward disabled individuals may be the product of both an 'aesthetic' anxiety, which narcissistically rejects marked deviations from 'normal' physical appearances, and of an 'existential' anxiety, which may find an implicit or projected danger of dehabilitating disability even more terrifying than the inevitability of death'. (Hahn, 1986, p.125)

These anxieties have undoubtedly contributed to the exclusion of disabled people from the mainstream of social and economic life and influenced policies that have placed people with impairments in segregated facilities such as residential homes, special schools and day centres.

They are further reinforced by the increased emphasis on consumer choice and options and the promotion of discourses within the media and the internet around healthy lifestyles and 'looking good' by the ever expanding health and beauty industry (Crawford, 1977). This includes the marketing of a wide range of pharmaceutical, surgical and technological products and services. Hence

> [T]he rise of consumer culture and healthism has resulted in the ageing body and disabled body becoming centres of great anxiety. A body that does not function 'normally' or appear 'normal', that is confined to a wheelchair or bed, is both visually and conceptually out-of-place as evidenced by the lack of public facilities for people with disabilities or the elderly. (Lupton, 1994, p. 38)

Consequently even where policy measures have espoused the language of community care, rights and independent living, the ideology of personal tragedy theory has continued to hold sway and so ensure that policies are by and large geared towards responding to the personal needs of disabled individuals rather than treating disabled people as a disadvantaged group.

But these definitions do not emerge solely based upon the contemporary understandings of politicians and policy makers themselves but are also shaped by the material forces of capitalist development. Therefore as capitalist economies have experienced a succession of fiscal crises over recent years (Harvey, 2010), so the ideology underpinning welfare provision for disabled people has changed. No longer does it reflect tragedy, anxiety and the influence of benevolent humanitarianism. Rather due to the growing priority placed on free market economics, it now reflects in various ways the economic burden that non-productive disabled people are assumed to be. The ideological climate in which this finds expression focuses upon the notion of dependency.

This is because the immediate post-war consensus on the need to ensure access to legal, civil and social rights for all as envisaged by Marshall (1950) and others has gradually given way to the monetarist doctrines of the neo-conservatives or New Right. From this perspective state-sponsored welfare systems are said to have discouraged individualism, self-reliance, voluntary action and private initiatives, and so tipped the balance in the development of social policy against competition and enterprise in favour of state planning and control (George & Wilding, 1994; Dwyer, 2000; Prideaux, 2005).

In light of the succession of global economic crises from the 1970s onwards, there have been extensive calls for cuts in government expenditure on welfare by politicians from both the left and right. The policies of the welfare state were now viewed as outdated and a major cause of, rather than a solution to these crises. It was the idea of dependency that was used to explain why state-provided welfare was part of the problem rather than part of the solution. An early example was cited in the first edition of this book:

> Everyone knows the sullen apathy of dependence and can compare it with the sheer delight of personal achievement. To deliberately set up a system which creates the former instead of the latter is to act directly against the best interests and indeed the welfare of individuals and society. (Moore, 1988, cited in Oliver, 1990, pp. 81–2)

Therefore the idea of dependency has been used ever since to socially construct, or perhaps, more accurately, socially reconstruct the 'problem of disability' (Oliver, 1990, p. 82) along with a whole range of other social problems which have been reconstructed in similar ways in many capitalist and late capitalist countries. In the UK, for example, policy initiatives during the 1980s and early 1990s emphasized the importance of self-help and individual enterprise, the need for cuts in public expenditure and a greater use of the private sector and voluntary agencies in the delivery of essential services (George & Wilding, 1994; O'Brien & Penna, 1998; Dwyer, 2000, 2004; Deacon, 2002; Prideaux, 2005).

Reconstructing the Disability Problem

The early 1990s produced much talk of a new 'third way' politics, most notably but not exclusively in the UK, that claims to go beyond the politics of the left and right. One of its chief proponents (Giddens, 1998, 2000) argues that welfare provision should be organized in order to generate and encourage an 'entrepreneurial culture' that rewards responsible risk takers. This new 'social investment state' fulfils the requirements of social justice and equality by means of the redistribution of 'possibilities', namely work and education rather than wealth. Central to this assertion is the reciprocal relationship between 'rights and responsibilities'. This approach can be seen as a direct challenge to 'universal entitlement derived from citizenship' as envisaged by Marshall and the architects of the post-war welfare state (Cox, 1998, p. 3).

The welfare society of the past which, theoretically at least, guaranteed a minimum of 'social rights' (Borsay, 2005) has been replaced by the 'active society' in which increasingly citizens can only access social rights if they are willing to become workers in the paid labour market. This is a radical shift from earlier universalistic policies that acknowledged a social obligation to those who make or had made a valid contribution to the general good. Increasingly, then, many of the assumptions about social obligations and consequential rights no longer apply. Policies that are based on unconditional entitlements to welfare benefits and support are perceived as promoting welfare dependency.

Consequentially the primary message of 'no rights without responsibilities' (Giddens, 1998, p. 65) suggests that welfare benefits and support should be available only to those who are active in the paid labour market and that: 'If necessary, reluctant individuals should be forced into activity by the application of benefit sanctions' (Dwyer, 2004, p. 268). Increasingly over the last two decades these ideas have gained extensive and enthusiastic support within Britain and have also had a major influence on policy development elsewhere in the world (Dwyer, 2000, 2004; Deacon, 2002; Prideaux, 2005, 2010).

This emphasis on rights and responsibilities and reduced access to state welfare systems, couched within a moral agenda, prioritizes government demands for cost-cutting exercises over and above the needs of citizens. This approach also legitimates the withdrawal or reduction of people's rights to state-sponsored welfare if they are unwilling or unable to meet the increasingly stringent state-endorsed standards or regulations. Furthermore:

> This enables politicians to place the blame for the predicament of those whose right to publicly funded welfare is reduced or removed firmly at the door of the individual concerned. Their exclusion from public welfare arrangements becomes less problematic for the government. (Dwyer, 2004, p. 266)

This reconstruction of the welfare problem in general and the disability problem in particular has been very successful at both the ideological and political level, giving rise to popular fears about the 'culture of dependency', and hence has made it possible to talk about not simply restructuring the welfare state but also reducing its size and costs. However we would suggest that this reconstruction cannot be understood just in terms of changing ideas about the role of welfare in society but as a crucial part of the process of disablement within an ever-changing capitalism. In order to do this we need to make clear our distinction between constructions and creationism within social theory.

Creating the Disability Problem

For us the essential difference between a social constructionist and a social creationist view of disability centres on where the 'problem' is actually located. With few exceptions both views have moved away from the core ideology of individualism. The social constructionist view remains rooted at the ideological level and sees the problem as being located within the minds and attitudes of able-bodied people, whether individually (prejudice) or collectively generated, through the manifestation of hostile social attitudes and the enactment of social policies based upon a tragedy view of disability.

Alternatively, the social creationist view sees the problem as located within the institutionalized practices of society, leading to the notion of institutional discrimination which has been used in a variety of different settings. It has helped to explain why, despite legislation and anti-sexist, anti-racist and anti-homophobic policies, discrimination against women, minority ethnic groups and lesbians and gay men persists. It is notable that following the distinction between constructions (attitudes) and creations (material forces) in Oliver (1990) this distinction has been blurred by Priestley (1998). In a discussion of the growing theoretical debates within disability studies, he links creationist approaches to the functional limitations of the body.

Indeed discrimination persists largely because the implementation of these policies has focused mainly on negative individual and social attitudes rather than on the policies and practices of powerful organizations and institutions. Consequently whilst the struggle for formal equality has been relatively successful, the structures of disadvantage remain largely unscathed and intact. Thus sexism, racism, heterosexism, ageism and disablism are institutionalized in the very fabric of society. They are real and socially created by a racist, sexist, heterosexist, ageist and disablist society. And as a consequence of globalization this is increasingly evident in both rich and poor countries throughout the world (Albert, 2006: Braedley and Luxton, 2010; Harvey, 2010).

Similarly the notion of institutional discrimination against disabled people has been used to support the case for anti-discrimination legislation in respect of disability in order to change behaviour rather than attitudes (Oliver et al., 1988; Oliver, 1990; Barnes 1991; Bynoe, Oliver & Barnes, 1991). The important advance that the social creationist approach makes over the social constructionist one, therefore, is that it does not assume that the institutionalized practices of society are nothing more, nor less than the sum total of individual and collective views of the people who comprise that society. To make the point again: ideas are not free-floating, they are themselves material forces.

We need to understand and to appreciate the complexity of institutional discrimination against disabled people which, elsewhere, we have defined as follows:

> Institutional discrimination is embedded in the work of contemporary welfare institutions and is present if they are meeting inadequately the needs of disabled people compared with able-bodied people. It is also present if agencies are regularly interfering in the lives of disabled people as a means of social control in ways, and/or to an extent not experienced by able-bodied people.

> Institutional discrimination operates both in society generally and in the state, and is supported by history and culture. It incorporates the extreme forms of prejudice and intolerance usually associated with individual or direct discrimination, as well as the more covert and unconscious attitudes which contribute to and maintain indirect and/or passive discriminatory practices within contemporary organisations. Examples of the influence of institutional discrimination on social policy include the way the education system is organised, and the operation of the labour market, both of which are influenced by government and both of which perpetuate the disproportionate economic and social disadvantage experienced by disabled people. It is evident therefore that within this frame of reference direct, indirect and passive discrimination are not easily distinguishable concepts but are intertwined in most contexts. (Barnes, 1991, p. 3)

But before focusing upon how institutional discrimination against disabled people operates and creates dependency, it may be helpful to discuss what is actually meant by the term dependency.

The Idea of Dependency

In common-sense usage dependency implies the inability to do things for oneself and consequently the reliance upon others to carry out some or all of the tasks of everyday life. Conversely independence suggests that the individual needs no assistance whatever from anyone else and this fits nicely with the current political rhetoric which stresses competitive individualism. In reality, of course, no human being is completely independent or, for that matter, never was. Human beings are, in common with other primates, social animals. We have neither the physical ability nor intellectual capacity to survive as truly independent, isolated individuals.

Hence as in all previous societies, we live in a state of mutual interdependence. In short: 'We rely on each other in a multitude of ways from the provision of the essentials of food, water, shelter to the complexities of self esteem' (Parker, 1993, p. 11). The dependence of disabled people, therefore, is not a feature which marks them out as different in kind from the rest of the population, but is different only in degree.

There is obviously a link between the common-sense usage of the term dependency and the way it is used in discussions of social policy, but these more technical discussions include at least two dimensions to the term. The first of these concerns the ways in which welfare states have created whole groups or classes of people who become dependent upon the state for education, health care, financial support and indeed, any other provision the state is prepared to offer. The second focuses on the supposed inability of particular individuals or groups to provide their own 'self-care' because of their assumed functional limitations or impairments.

Besides young children and very old people, people with impairments and especially those labelled with 'learning difficulties', 'mental health' problems and 'complex support needs' are particularly vulnerable to this form of rhetoric. Both of these dimensions of dependency have figured large in recent debates about the restructuring of welfare states by attempting to reduce the size and scope of state benefits and services and by shifting existing provision away from institutions and into the community.

These two assertions have helped facilitate the development of reductionist explanations of the phenomenon of dependency. Psychological reductionism has focused upon the way the self-reliance of individuals and families has been eroded by the 'nanny state' and has thereby created 'pathological individuals'. Sociological reductionism has tended to focus upon the common characteristics of different groups, of which dependency is a major feature, thereby creating 'pathological groups' (Oliver, 1990, p. 85). Social science has often been actively engaged in the creation of these reductionist explanations to the point where social scientists have been criticized for reflecting a particular set of 'values and ideologies' and 'treating the concept of dependency as non problematic' (Wilkin, 1987, p. 867).

Since the early 1980s feminist critiques of welfare provision have come to prominence (see, for example, Finch & Groves, 1983; Finch, 1984; Dalley, 1988; Ungerson, 1997, 2004). But whilst they have addressed the issue of dependency amongst disabled people, unfortunately they have done it in an uncritical way. They have reinforced discriminatory stereotypes of disabled people as passive and dependent in their efforts to emphasize the emotional and physical costs of 'caring' and to provide alternative approaches to the problem (Morris, 1991, 1997; Thomas,1999, 2007). None has sought to examine the concept of dependency critically or to suggest that the dichotomy dependence/independence is a false one. Nor have they drawn on the growing body of work within disability studies that has shown how disablement, and hence dependency, is not an intrinsic feature of impairment but rather a socially created phenomenon produced by a disablist society.

Furthermore, approaches that examine disability as a specific form of social oppression that creates dependency have often been ignored or dismissed. However, it is to some of the ways in which this dependency is created by the institutionalized practices of late capitalist society that the rest of this chapter will now turn.

Creating Economic Dependency

As will be evident from the arguments above and in previous chapters, we believe that work in the paid labour market is central to all capitalist societies simply because labour power produces the goods to sustain life. It also generates particular forms of social relations. For most people therefore exclusion from or marginalization within the labour market will almost certainly result in poverty, social isolation and alienation. Moreover in the past the mechanism for controlling people considered economically unproductive was the workhouse, the asylum and a whole host of other specialist institutions which grew up to contain and control these 'social deviants'. These establishments were successful in controlling individuals who would not or could not work.

It was soon recognized that these institutions not only created dependency in individuals but also created dependent groups. This led to fears about the 'burdens of pauperism' in the nineteenth century (Borsay, 2005). In order to discourage 'the poor' from seeking publicly funded support and hence becoming dependent on the state, the workhouse was designed to be as unpleasant as possible to deter anyone from entering it willingly or extending their stay any longer than absolutely necessary. However enforced institutionalization became the favoured policy for dealing with 'infirm' and 'incapacitated' individuals who simply could not compete in the new labour markets or work in the new factories.

The result was the growth of a plethora of disability charities and segregated institutions including hospitals, asylums and special schools. Children and older people with impairments were mostly represented as part of the 'deserving poor'. Notwithstanding that, expectations of a less harsh institutional regime, compared to their 'undeserving' counterparts, were rarely fulfilled, and there was a general stigmatization of recipients of social welfare (Borsay, 2005). As indicated above, this legacy remains with us today, although, of course, the language has changed.

The reason for going over this again here is that the issues are still the same the world over: people with impairments are much more likely to encounter exclusion from the workforce because of their assumed inabilities and hence dependency is still being created (Russell, 1998, 2002; Barnes, 2003b; Roulstone & Barnes, 2005). And even where attempts are made to influence the work system, they do not have the desired effect because, on the whole, they tend to focus on labour supply. Examples include 'job introduction' schemes, 'workfare' and 'access to work' programmes.

The stated aim of these policies is usually to make individual disabled job seekers more attractive to employers, but whilst they may succeed in individual cases, they also have the opposite effect. By packaging and selling workers with impairments as a special case, the idea that there is something different and 'wrong' with them is reinforced and can lead to exclusion rather then inclusion. Yet while it has been increasingly recognized that it doesn't have to be this way, little has been done to remove the barriers to work, despite the recent fashion for anti-discrimination legislation.

Most governments have failed to recognize that institutional discrimination against disabled people in the labour market and the work system can only be really addressed by refocusing their economic polices. As two critics of such policies put it many years ago:

> The alternative, or more properly the supplement, to these programs is a focus on the demand side of the market, making people more employable and more a part of general social life by changing the social organisation of work and of other aspects of everyday life, through the removal of architectural barriers, nondiscrimination and affirmative action programs, mainstreaming in the schools, and so on. Until recently, there has been almost no concern with these possibilities (Erlanger & Roth, 1985, p. 339).

In other words, reducing the economic dependency of disabled people can only be satisfactorily addressed by changing the way the labour market operates and the ways in which work is organized.

In short, there are virtually no serious attempts within late capitalist societies targeted at the social organization of work and the demand side of labour. And given the size of what Marx termed the 'industrial reserve army of labour' in rich and poor countries alike, it is unlikely that such targeting will occur in the foreseeable future. In the globalized world of the twenty-first century: 'labour reserves exist everywhere and there are few geographical barriers to capitalist access to them' (Harvey, 2010, p. 66).

In light of this it is hardly surprising that there is a general assumption amongst politicians, policy makers and the general population that people with impairments and labelled 'disabled' are economically unproductive and therefore financially and socially dependent. The reality of course is quite the opposite. Although the numbers of people claiming disability related welfare benefits is rising in all high-income states (Marin, Prinz & Queisser, 2004), the majority of disabled people of working age do have jobs and hence are economically productive.

In the UK, for example, figures from the period 1999–2006 show that around 53 per cent of disabled workers were in paid employment compared to 84 per cent for non-disabled peers (ONS, 2006). However disabled workers are over-represented in low-skilled, poorly paid, part-time jobs with few opportunities for promotion. Unemployment and underemployment is especially high amongst disabled young people and those over 50 years of age (Burchardt, 2003, 2005; ONS, 2006). A similar situation exists in other high-income states such as the USA, Canada and Europe (Marin, Prinz & Queisser, 2004). Moreover, 'as documented by several studies, both in developing and developed countries, working age persons with disabilities experience significantly lower employment rates and much higher unemployment rates than persons without disabilities' (WHO, 2011, p. 235).

Legislating for Dependency

As we have already argued, policies enacted through the legislative process have the effect of creating dependency and the current restructuring of state welfare systems is legitimated by the desire to reduce our 'culture of dependency'. In the UK, for example, services for people with impairments were established with the introduction of the National Assistance Act (1948) and the Chronically Sick and Disabled Persons Act (1970) but in doing so they reinforced 'the notion that people who happen to have disabilities are people who are "helpless", unable to choose for themselves the aids to opportunity they need' (Shearer, 1981, p. 82).

This assumption continues to underpin government thinking despite the rhetoric of equality and rights that has permeated legislation and policy documents since the mid-1990s. Indeed the Disabled Persons (Services, Consultation and Representation) Act (1986) and the Community Care Act (1990) both acknowledged the inadequacies of previous provision as well as a wish to involve disabled people more in shaping their own destinies. Yet in common with previous legislation both were noticeably silent on how services were to be obtained and how the right to self-determination could be achieved in the face of recalcitrant local authorities.

The need to address the problem of dependency was brought about by a combination of factors including successive economic crises, growing concern over the rising cost of state welfare in the post-war period, combined with intensive campaigning by disabled people and their organizations since the 1970s. All this led to an apparent change of policy by the British government. Formal acknowledgement of disability as an equal opportunities and human rights issue came with the introduction of the Disability Discrimination Act (DDA) (1995) and the Community Care (Direct Payments) Act (1996) one year later.

Even so the DDA and subsequent amendments remain based on an individual medical definition of disability and despite the establishment of a Disability Rights Commission (DRC), which adopted a social model definition, the legislation has proved largely ineffective in abolishing institutional discrimina-tion against people with impairments (Harwood, 2005; Miller, Gillinson & Huber, 2006; Crowther, 2007). Furthermore neither the DDA nor the various direct payment schemes have substantially challenged the dependency-creating tendencies of state-provided welfare.

There are several factors which have contributed to this failure. These include lack of funding, lack of clarity in government guidelines, a reluctance amongst managers and professionals to devolve power to users, inter-professional rivalry, negative assumptions concerning the capabilities of service applicants and a lack of information and support for potential users (Barnes & Mercer, 2010, pp. 147–8). In short the legislative framework remains locked into a professional and administrative approach to service delivery.

Dependency is continually reinforced by the ways in which the discourse surrounding disability and social policy is presented and conducted. This is evident in the patronizing and demeaning way politicians discuss disability in Parliament and the ways in which civil servants, lobbyists, policy analysts and political commentators fail to examine the concept of disability critically. It is particularly evident in the discourses associated with 'social and community care' and organizations representing 'carers' groups'. Yet as noted in Chapter 2, the phrases 'social care' and 'community care' have been criticized for their lack of clarity for many years now. Moreover for many disabled people the concept of 'care' represents 'a tool through which others are able to dominate and manage our lives' (Wood, 1991, p.199).

Such language perpetuates traditional assumptions that disabled people are helpless and that things have to be done to them 'for their own good' (Hunt, 1966; Rae, 1989; Barnes, 1992; Morris, 1993; Clark & Marsh, 2002). In short, the underlying ideology of the 'care' discourse is 'oppressive and objectifying' (Fine & Glendinning, 2005, p. 602). Additionally this discourse obscures the reality of unequal power relations as disabled activists have consistently pointed to the negative consequences that flow from community care policies on those involved. It is

> the most exploitative of all forms of care delivered in our society today for it exploits both the carer and the person receiving care. It ruins relationships between people and results in thwarted life opportunities on both sides of the equation. (Brisenden, 1989, p. 10)

The political sphere thus plays a significant role in the social creation of dependency amongst disabled people in terms of both its legislative enactments and the way it conducts its discourse about policy. It lays the foundations for the ideological climate within which services are provided and professional practices are organized and carried out. This is the focus of the next section.

Promoting Dependency in Practice

The post-1945 period has been characterized as the age of 'disabling professions' (Illich et al., 1977). The terms professions and professional are generally used to refer to highly skilled, high-status occupations which claim, or aspire to claim, access to and control of a particular area of expertise (Wilding, 1982). The creation of dependency-creating services in capitalist societies such as the UK and the USA is partly due to the rapid decline in manufacturing industries in the latter half of the last century. This was accompanied by a comparable growth in service sector employment in order to minimize unemployment and social unrest (Wolfensberger, 1989). For example, the UK's National Survey of Day Services conducted between 1974 and 1978 estimated that in 1959 there were just 200 day centres operating in England and Wales. In the following ten years, what Gough (1979) termed 'the golden age of the welfare state' the number increased fourfold. In 1976 there were 2,600 known day centres operating up and down the country. Whilst this study bears witness to the lack of jobs available to service users – 'all users of day services are outside the jobs market for one reason or another' (Carter, 1981, p. 4) – it also provides an indication of the expansion of employment in the service sector during the 1960s and 70s. Nearly a quarter of day centre personnel had transferred from 'blue collar and manual trades occupations into the health and personal social services'. A key finding was that 'many of the staff are as unqualified as the users. Half had left school at age of 15 (the then school leaving age) or before' (p. 5).

However, due to the rising cost of welfare there was a concerted effort during the 1980s to 'roll back' the state following the election in 1979 of a 'New Right' Conservative government. This was justified with reference to several reports on community care policies that identified significant inefficiencies and poor quality services for service users (Audit Commission, 1986). There followed Government directives to enhance market forces and competition within health and social support services. By emphasizing the importance of 'economy, efficiency and effectiveness' (Exworthy & Halford, 1999), the aim was to deliver 'better value for money' and enhance 'consumer choice' (Griffiths, 1988).

This 'mixed economy of welfare' approach, with quasi-market competition between the public, private and voluntary sectors to enhance individual choice, underscored the National Health Service and Community Care Act (1990). Multi-agency working and social partnerships were encouraged (Clarke, 2004). The outcome was a blurring of the boundaries between state, private and voluntary provision, and formal and informal 'care' (Glendinning et al., 2000). Further, despite the rhetoric of consumer choice and control, these reforms reaffirmed the role of local authority managers in assessing individual support needs, designing a 'care plan' and buying packages of care on behalf of service users (Wood, 1991). And as noted above, these policies have been further endorsed by successive British governments.

What is equally striking is the fact that choice remains limited and the private sector has proved no more efficient in providing better quality services than the state sector. For example, a recent review of 'care homes' managed by Southern Cross Healthcare, the UK's largest private 'care' operator, found that over half their homes provided a 'poor standard of care' due to a chronic shortage of 'competent, trained staff'. Also due to substantial financial losses the company announced a 'slimming-down' of its operations and further job cuts in order to avoid bankruptcy. Hence many of their homes were to be taken over by other private and public providers, including local authorities who have a legal duty to provide 'care' for those who need it (Wachman, 2011, unpaged).

Since the 1980s the privatization of health and social support services has gathered considerable momentum across rich and poor countries alike due largely to the activities of transnational funding agencies such as the International Monetary Fund (IMF) and the World Bank. Yet an Oxfam report, *Blind Optimism: Challenging the myths about private health care in poor countries* (2009), asserts that the Bank's policies over the last two decades have weakened public health systems through enforced public spending cuts and widescale restructuring of the sector in favour of privatization. Moreover, an independent World Bank Evaluation Group has produced a damning report on the Bank's lending policies regarding its continued push for the privatization of health and related public services, particularly in Africa. The report covers projects from

1997 to 2008 across the world totalling $18 billion:

> It rated 220 projects according to how well they met stated objectives, regard-less of how good these objectives were. Highly satisfactory outcomes were almost unheard of and only about two thirds of projects had moderately satis-factory or better outcomes. Projects in Africa were 'particularly weak' with only 27 per cent receiving satisfactory outcomes. (Bretton Woods Update, 2009, p. 1)

However, as we have already detailed, whilst there have been some significant changes to the role of welfare services in the UK, most service users remain reliant on traditional professionally led provision. Consequently there are several ways that professional helpers generate and maintain dependency, albeit often unintentionally. For instance, the continued use of residential and nursing homes of varying kinds, segregated special schools, day centres and other institutional facilities in both the public and private sectors has ensured that, for the most part, an 'enlightened guardianship model of care' (Miller & Gwynne, 1972) has dominated. This has served to institutionalize service users and so create and sustain dependency. Notwithstanding that over recent years some attempts have been made to address this problem, it remains unfortunately true that power and control continue to be firmly in the hands of professionally trained staff.

Many community services are delivered in similar ways and reinforce dependency. Hence disabled people are usually offered little meaningful choice about aids and equipment; times at which professional helpers can attend to help with matters like toileting, dressing or preparing a meal are often predetermined; and the range of tasks that professionals can perform is limited because of professional boundaries, employer requirements or trade union practices (Oliver & Sapey, 2006; French & Swain, 2008).

The 'professional-client' relationship can itself be dependency-creating and the very language used suggests that power is unequally distributed within this relationship. Recent attempts to address this problem by changing the termi-nology from 'client' to 'consumer' and now on to user' have done little to change the structural context in which these power relations exist. Consequently the various economic structures that determine the roles of professionals as gate-keepers of scarce resources remain firmly in place. They are supported by politically sanctioned and legally binding frameworks and formal ethical codes that specify their controlling functions as administrators of services. Career structures and pathways also influence their decisions about whose side they are actually on (Abberley, 1995, 2004; Begum, 1996; Finkelstein, 1998; Exworthy & Halford, 1999; Beresford, 2004; Truman, 2005; French & Swain, 2008).

All of this is reinforced by a knowledge base founded upon traditional individual, medical models of 'care' which suggest that disabled people need help ' – otherwise why would they be employed to help them?' (Oliver, 1990, p. 91). The economic and social relations of professional practice trap both professionals and users into dependency-creating relationships. However ideology serves to obscure the real nature of these relations because, in a fundamental sense, it is professionals who are dependent upon users for their jobs and careers.

A central problem in all of this has been the goal of 'independence' which both disabled people and professionals usually endorse. Advancing the idea of 'independent living' has become extremely problematic in that professionals and disabled people have not been talking about the same thing. Professionals, for example, have tended to define independence in terms of self-care activities such as washing, dressing, toileting, cooking and eating without assistance, with the result that:

> The practice of care assessment and management is not simply a technical gate keeping mechanism – it defines disabled people's needs in a very particular way. Value laden purchasing decisions can perpetuate the myth of 'care' over independent living by focusing resources on personal care and limited domestic chores at the expense of support for social integration. Thus, care assessments all too frequently consolidate the social segregation of disabled people in their own homes rather than challenging their enforced dependency. (Priestley, 2004, p. 259)

Disabled people, on the other hand, have defined independence differently. As a disabled women points out:

> We have to gain control over our lives even when we need help from others to function. Unless we do this, we can never make a real contribution to society because our own thoughts will never be expressed through our actions, only through those of other people, our 'carers'. Having no control over your life also makes you totally vulnerable to abuse, the evidence of which is all around us. Therefore we define independence to mean having control over your life, not 'doing things without help'. (Mason, 2000, p. 66)

Hence for the international disabled people's movement the ideas of 'independent living' is based on two fundamental assumptions:

> Human beings, regardless of the nature, complexity and/or severity of impairment, are of equal worth, and have the right to participate in all areas of mainstream community life.

Therefore

> Whatever the character and severity of an impairment, individuals must be empowered to make choices and exercise control in their everyday lives. (Barnes and Mercer 2006, p.184)

Consequently if disabled people and professionals are ever going to engage in dependency-reducing rather than dependency-creating relationships, then the following advice from a disabled sociologist written over three decades ago must be taken into account.

> We must expand the notion of independence from physical achievements to socio-psychologic decision-making. Independent living must include not only the quality of physical tasks we can do but the quality of life we can lead. Our notion of human integrity must take into account the notion of taking risks. Rehabilitation personnel must change the model of service from doing something to someone to planning and creating services with someone. In short, we must free ourselves from some of the culture-bound and time-limited standards and philosophy that currently exist. (Zola, 1982, p. 396)

There are, of course, many other ways in which dependency is created, whether these are patronizing social attitudes or the inaccessibility of the built environment, which consistently force disabled people to seek help. There is no need to consider them here, though, as we shall return to them in the following chapters. Finally in this chapter we need to consider how the economic, political and professional dependency-creating processes impact on individuals with impairments and render them disabled.

Internalizing Dependency

It is not difficult to understand why, given all of the factors we have discussed in this chapter, most disabled people and their families come to the point where they accept and even internalize this notion of dependency. This is clearly reflected in the general view that the birth of a disabled child is a traumatic and shattering experience for a family, a view perpetuated by the activities of 'professionals and researchers' (Oliver & Sapey 2006, p. 90). It has long since been acknowledged that the presence of impairment within the family has 'an important effect on the relationships and opportunities of the family as a whole' (Topliss, 1979, p. 129).

Indeed, one direct consequence of having a disabled child is that one or both parents' ability to participate in the paid labour market will be adversely affected. When coupled with the additional costs of impairment, this can have a substantive impact on the family income. One study found that only 3 per cent of mothers of disabled children are in full-time employment compared to 22 per cent of mothers of non-disabled children, while the costs of bringing up a disabled child are three times higher than for a non-disabled child (Gordon et al., 2000). Invariably the family then becomes dependent upon welfare benefits in one form or another.

Indeed disabled children and young people are especially vulnerable to the dependency creation process. In the UK, as in most developed countries, the individual model is still dominant within education systems. For example, '"special educational needs" (SEN) has a legal definition, referring to children with learning difficulties or disabilities that make it harder for them to learn or access education than most children of the same age' (Directgov, 2010, p. 1).

Instead of focusing on the failings of an education system that consistently does not accommodate the educational needs of all children, this approach continues to rely on what many educationalists would call the deficit model, but which we would more appropriately for our purposes here call the individual model.

This approach often leads to a lengthy process of assessment, diagnosis, individual education packages, specialist help, and possible removal from a mainstream school environment into a segregated special school or unit. This marks children with SEN out as somehow different from 'normal' children. Small wonder, then, that many of these children come to believe that they have something wrong with them. Furthermore, 'It is the professional status of those involved in assessment processes that legitimates the complex procedures which have been developed to exclude or marginalise young people from mainstream education' (Tomlinson, 1996, p.175).

The consequences for those who are excluded remain, as has been the case for many years:

The special education system, then, is one of the main channels for disseminating the predominant able-bodied/minded perception of the world and ensuring that disabled school leavers are socially immature and isolated. This isolation results in passive acceptance of social discrimination, lack of skills in facing the tasks of adulthood and ignorance about the main social issues of our time. All this reinforces the 'eternal children' myth and ensures at the same time disabled school leavers lack the skills for overcoming the myth. (BCODP, 1986, p.6)

By producing educationally and socially disabled individuals, the special education system also instils in non-disabled children and adults the notion that people with special needs are somehow inadequate and unable to participate and contribute to familial or community life. In so doing it legitimates and perpetuates exclusionary policies and practices in all other areas of life and particularly in employment as the child grows up.

Being excluded from some of the main areas of life such as education and work inevitably results in poverty and many disabled people come to rely on welfare payments from either the state and/or charitable organizations. More-over, in order to access these payments disabled individuals must emphasize their limitations rather than their strengths, a process that is both psychologically and socially demeaning. All of this adds weight to the view that disabled indi-viduals are a burden to themselves, their families, their communities and the state.

Perhaps inevitably, then, the overwhelming majority of the population with and without impairments internalize the personal tragedy view of disability. Given all this, it is hardly surprising that many disabled people experience what has been referred to as 'felt stigma' (Scambler, 2004), 'internal oppression' (Rieser, 1990; Mason, 2000) and 'psycho emotional disablism' (Thomas, 1999, 2007; Reeve, 2006). The net effects are often profound, resulting in chronic feelings of low self-esteem, limited self-confidence and personal insecurity. In short, individuals with impairments are socialized into viewing themselves as worthless, useless, of lesser value than non-disabled peers and therefore completely dependent upon the good will of others for their very existence and survival.

Conclusion

In this chapter we have suggested that social policies in respect of disability have been influenced, albeit unknowingly, by the core ideology of individualism. However, recently peripheral ideologies have shifted away from the ideologies of disability as personal tragedy and towards disability as dependency. This dependency is created amongst disabled people, not because of the effects of their functional limitations on their capacities for self-care, but because their lives are shaped by a variety of economic, political and social forces which produce it. Dependency is not a problem simply for the dependent individual but also for politicians, planners and professionals who have to manage (control) this dependency in accord with current social values and economic circumstance.

This problem and the political responses to it, both on the part of the state and of disabled people themselves, will be the subject of the next two chapters. It is only through a proper understanding of the politics of disability that disabled people can be seen as not simply constituted by the variety of structural forces already considered in this book, but also as active agents in the process of constituting society in its totality.

Part III

Agendas and Actions

7

Dealing with the Disabling Society

Introduction

Whilst there have been some significant improvements in the quality of life for some disabled people in some parts of the world, exclusion, poverty and dependence are everyday experiences for the overwhelming majority of people with impairments in rich and poor countries alike (WHO, 2001, 2011; Sheldon, 2005, 2010; Barron & Ncube, 2010). Consequently in this and the following chapter we aim to provide a broad-based discussion and analysis of the recent changes in the general areas of disability politics and policy with particular emphasis on developments since the early 1990s.

In the first edition of this book we suggested that change was necessary in order to ensure that disabled people were fully included in the societies in which they lived. In capitalist societies which were, and are, the main focus of our analysis, we suggested that there were three main ways to achieve the needed changes: through the provision of non-disabling welfare services, by exerting pressure on governments through political party and pressure group activities and by disabled people acting on their own behalf through organizations which they control.

Originally we were pessimistic about the first two ways and hopeful that disabled people could shape their own lives by taking matters into their own hands. In the intervening 20 years there have been some significant changes, particularly in capitalist societies, and there is no doubt that organizations controlled by disabled people have been in the vanguard of many of those changes. However, we have to conclude that the pace and extent of these change have been disappointing. Our aim in the rest of this book will be to consider the whys and wherefores of this and to look at what we can expect for the future.

We will contextualize our discussion within recent debates about the succession of economic crises that have characterized capitalist development since the early 1970s and their implications for state-sponsored welfare. We will then consider the market based responses that have been utilized as a way of dealing with these crises. We will then turn to recent developments within the disabled people's movement and its influence on mainstream political agendas, particularly in terms of its advocacy of rights-based solutions. Finally we will look at international responses and mechanisms relevant to the recent rise in global capitalism.

Capitalism in Crisis

Ever since capitalism replaced feudalism it has been subject to periodic crises which have threatened its economic and political stability. However it has always managed to survive these varying crises and move on to new stages in its development. Our purpose here is not to provide a commentary on these periodic crises but to examine the ways in which the crises from the end of the Second World War onwards have impacted on the lives of disabled people in the here and now.

When the War ended a post-war settlement between 'capital and labour' precipitated widespread institutional change and the emergence of the modern welfare state (Oliver & Barnes, 1998). Indeed, following the atrocities of the 1939–45 conflict many western industrial nations introduced some form of state-sponsored welfare system. Several factors were responsible for this unprecedented development.

To begin with there was an urgent need for a healthy, well educated workforce to facilitate a technically advanced and competitive economic recovery following the economic depression of the 1930s and the devastation of the 1939–45 war. Additionally the spread of communist and socialist ideas across Europe posed a significant challenge to western style neo-liberal democracies. Finally there was also a general concern over the growing numbers of disabled people due to war injuries, medical advances and ageing populations. It was not long, however, before both the idea of state-provided welfare and its spiralling costs were called into question. Indeed since the end of the 1950s there has been a growing retreat from state-sponsored provision as characterized by the social democratic models of welfare provision towards a more market led 'liberal'-type system (Esping-Andersen, 1990).

This retreat has been due to a combination of factors including the growing cost of provision, the coming to power of right-of-centre governments in the USA and UK respectively in the 1980s and 1990s, and a succession of escalating economic crises that have plagued the world economy since the 1970s. Until recently welfare provision of all kinds has been indicted as a key cause of these periodic crises: 'The crisis definition is now being used as an ideological basis for reducing social expenditure, changing redistributive patterns in disfavour of marginal groups and reducing government responsibility in social policy' (Oyen, 1986, p.6).

The most recent recession, described as the 'mother of all crises', is the worst recession since the 1930s (Harvey, 2010, p. 6) and was different from the previous ones in that welfare provision was not seen as its main cause. It began in 2006 with the reckless lending practices of financial institutions and banks, encouraged by American and British governments. By 2009 the US and UK economies were in deep trouble with declining consumer confidence, a rapidly deteriorating property market, plunging retail sales, businesses large and small closing down or going into bankruptcy and rising unemployment.

The European Union (EU) was also affected, although unevenly. Greece, Ireland, Portugal and Spain along with several eastern European states that had recently gained EU membership were particularly impacted. This had major financial repercussions across the world. Foreign financial institutions and investors which had speculated heavily in these markets made substantial losses and some, such as banks in Iceland, went bankrupt (Harvey, 2010).

In subsequent debates about this particular crisis, little attention has been paid to the fact that it is merely the latest of many crises that have beset capitalism:

> The idea that the crisis had systematic origins is scarcely mooted in the mainstream media. Most of the Government moves so far in North America and Europe amount to the perpetuation of business as usual, which translates into business as usual for the capitalist class. (Harvey, 2010, p. 218)

Solutions to this crisis have thus prioritized policies to support finance capital and the capitalist classes. Such policies are accompanied by a plethora of discourses about the importance of 'individual freedom, liberty, personal responsibility and the free market' which are designed to legitimate draconian policies with which to sustain and consolidate capitalist class interests and power. This is underpinned by assertions that future prosperity depends on the creation of a good business climate in which financial institutions can generate and maximize profit.

Moreover, the scramble by national governments to bail out banks and financiers by borrowing money from transnational financial institutions and investors such as the World Bank (WB) and International Monetary Fund (IMF) reaffirms the fact that the links between state and capital are as tight as ever and remain largely unchecked. As a result the economic recovery of many wealthy nations including the USA and Britain is now solely dependent on their ability to repay these loans.

Given that international money markets have never looked favourably on countries that support state-sponsored welfare, the future of the welfare state is now open to serious question and now more than ever in jeopardy. Ironically while welfare states have not been blamed for causing this particular crisis, it undoubtedly poses a serious threat to their continued existence. The debates about whether state-provided welfare is a good thing or not no longer figure on the political agenda. Everyone seems to agree that we have no choice but to severely cut back state-provided welfare programmes. The only issues left to debate appear to be how much should be cut and how quickly.

There is, of course, an ideological basis for severely reducing the size and costs of welfare that centres on the issue of dependency. Reductions in expenditure, changes in redistribution and the gradual withdrawal of the state from people's lives, have all been legitimated on the grounds of the need to reduce dependency. Yet as was discussed in the previous chapter, this issue of dependency is itself problematic and means different things to different people and groups.

There is no doubt that despite the problematic nature of the issue of dependency, the withdrawal or severe reduction of state funding of welfare will almost certainly condemn many disabled people to isolation and loneliness within the community or incarceration in residential institutions as is the case in many low income developing states where state-sponsored welfare is non-existent (DfID, 2000; Yeo, 2001, 2006; Clements & Read, 2003; Holden & Beresford, 2002; Coleridge, 1993; Barnes & Sheldon, 2010; Barron & Ncube, 2010). Given the enormity of the recent global fiscal crisis and the ensuing political climate within capitalist societies, there appears to be little scope for intervening in the economy as social policy is assigned the role of supporting an assumed 'natural order of economic relationships' (Walker, 1984). Put crudely, in practice this means 'privatise profits and socialise risk; save the banks and put the screws on the people' (Harvey, 2010, p.10).

Tackling the Crisis – the Market

From the previous analysis it would be easy to assume that we are adopting a fatalistic economic determinist position. However, while we are pessimistic about the situation for the immediate future, we remain convinced that:

> [W]hile the economic may be determining 'in the last instance', there is considerable scope within what Gramsci called the state (conceptualised as a social relation) and civil society for individuals, groups, interests or classes to act autonomously. The point being made here is not that economics determines politics, but the more limited one that the politics of social policy is circumscribed by economic considerations. (Oliver, 1990, p. 97)

Apart from bailing out failed financial institutions with a view to returning them to the private sector once they become profitable, most capitalist societies have shown little inclination to interfere in the workings of the market. In terms of social policy this has meant what has been referred to as the 'marketization' of welfare which has been achieved by a general drift toward privatization in one form or another. Such policies have been legitimized by the rhetoric of targeting, consumer choice and dependency reduction (see, for example, Priestley et al., 2009; Duncan Smith, 2010) which emphasize the need to give consumers more choice and control over services.

As yet no capitalist society has suggested that all welfare services should be provided exclusively by the third sector – private or voluntary agencies – although this may be a distinct possibility if the global economy does not improve and governments find that they are unable to meet their debts. At present, however, apart from those on the extreme right, the main goal of politicians and policy makers in most high-income wealthy states is a commitment to a substantial reduction of state spending on services but within what is often called a mixed economy of welfare.

As far as disabled people and their services are concerned, privatization is not a new phenomenon. In the UK, for instance, since the inception of the post-war welfare state services such as residential institutions, special schools and community-based supports such as home helps and meals on wheels have been provided by third-sector agencies and charities large and small. Well known examples include the Leonard Cheshire Foundation, Scope (formerly known as the Spastics Society) and the Women's Royal Voluntary Service (WRVS). All the evidence suggests that these services create dependency in exactly the same way as state-sponsored services (Oliver, 1990; Barnes, 1991; Wood, 1991; Morris, 1993; Priestley, 1998b; Oliver & Barnes, 1998; Oliver & Sapey, 2006; French & Swain, 2008).

Moreover, in other capitalist countries such as the USA, Australia, New Zealand and Sweden, since the mid-1980s the introduction of market forces into state welfare systems has gathered considerable momentum. A similar situation is also evident in low- and middle-income countries where governments have neither the inclination nor resources to pay for disability services as these are usually provided by non-government organizations (NGOs) and inter-national charities. The recourse to such policies simply re-affirms traditional assumptions about disabled people's assumed dependence on others and as burdens of charity.

Tackling the Crisis – Rights

A second response to the crisis, at least for the marginal groups worst affected, has centred on the discourse of rights. Although a rights discourse entered and asserted itself within the political landscape internationally and nationally in the aftermath of the Second World War, its impact has been minimal, particularly with reference to disabled people. In 1948 the United Nations (UN) produced the Universal Declaration of Human Rights, which states:

> Everyone has the right to a standard of living adequate for the health and well being of himself and his family, including food, clothing, housing and medical care and the necessary social services and the right to security in the event of unemployment, sickness, disability, widowhood, old age or other lack of liveli-hood in circumstances beyond his control. (UN, 1948, Article 25)

The reference to 'disability' and 'old age' may be interpreted as an appreciation of the disadvantages associated with the experience of 'impairment' (Borsay,

2005). Yet the widespread exclusion of people with impairments from a mainstream rights agenda during the 1950s and 60s prompted the elaboration of a disability rights discourse with the passing of the UN's Declaration on the Rights of Mentally Retarded Persons (1971) and the Declaration on the Rights of Disabled Persons (1975). The latter states clearly that:

> Disabled persons, whatever the origin, nature and seriousness of their handicaps and disabilities, have the same fundamental rights as their fellow-citizens of the same age, which implies first and foremost the right to enjoy a decent life, as normal and full as possible. (UN, 1975, Article 3)

These declarations were followed by the UN's International Year of Disabled Persons in 1981 and the Decade of Disabled Persons 1983–1992. There followed a series of similar initiatives. These included the first and second Asian and Pacific Decade of Disabled Persons (1993–2002 and 2003–2012), the African Decade of Disabled Persons (2000–2009) and the Arab Decade of Disabled Persons (2003–2012), largely as a result of persistent lobbying by disability activists and their organizations in developing countries. This was because the first UN Decade tended to underplay the issues faced by disabled people in poor nations (Takamine, 2006).

Since the 1990s, anti-discrimination legislation for disabled people has been enacted in a growing number of countries around the world including the USA (1990) and UK (1995) (Doyle, 2008). Other international initiatives recognizing the social exclusion of disabled people soon followed. In 1993 the UN issued the Standard Rules on the Equalization of Opportunities for People with Disabilities. It comprises twenty-three rules to facilitate full participation and equality for 'persons with disabilities'. These cover aspects of daily living including awareness raising, medical and support services, education, employment, leisure and cultural activities (UN, 1993).

The UN Convention on the Rights of Persons with Disabilities and its Optional Protocol was adopted in December 2006. It was negotiated over eight sessions of an ad hoc committee of the General Assembly from 2002 to 2006 that included representatives of disability organizations and marks the first human rights treaty of the twenty-first century. With 50 articles, the Convention is the most comprehensive document yet produced on the rights of disabled people. Article 1 states that:

> The purpose of the present Convention is to promote, protect and ensure the full and equal enjoyment of all human rights and fundamental freedoms by all persons with disabilities, and to promote respect for their inherent dignity. (UN, 2006)

Designed in an international law context, the Convention sets out the duty of nation states to protect human rights. It is said to be legally binding on any country that ratifies it. At the time of writing it has been signed by 149 countries and ratified by 101 states (UN Enable, undated).

Whilst the Convention may be seen as a major step forward in the struggle for equality as it provides a comprehensive list of what needs to be done to eliminate disablism, there is little on how this is to be achieved by way of enforcement. As yet there is little sign that it has had any significant impact on securing disabled people's individual or social rights within and across nation states. Consequently initial enthusiasm amongst disabled activists and their organizations for the Convention has started to wane (Jolly, 2010).

Examples of its problems are not hard to find. The UK, for example, signed the Convention and ratified it in 2009. But the British government has opted out of several parts of the Convention, including education, immigration and the armed forces. Disabled people may not therefore have the right to a mainstream education; disabled migrants wishing to stay in or enter the UK may be subject to wider health checks; and disabled people may be barred from working in or for the armed forces (Peck, 2009, p.7). The USA has only signed the Convention. It has not ratified it nor signed and ratified the optional protocol (UN, 2010; UN Enable, undated).

Consequently the rights-based approach to securing social justice has been rejected by many critics. For instance:

> A rights-based approach to legal development has been rejected by many modern critical legal scholars. They raise a number of concerns about rights. These include a misuse and abuse of the concept of rights; the indeterminism of rights; the fact that rights are unstable and context bound; the fact that rights cannot determine consequences; and the fact that rights formalise relationships and thereby separate us from each other. (Jones & Marks, 1999, p. 22)

In short, however they are defined, individual, social or human, rights are open to interpretation and context-bound. What is right for some may not be right for others. Furthermore the idea of individual and social rights is the outcome of neo-liberal thinking and has little relevance to those living in non-western cultures (Miles, 1995, 2006; Ingstad, 1999; Stone, 1999; Baylies, 2000; Katsui, 2006). Even where appropriate legal frameworks exist, challenging the denial of rights through the law courts is costly in terms of resources and time. As indicated earlier, the overwhelming majority of disabled people and their organizations in both rich and poor nations rarely have either.

Indeed, the emphasis on human and civil rights within existing legal frameworks has not brought about equality for disabled people or other oppressed groups across all nation states. This is simply because the pursuit of legal protection through the law courts does not overtly challenge the established political and economic structures in capitalist societies. Therefore such an approach is unlikely to bring about the radical environmental and cultural changes needed to eradicate structural inequalities (Jones & Marks, 1999; Hahn, 2002; Oliver & Barnes, 2006).

As we have stated elsewhere, the pursuit of a single aim or goal in disability politics was and is a mistake and was bound to lead to a dilution of the collective energy and commitment of disabled people and their organizations and would ultimately achieve relatively little (Oliver, 1990; Barnes, 1991; Barnes & Oliver, 1995; Oliver & Barnes, 2006). Focusing on a rights route to emancipation as an end in itself rather than as a means to an end was always likely to be counter-productive. It is becoming increasingly apparent that having legal rights does not mean that they will be enforced and even if they are, that enforcement will achieve the desired aims.

In previous chapters we have argued that the rights of disabled people to be included in the economic, political, cultural and social aspects of the societies in which they live are essentially individualistic in nature and therefore can easily be incorporated and effectively neutralized within capitalism. We also need to consider rights in a much more fundamental sense, notably rights to exist, or to put it more explicitly, rights to be born and rights not to be killed off. New developments in biotechnology offer capitalist societies new solutions to the problems of disability, or rather old solutions dressed up in new clothes.

We are now living in the 'century of the gene' and current and future developments in biotechnology will have as significant an impact on the global economy, politics and culture as did the recent advances in information technology (Kerr & Shakespeare, 2002). In areas such as agriculture and medicine unsubstantiated claims are made for genetic technologies in terms of eradicating famine, eliminating poverty and reducing disease, and increasing longevity. In the interests of the 'common good', it is claimed that this revolutionary new science will enable us to take control of our 'evolutionary destiny' (Goble, 2003, p. 46).

There is, however, growing concern about the use and control of these technologies, particularly with regard to genetically modified crops and their impact on the environment. Environmental activists warn that although genetic modification may have some benefits, the risks involved are difficult to calculate as, once released into the environment, genetically modified organisms 'may set off a string of knock on effects that will be difficult to monitor and control' (Giddens, 2006, p.963).

Similar concerns are expressed by disabled activists and their organizations regarding the claims made by advocates of bio-medicine as a solution to the problem of disability. Their fears revolve around the frequently repeated assertion that the recent advances in biotechnology or 'new genetics' will enable doctors to identify and eradicate impairment and disease. All of this reinforces the traditional individualistic, biological and determinist explanation for disablement; threatens eugenic elimination of impairment; 'undermines the authenticity of disabled lives'; and 'reinforces the hegemony of biomedicine over disability' (Shakespeare, 1995, p.24).

Genetic screening takes many forms, but the most common in the UK and USA is prenatal screening, which is widely available and especially to families with a history of conditions such as cystic fibrosis, Huntington's disease and Duchenne muscular dystrophy. Whilst there is widespread consensus that such conditions are undesirable, the promise of genetic medicine is that it gives us the possibility of selecting those characteristics that we view as valuable and eliminating those that we do not. Not everyone, however, sees these developments in an entirely positive light. For example, Disabled People's International (DPI) posed the question:

> How can we live with dignity in societies that spend millions on genetic research to eradicate disease and impairment but refuse to meet our needs to live dignified and independent lives? We cannot. We will not. The genetic threat to us is a threat to everyone. (DPI, 2000, p.4)

As we have said, fundamental human rights to be born are just one end of the spectrum; the other is not to be killed off, even if it is cloaked in neutral language and caring ideology. For many disabled people, recent debates about how and when to end life because of impairment and disability are especially poignant as they appear to threaten directly their very existence, possibly even more so than biogenetic medicine and pre-natal screening (Shakespeare, 2006).

These concerns have intensified over recent years as the euthanasia debate has assumed a particularly high profile in many western societies. Voluntary and non-voluntary euthanasia was legalized in the Netherlands and Belgium in 2002 (Priestley, 2003). There has been a concerted campaign to introduce similar legislation in the UK over recent decades. This campaign is bolstered by the support of high-profile and respected public figures. Furthermore, notwithstanding that there is clear opposition to this within the international disabled people's movement by organizations such as America's Not Dead Yet and DPI, attitudes to this issue within the disabled population as a whole are said to be divided (Campbell, 2009; Shakespeare, 2009).

The end result of all this is that the decision to eradicate those considered unworthy of life and/or an economic and social burden to themselves, their families and the state remains largely unchecked. It is evident in the rhetoric surrounding recent developments in biotechnology, the policies and practices of those charged with life and death decisions at the beginning and end of life, and the general view that living with impairment is no life at all as exemplified in the leniency accorded those responsible for the mercy killing of disabled relatives (Barnes & Mercer, 2010).

Taken together these tendencies serve only to reinforce the traditional personal tragedy view of impairment and disability and in so doing undermine disabled people's calls for effective political and social change with which to bring about a more equitable and just society that acknowledges, supports and indeed celebrates the reality of human diversity, difference and frailty. Clearly such an approach fits snugly into the social and economic relations of capitalism in seeking to eradicate the 'abnormal' and those who become, or even might become, an economic burden.

Tackling the Crisis – Politics

Politics is about the struggle for power and influence. In 'representative liberal democracies' which almost all capitalist societies claim to be, government is said to be 'of the people, by the people, for the people'. National and local representative bodies such as Parliament, the Senate and local councils are accountable to the people by means of periodic public elections. In addition politicians and political parties may be influenced through individual contact, pressure group activity and public campaigns. This implies a high level of public involvement. Yet this is rarely achieved.

Political power and influence is distributed unevenly, with some groups better placed than others to secure their interests. Wealth, status and power are closely linked and historically power has been dominated by the upper and upper-middle classes. Consequently the ideological hegemony of a capitalist world view has been secured by a combination of 'repressive' and 'ideological' state apparatuses (Althusser,1971). Legitimacy is also justified by the assertion that individual citizens may participate in all aspects of the political process.

However participation for disabled people is often difficult to secure due to a variety of environmental, cultural and social barriers. For example, there is a wealth of evidence indicating that disabled people encounter environmental, political and cultural barriers when attempting to exercise their right to vote in local and national elections in both wealthy and poor states (Barnes & Mercer, 2010). This is despite the fact that by the middle of the 1990s, we saw the rise of many organizations controlled and run by disabled people at local, national and international levels to the point where it was possible to suggest that these organizations constituted a disabled people's movement with the potential to exert a powerful influence on political and social change (Campbell & Oliver, 1996; Barton, 2001).

Yet even at the high point of this development we were cautious about just how powerful the movement was and we pointed to some of the dangers it might encounter:

> To get too close to government is to risk incorporation and end up carrying out their proposals rather than ours. To move too far away is to risk marginalisation and eventual demise. To collaborate too eagerly with the organisations for disabled people risks having our agendas taken over by them, and have them

presented both to us and politicians as theirs. To remain aloof risks appearing unrealistic, and denies access to much needed resources. (Barnes and Oliver, 1995, p. 115)

Unfortunately this caution has proved to be justified. Since the mid-1990s there has been a growing professionalization of disability politics and a corresponding gradual downgrading of the role of organizations controlled and run by disabled people at the local, national and international levels by successive governments and international agencies, despite rhetoric to the contrary. As a result we no longer have a strong and powerful disabled people's movement and the struggle to improve disabled people's life chances has taken a step backwards. There can be little doubt that since the mid-1990s Britain's disabled people's movement has been in decline to the point where some have predicted its inevitable demise (Christie, 2000; Hudson, 2000; Shakespeare, 2006).

It is certainly true that the optimism we felt when writing the first edition of this book has dissipated somewhat. In 1991 the British Council of Organisations of Disabled People (BCODP) had 80 national and local member organizations representing 200,000 disabled individuals (Barnes, 1991, p.134). It was responsible for initiating the research which forced the Government's about-face on the need for a disability discrimination law, resulting in the Disability Discrimination Act (1995). It had forced the government to introduce direct payments legislation to facilitate independent living, the Community Care (Direct Payments) Act (1996). It had promoted the social model of disability to the point where it was not just a consciousness-raising device for the disabled people's movement but also a way of understanding the nature of disablement amongst politicians, policy makers and charities.

For many people these developments signalled the coming of age of disability politics and that future progress would ensure that disabled people would finally achieve their goal of full inclusion into mainstream society. But as the contents of this book clearly indicate, this optimism was and remains premature. The coming to power of a new government seemingly more willing to listen to the voice of disabled people in 1997 was a problem in itself. This was because the disabled people's movement which had cut its teeth on oppositional politics had little experience of participating and dealing with politicians and the political system.

The big charities, however, were only too willing to step in and fill the void.

Consequently since the late 1990s the combination of successive progressively right-wing governments and the big charities have successfully adapted and adopted the ideas of the disabled people's movement, usurped its language, and undertaken further initiatives which promise much but as yet have delivered relatively little. This changing landscape of disability politics has recently been referred to as 'disabling corporatism' (Oliver, 2009).

There are other dimensions to this phenomenon also. Centres for Independent, Integrated or Inclusive Living (CILs), which provided a focal point for political activity at both the local, national and international levels were also in decline from their heyday due to the increased emphasis on market forces and unprecedented competition from non-user led agencies and the big charities for local authority contracts. Hence there has been a marked decline rather than an expansion in the numbers of CILs operating across the UK over recent years (Barnes & Mercer, 2006, 2010; Oliver & Barnes, 2006).

Further, leading organizations from within the disabled people's movement including the BCODP, renamed the United Kingdoms Disabled People's Council (UKDPC) in 2006, and the National Centre for Independent Living (NCIL), have been marginalized still further within the corridors of power over recent years. Instead UK governments have supported their own initiatives such as the Disability Rights Commission (DRC), the Office of Disability Issues (ODI), established in 2005, and the Equality and Human Rights Commission (EHRC), the successor to the DRC which was abolished in 2006. Hence disabled people's organizations have found it increasingly difficult to attract core funding. Further policy changes in the way government funds for voluntary agencies are missing have also meant that these organizations have had to enter into partnerships and mergers with the big disability charities.

The Direct Action Network (DAN) which had been the enforcement arm of the disabled people's movement in its heyday in the 1990s has also gone into decline. DAN's most spectacular achievement was a demonstration outside 10 Downing Street – the home of the UK Prime Minister. A small group of disability activists got as far as the front door and threw red paint over it, symbolizing the blood of disabled people that would be shed as a consequence of Government plans to cut disability welfare payments. This demonstration attracted widespread international attention, including as far away as New Zealand and America, and the plans were quietly dropped. While this was a success for DAN in one sense, it left it with a difficult legacy to follow. As the organization is committed to peaceful direct action it was virtually impossible to organize something bigger or better and while DAN has continued in existence, particularly via its internet presence, its influence has steadily declined.

Another factor in the decline of the disabled people's movement is the very real toll that impairment takes on both the leadership and other activists within the movement. Through untimely deaths and emotional burn-out, the movement has been robbed of many important members long before their contributions have been completed. Of course, all political movements suffer from this but, we would argue, not to anything like the same extent (Oliver & Barnes, 2006).

It is also evident that a similar situation exists in many countries both rich and poor across the world. Disability activism in countries as diverse as Japan, South Africa, Sweden and the USA can be traced back to the middle of the last century. Hence, disabled activists have been incorporated into the government and the rhetoric of rights and inclusion has found its way into government policy statements and legislation. But, as indicated in previous chapters, the rhetoric has yet to be matched by reality and the majority of the disabled population in all countries remain in poverty (DfID, 2000; Yeo, 2001, 2006; Hurst & Albert, 2006; Barnes & Sheldon, 2010; Barron & Ncube, 2010; WHO, 2011).

Tackling the Crisis – Internationalism

At the international level we have already discussed the UN response in the section on rights, but global capitalism has developed a number of other key trans-national mechanisms for ensuring that its interests are protected. The two of particular relevance to our considerations here are the World Health Organization (WHO) and the World Bank (WB) both of whom have a key role to play in managing the increasingly global crises of capitalism as they occur. Their roles in identifying and controlling the costs and consequences of global disabling policies and practices are crucial to the interests of international capital.

The WHO, for example, has had some success in drawing disabled representatives of disability organizations into discussions about the development of the *International Classification of Functioning and Health* (ICF) which, as discussed In Chapter 1, is like its predecessor, the *International Classification of Impairments,*

Disabilities and Handicaps (ICIDH), overtly apolitical and has limited use beyond the measurement of impairment. Also the growing use of the phrase 'persons with disabilities' in place of 'disabled persons' in international documents reaffirms in the public mind that it is individuals, 'persons', who have 'problems' ('disabilities'), and not society.

In addition, due to the critique of its activities from disabled people and their organization (Hurst & Albert, 2006) and the appointment in 2004 of Judy Heumann, a key activist in America's disabled people's movement, as principal advisor on disability and development (Coleridge, 2006), the World Bank has since adopted a policy of 'mainstreaming disability' in all its programmes. In 2007 it published its *Social Analysis and Disability:* a Guidance Note which 'offers a practical guide to integrating social analysis and disability inclusive development into sector and thematic projects and programs of the World Bank' (p. 1).

However, although this document focuses on the importance of disability rights and institutional change the guidelines therein are not binding. Hence their impact will depend on a variety of factors, including the project or programme, local context and, most importantly, 'available resources' (p. 2). These must come from other sources such as international non-government organizations (INGOs), non-government organizations (NGOs) and other agencies, as the Bank is not a charity or human rights organization, nor is it concerned with equality. Its policies are heavily influenced by a neo-liberal/ capitalist philosophy that strongly upholds the interests of big business and trans-national corporations. Its primary function is to provide loans for economic development which have to be repaid.

The Bank's policies are determined by shareholders' votes. The United States of America is the Bank's largest shareholder followed by Japan, Germany, the UK and France. 'The poorer the country the fewer votes it has and the less influence over the Bank's agenda' (Yeo, 2006, pp. 75–6). Despite the apparent inclusion of disability issues into its Millennium Development Goals, the Bank has yet to allocate substantial amounts of funding into medium- and low-income countries with an overtly disability-inclusive philosophy and policy programme, such as South Africa and Uganda (Yeo, 2006,p.76), or indeed any country that supports an extensive welfare infrastructure. All of this has important implications for states which have hitherto supported state-sponsored welfare systems and are struggling to meet their international debt obligations, for example, the UK.

It is difficult not to conclude therefore, that in an increasingly globalized world, the international economic, political and social institutions that exist are likely to continue to function to ensure that the needs of global capital will continue to have priority. This inevitably means that the needs of marginalized groups throughout the world are unlikely to be adequately met whatever charters, rules and laws promise.

Conclusion

In this chapter we have attempted to provide an overview of the politics of disablement with particular reference to the ways in which developing capitalism has managed its own internal crises since it replaced feudalism. Our specific focus, however, has been on the succession of deepening fiscal crises that have dogged the capitalist world economy since the 1970s which has had a major impact on the struggle for a more equitable and just society. This has resulted in a gradual but intensifying shift to the right in political circles at both the national and international levels and led to the systematic erosion of the post-1939–45 war consensus regarding state-sponsored welfare amongst politicians, policy makers and disabled activists and their allies within and across the rich nations of the west.

Clearly the optimism that surrounded the growth and achievements of the disabled people's movement during the last decades of the last century has ebbed away, due in part to the movement's incorporation into mainstream politics and its support for the rights route to emancipation and equality. The result has been a strident re-affirmation of capitalist hegemony at the global level and the introduction of drastic cuts in state-sponsored welfare with a particular emphasis on services and support for disabled people in many rich countries such as the UK.

There is little room for doubt that the forces which sustain economic, political and social inequality within global capitalism have not been seriously challenged by the mechanisms, activities and organizations which we have discussed herein. Instead we all, and disabled people in particular, face a return to a world dominated by personal tragedy theory, philanthropy, charity and uncertainty of provision and outcome. Consequently without radical change, the future for disabled people, their families and indeed all other economically and socially disadvantaged groups looks especially bleak. How this unfortunate and alarming situation might be addressed and reversed is discussed in the final chapters of this book.

8

Resisting the Disabling Society

Introduction

We hope that it is clear from the general tone of this new edition that the optimism we felt when producing the first edition of this book has waned somewhat. However this is not meant to imply that disabled people must inevitably accept the disabling practices of global capitalism and relinquish the possibilities of hope or the potential of resistance. We agree with a recent comment made by Harvey that:

> To say that the capitalist class and capitalism can survive is not to say that they are predestined to do so, nor that their future character is given. Crises are moments of paradox and possibility out of which all manner of alternatives, including socialist and anti-capitalist ones, can spring. (Harvey, 2010, p. 216)

Historically it has usually been assumed that the working class and organized labour will one day fulfil its historical mission to transform the economic and social relations of capitalism. However the apparent disappearance of the working class and the emasculation of trade unions in recent times have rendered this task increasingly unlikely. That does not mean that resistance is no longer possible but that the rise of 'movements of dispossession' offer different possibilities:

> The general effect of such movements has been to shift the terrain of political organisation away from traditional political parties and labour organising in factories into what was bound to be in aggregate a less focused political dynamic of social action across the whole spectrum of civil society. (Harvey, 2010, p.252)

In the last chapter we looked at the way capitalism has managed to respond to and survive the many crises that have beset it since its inception and suggested that it has proved adept at absorbing and incorporating many of the challenges it has faced. In this penultimate chapter we want to revisit some of these challenges particularly in the context of disability and suggest that they may offer the potential for resistance and even transformation instead of absorption and incorporation. Accordingly we will consider the possibility of the social model of disability still becoming a tool of resistance and even transformation for disabled people; whether independent living can become liberating not just for some but for all; and the political possibilities of disabling corporatism, identity groups and new social movements.

Transformation or Resistance

There is no doubt that since the first edition of this book was published capitalism has become the dominant, if not only, social formation in the globalized world of the twenty-first century, particularly with the collapse of the Soviet Union and the subsequent rush of Russia, China and India into the capitalist marketplace. These big players, along with the United States, dominate the world and are able to impose their economic, cultural, political and social values almost everywhere. Given its almost universal popularity, there seems little prospect of transforming capitalism in the foreseeable future

In these circumstances it is not perhaps surprising that revolutionary social theory based upon Marxism has almost disappeared from view and not just in academia. This is serious for our understanding of disablement in society for, as one disability scholar has put it:

> If we conceptualise disablement as the product of the exploitative economic structure of capitalist society, one which creates the so-called disabled body to permit a small capitalist class to create the economic conditions necessary to accumulate vast wealth, then it becomes clear that anti-discrimination legislation, by failing to acknowledge the contradictions of promoting equal opportunity in class-based (unequal) society, is insufficient to solve the unemployment predicament of disabled persons. (Russell, 2002, p.121)

This is not just a criticism of rights-based mono-causal approaches to disability but goes to the heart of industrial capitalism: the body and for our purposes herein, the disabled body. As we put it elsewhere:

> The social oppression of disabled people is immersed in a complex and uneven historical repression of certain forms of embodiment, capitalist development, and the inability of people with impaired bodies to sell their labour. In capitalism

the embodied characteristics of certain individuals disqualify their claims to social legitimacy, and therefore the social construction of abnormality is legitimised. (Barnes & Mercer, 2010, p. 85)

Hence, if capitalism is not to be transformed, the prospect of disabled people, as a group or class, becoming fully included in capitalist society is remote. The historical and contemporary statistics show, not just that far more disabled people are unemployed than their non-disabled peers, but that far fewer disabled people also have jobs (Marin et al., 2004; OECD, 2006, 2010; WHO, 2011). This is an unchanging picture regardless of the measures that governments take to alleviate this problem, whether it is through quota schemes, anti-discrimination legislation, individual support programmes or employer incentives and the like. Consequently all capitalist societies have periodic concerns about the size and costs of unemployment for disabled people especially if they run financial benefits programmes.

Given the current situation, we reluctantly accept that the idea of 'resistance' may be the best approach for political activists committed to confronting disablement. Resistance theory emerged in the social sciences to fill the vacuum left by retreating Marxism and was developed by a number of critical theorists (Touraine, 1981; Giroux, 1997). It has been taken up by a variety of post-structuralists and postmodernists and used as a way of challenging dominant discourses including those on disability (Mitchell & Snyder, 1997; Corker & Shakespeare, 2001; Shakespeare, 2006; Kristiansen, Velmas & Shakespeare, 2009). For them resistance is not about challenging the material relations of capitalism but rather its political and cultural discourses.

For most disability scholars working within this framework has led to their work being considered apolitical and of little use for disability activists seeking radical structural change. One notable exception, however (Peters, Gabel & Symeonidou, 2009), has attempted to use resistance theory both as a way of understanding past events in disability politics and as a means of developing tactics and strategies for confronting the disabling society. We shall try to build on this important work but temper our discussions with our fears about capitalism's ability to incorporate such examples of resistance into its own agenda and hence neutralize it. We shall begin with the most discussed concept in disability studies and politics.

The Social Model

During the 1970s and 1980s, disabled activists and their organizations in Europe and North America became increasingly vocal in their dismissal of the individual, medicalized understanding of disability, and its psychological and social welfare implications. Reflecting on their experiences of discrimination, disabled people focused on the organization of society rather than individual functional limitations or differences. Modern society failed to recognize or accommodate the human diversity associated with impairment (Bowe, 1978; Oliver, 1981; Zola, 1982). It was the Union of the Physically Impaired Against Segregation (UPIAS) (1975) that codified these concerns into the 'fundamental principles' document declaring that people were disabled by society and not their impairments. This led to the formulation of what came to be called the social model of disability (Oliver, 1981, 1983).

Early disability research inspired by a social model account concentrated on structural aspects of the social and material conditions experienced by disabled people in the family, education, income and financial support, employment, housing, transport and the built environment (Barnes, 1991). This was considered central to building explanations of how far, and in what ways, 'society disables' people with impairments, and analysing the structures and processes associated with social oppression and discrimination, whether at the level of social policy and the state or in everyday social interaction. Key contributors to the development of a social model approach strongly favoured a 'materialist' or 'social creation' approach over an 'idealist' account that prioritized cultural values and representations (Finkelstein, 1980; Oliver, 1990; Barnes, 1991).

Debates on disability now routinely acknowledge the influence of social model thinking. What is particularly striking is its impact on current policies across a diverse range of organizations, including central and local governments, charities and voluntary agencies. Indeed, some disabled activists and disability theorists have been unsure whether this has always been a positive development (Oliver, 2004). At the same time, attacks by social scientists on the social model have multiplied (Bury, 1997; Williams, S., 1999; Williams, G., 2001) from 'without' with additional criticism 'from within' (Shakespeare, 2006; Shakespeare & Watson, 2001). The problem with much of this criticism is that: 'Sadly a lot of people have come to think of the social model of disability as if it were an explanation, definition or theory and many people use the model in a rather sterile formalistic way' (Finkelstein, 2002, p. 6).

We do not intend to reprise debates about the social model here, as in our view too much time and too many words have been expended in discussing it. However Peters, Gabel & Symeonidou (2009, p. 544) have been happy to incorporate it into their work on resistance: 'The social model, then, has been particularly useful as a tool in that it raises awareness of oppression – a critical first step needed in order to challenge oppression through action.'

While this is undoubtedly so, this is not the whole story. As we have pointed out, the social model has been incorporated into the agendas and practices of governments, welfare agencies, 'quangos' (quasi-non-government organizations), charities and a variety of other organizations worldwide. All this has occurred often without any of these agencies making any substantial changes to their practices; we still have international charities who incarcerate disabled people all over the world claiming to work to the principles of the social model and governments who endorse it yet continue providing individualizing responses to the problems of unemployment and discrimination.

There are other problems as well, particularly the way in which the social model has become a talking shop for many academics leading to claims that it has failed to bring about meaningful change, that it should be abandoned or that it needs to be reclaimed (Oliver, 2009). Thus rather than being a symbol of resistance, for some it now represents the wrong direction and for others it has become counter-productive. Most importantly of all for us, the social model connection with the material circumstances of disabled people has been lost. Any reference back to the *Fundamental Principles of Disability* document (UPIAS, 1976) shows that members of UPIAS were fully aware of the need to address this, because much of the document is devoted to a debate with the Disability Alliance over whether there should be a national disability income. The UPIAS members were always clear that this form of 'state-sponsored charity' would merely lock disabled people further into relations of poverty and dependency and it was these material circumstances which needed addressing.

Independent Living

Peters, Gabel and Symeonidou (2009) suggest that the rise of the Independent

Living Movement (ILM) in America, with its emphasis on 'self-empowerment' (De Jong, 1983; Hahn, 1986) can be seen as a 'critical incidence of resistance'. Throughout the 1960s and early 1970s a number of disabled students at the University of California at Berkeley began lobbying for the support necessary to enable them to carry out and complete their studies. So successful were they that their numbers expanded noticeably with the increasing accessibility of the campus and generally supportive culture.

Their experience inspired the development of a Centre for Independent Living (CIL) in the local community, with similar initiatives elsewhere in America (Zola, 1994). Services offered ranged widely, from political and legal advocacy, peer counselling, screening and training personal assistants, wheelchair repair and ramp construction, to moving into accessible housing. By the late 1980s, over 300 CILs had been established across America. These user-led services offered an example of disability praxis – with the integration of a socio-political analysis of disability and practical support for independent living. Besides providing services, they became a site for consciousness raising and political organization, 'although not all have been unambiguously controlled by disabled people' (Scotch, 1989, p. 394).

In Britain these experiences and developments were monitored closely by a number of disabled people who were either struggling to escape from residential institutions or struggling to stay out of them. They used them as a means of establishing their own community support programmes and provided the momentum for developing Britain's first two CILs in Derbyshire and Hampshire in 1985. From the outset these CILs realized that there were problems with the American approach which was essentially individualizing and supportive of capitalism's market ideology.

The Derbyshire Centre for Integrated Living (DCIL) opted to deliver a wide range of services supporting inclusive living (Davis, 1990; Davis & Mullender, 1993). These included information and advice (know what options exist), counselling and peer support (for encouragement and guidance from other disabled people), housing (appropriate place to live), technical aids and equipment (to generate more self-reliance), personal assistance (controlled by the disabled person as employer), transport (mobility options) and access to the built environment (adapted from Davis, 1990, p. 7). By contrast Hampshire Centre for Independent Living (HCIL) concentrated initially on personal assistance and

training in 'independent living skills' but in 1989 added four more needs: education and training, employment, income (to cover the additional costs of living
with impairment) and advocacy (Barnes & Mercer, 2006, p. 48). For both organizations the priority was to provide appropriate and accountable support as the
necessary foundations to enable disabled people to live independently and on
equal terms in mainstream society (Oliver, 1990; Morris, 1993; Barnes & Mercer,
2006). While some European countries, particularly in Scandinavia, were influenced by the philosophy of independent living, their strategic priority was to
enhance existing state-sponsored welfare systems to meet disabled people's needs.

In Europe at least, state-provided welfare programmes were regarded as essential
to overcome the perceived shortcomings of market provision and heightened
barriers experienced by poorer disabled people. Nonetheless, despite these
reservations the philosophy of independent living has had a profound influence
on the provision of services for disabled people. And in concert with the increasing
penetration of the market into welfare provision during the 1980s, giving
people money, whether individually or through organizations, has become the
main, if not the only, mechanism for delivering independent living-type services
across Europe (Ungerson, 2004). In the UK the Community Care (Direct
Payments) Act (1996) and subsequent amendments (2000 and 2003) provides
but one example of this cash mechanism (Barnes & Mercer, 2006).

There is no doubt that this approach has given thousands of disabled people
back substantial measures of control over their own lives and been personally
empowering, but at what cost? Can independent living be seen as 'a critical incidence
of resistance' as some claim (Peters, Gabel & Symeonidou, 2009) or are the
worries about its connections to individualization and marketization evidence of
its incorporation into capitalist social and welfare relations?

The disability activist and writer Finkelstein has no doubt that:

> The promoters of 'independent living' in a market economy can't complain that
> they get what they wanted. When disability groups became 'independent' they
> needed to get on with the job and compete against other 'independent living'
> service providers ... That's what 'independence' means in the capitalist system.
> It's all about 'efficient' service provision (meaning who has the cheapest
> product to sell). (Finkelstein, in Oliver 2009, 150, p.1)

But he goes further and asserts:

> This is a capitalist dream come true – every single disabled person becomes an

employer, pays personal assistants for their labour, is responsible for working conditions, ensures annual leave is provided, does the obligatory paperwork and checks taxes, etc. The only trouble is – capitalism doesn't stop here – competition means successful companies gobble up weaker groups, companies merge forming larger groups and those that fail, well, they go bankrupt and disappear. No surprise, surely, that entrepreneurs are setting up companies to relieve stressed disabled people from managing their 'direct payments' funding. (Finkelstein, 2009, p. 151)

Furthermore the penetration of the market into state-sponsored welfare may not end there. In Britain, for example, government has eagerly seized upon the idea of giving people cash instead of services and is currently rolling out a programme of personalized health budgets with considerable enthusiasm (Lednetter, 2004; Department of Health, 2010). Coupled with their other plans for privatizing health care provision, these developments could effectively mean the demise of 'health care for all, free at the point of delivery' in Britain. Given these developments we are reminded of the old saying 'be careful what you wish for because you might just get it'.

To reiterate, the marketization of welfare has undoubtedly caused great difficulties for many disabled people, but the introduction of independent living-type services has also transformed the lives of some, but not all. In the UK, for example, the number of people receiving 'cash for care' remains small relative to the total service user population. Access varies considerably between local authorities and is especially low for 'parents of disabled children, mental health systems users, and people with learning difficulties' (CSCI, 2006). We supported these policies because professionalized welfare has regrettably proved to be incapable of giving disabled people control over the services needed to live a decent life. But we are also clear that it is too simple an argument to present independent living as either an example of resistance or an exemplar of the capitalist market penetrating ever deeper into our lives. It is of course both, which is why we should support it and be critical of it. And without wishing to sound too self-righteous, in our view, the only way to be able to deal with this is to have a proper understanding of the real nature of disablement in a neo-liberal, capitalist world economy.

Disabling Corporatism

The remarkable politicization and mobilization of disabled people and their organizations around the world over recent years has been extraordinarily significant in challenging myths and misconceptions about disabled people's supposed passivity. This mobilization is especially remarkable in light of the fact that it has been achieved with few resources and poor access to the electoral and political processes as political environments all too frequently make voting difficult due to poor access (ADD, 2005; Barnett, Scott & Morris, 2007; Keeley et al., 2008) and engaging in political activities and procedures difficult due to negative attitudes and discriminatory practices (Scott & Crooks, 2005; Barnes & Mercer, 2010).

Until the 1990s, disability politics in most Western societies was dominated by professionally led impairment-specific organizations that perpetuated a traditional paternalistic understanding of disability and disabled people. The upsurge of disability activism amongst grassroots organizations has had a significant influence on these organizations but also on mainstream political parties, policy makers and the general population. A significant illustration of this impact is demonstrated by the growth of anti-discrimination legislation in many countries around the world (Doyle, 2008) and the growing focus on disability rights among international organizations as diverse as the World Health Organization, the World Bank and the United Nations (WHO, 2011).

While there have been significant advances in placing disability issues firmly on national and international political agendas, this has not generated the changes necessary to bring about a more equitable and just society either within or across nation states. Indeed, there are concerns amongst some disability activists that the assimilation of disability politics into mainstream political agendas will undermine the more radical aims and political struggles by disabled people and their organizations for social justice.

Moreover there is no doubt that over the last decade the big charities have experienced a resurgence, while the power and influence of the disabled people's movement has undoubtedly declined. These two things are not unconnected, both because the greater resources of the big charities have enabled them to compete more effectively for government and local contracts, and because they have unashamedly adopted and adapted the ideas and language of the disabled people's movement. This has been helped by the increasing numbers of people with impairments who have moved into key positions in many of these organizations. Ironically many of those people would not have 'touched any of these organisations with the proverbial barge pole' ten years ago (Oliver & Barnes, 2006).

As well as this resurgence, as noted earlier, the government in the UK has created a number of semi-independent organizations or quangos, such as the Disability Rights Commission, (DRC) the National Centre for Independent Living (NCIL) and the Office for Disability Issues (ODI), all of which draw funding away from the disabled people's movement. This trend has become so prominent in the twenty-first century that we have called it disabling corporatism (Oliver, 2009). It has also manifested itself in European and international agencies, again aided by prominent disabled activists who have joined these organizations, usually called International Non-Government Organizations (INGOs) in this context. The historical record of disabling corporatism at national and international levels is patchy and for our purposes here does nothing to confront the economic and social relations of capitalism. One commentator sums this up as follows:

> While there are many radical and dedicated practitioners in this NGO world, their work is at best ameliorative. Collectively, they have a spotty record of progressive achievements, although in certain arenas such as women's rights, health care and environmental preservation they can reasonably claim to have made major contributions to human betterment. But revolutionary change by NGO is impossible. They are too constrained by the political and policy stances of their donors. So even though, in supporting local empowerment, they help to open spaces where anti-capitalist alternatives become possible, and even support experimentation with such alternatives, they do nothing to prevent the re-absorption of those alternatives into the dominant capitalist practice; they even encourage it. (Harvey, 2010, pp. 253–4)

While some disability theorists now argue that we should put our trust in these organizations because they have changed significantly (Shakespeare, 2006) others see identity politics as a way of resisting and transforming the disabling society.

Identity Politics

Initially some disability scholars viewed the politicization of disabled people as a response to their common experience of oppression (Finkelstein, 1980; Oliver, 1983). This provided a unifying group identity and interest while identifying the source of these grievances in the structures and processes of a market-led disabling society. For many people with impairments, engaging in collective action was liberating and empowering psychologically and a source of a positive identity:

> Not only is the fashioning of collective identity an explicitly articulated goal of the politicised disabled people's movement, but the very act of political partic-ipation in itself induces others to impute certain characteristics to the activist. (Anspach, 1979, p. 766)

The assertion of a positive cultural identity and a 'politics of difference' have become favoured political strategies for a number of protest movements, not just those based on disability. The initial goal of such movements is the recog-nition and celebration of difference. Therefore just as 'self-identity' is a central issue in considering the emergence of disability culture, so too it is at the heart of disability politics. Yet many individuals with impairments do not 'self-identify' as disabled people or get involved in political activity of any kind (Watson, 2002).

In common with all social categories and groupings people with impairments and labelled 'disabled' are not necessarily an homogenous group. They may divide along impairment-specific grounds such as 'learning difficulties' (Chappell, 1998) or mental health systems users and survivors (Sayce, 2000), for example, or ethnicity (Hill, 1994), gender (Fine & Asch, 1988), sexuality (Shakespeare, Gillespie-Sells & Davies, 1996) or social class. Indeed, those in a middle- or upper-middle class position with access to financial and other resources which mitigate some of the worst effects of disability, may distance themselves from their poorer contemporaries (Russell, 1998).

But this factionalism may not be the only difficulty for identity politics. As the disabled people's movement has discovered with respect to deaf people, disabled identities are sometimes contested, and critics of this 'politics of identity' approach, such as Fraser (1997, 2000), have suggested it signals a retreat from a vision of a 'just social order', and a shift away from struggles over redistribution to a focus on winning 'recognition' of social collectivities in a distinctive cultural and political struggle. She argues that, whatever its claims, an essentially 'cultural politics of identity and difference' fails to connect with a 'social politics of justice and equality' (1997, p.186).

As Russell argues, the challenge for disability politics is to

> build upon mutual respect and support *without dismissing or diluting difference*. For instance, to *move beyond ramps, we must first agree that ramps are indisputably necessary*. That would be making a common political 'home', blending difference into commonality'. (Russell, 1998, p. 233, original emphasis)

A further issue that generates intense debate is how far disability politics should reflect the wider flow of identity politics and the celebration of difference. This has focused attention on cultural politics, both as forms of domination and resistance, and the significance of attending to diversity among disabled people. What is at risk is that the material bases of economic inequality are set aside or marginalized, along with the goal of political-economic redistribution.

New Social Movements

While conventional politics remains central to political campaigns by disabled people and their organizations, the failures of pressure group, identity and electoral politics to win significant policy reforms have encouraged a more radical disability politics. This has given rise to suggestions that the disabled people's movement may lay claim to be a 'new social movement' (NSM) (Oliver, 1990, 1996), or a 'liberation struggle' (Shakespeare, 1993). The polarization of 'old' and 'new' forms of social protest runs parallel to claims that there have been major re-alignments in the late twentieth century social and economic order which herald the emergence of what has been variously termed 'post-industrial', 'postcapitalist', or 'post-modern' society (Fagan & Lee, 1997).

A shift towards consumption rather than production (Bauman, 1990), consequential changes in the division of labour and social structure, with deepening social and cultural disorganization and crises in capitalism have all been identified as key features. In turn, changing class configurations and other emerging social divisions and conflicts have encouraged new forms of social protest. Some now see progressive social change stemming from the emerging range of new protest movements of the 1970s and 1980s that included the women's movement, peace and environmental groups (Touraine, 1981; Scott, 1990).

In the previous edition of this book (Oliver, 1990) we argued that the disabled people's movement was a new social movement, because it was peripheral to conventional politics; it offered a critical evaluation of society; it embraced 'post-materialist' or 'post-acquisitive' values; and it adopted an international perspective (Oliver, 1990, 1996). The emphasis of the movement was on self-organization and a commitment to radical political action to promote change and to improve the quality of disabled people's lives and promote their full inclusion into society.

A key feature of the disabled people's movement has been its focus on social exclusion and oppression. It argues that the barriers to disabled people's inclusion are embedded in policies and practices based on the individualistic and medical approaches to disability. The removal of such obstacles involves gaining control over material resources and the range and quality of services. Previously we have suggested that the aim of the movement was to be 'consciously engaged in critical evaluation of capitalist society and in the creation of alternative models of social organisation at local, national and international levels, as well as trying to reconstruct the world ideologically and to create alternative forms of service provision' (Oliver, 1990, p. 113).

A further aspect of this approach was the adoption of unconventional political tactics, including demonstrations, direct action and civil disobedience. These attracted particular attention in the United States, where disability protests often took their cue from the actions of other social protest movements of the late 1960s and early 1970s: 'When traditional legal channels have been exhausted, disabled people have learned to employ other techniques of social protest' (De Jong 1983, p. 12). This engagement in 'direct action' represents a shift in the balance from 'old' to 'new' style political protests and campaigning.

Another element claimed as a distinguishing feature of new social movements is their adherence to 'post-materialist' or 'post-acquisitive' values – over those that have to do with income, satisfaction of material needs and social security (Inglehart, 1990). This is particularly evident in environmental and peace groups, but evidence of this 'value switch' is far from compelling when applied generally to disabled people, women, lesbians and gay men or black and minority ethnic groups. All these groups have stressed the importance of overturning disadvantages in the distribution of income and wealth, welfare benefits and the labour market.

Similarly, the demand for more resources and service support typifies disabled people's demands around the world. However, the disabled people's movement has also struggled to incorporate counter-cultural shifts, such as those identified in a disability culture which has confronted the 'stigmatisation of difference', and presented an altogether more positive 'disabled identity' (Oliver, 1996, p.157). Other accounts of new social movements stress the tension between what Fraser (1997) terms a politics of 'distribution' and of 'affirmation'.

Certainly, the disabled people's movement, as with feminist politics, has committed itself to a more expressive politics in seeking empowerment and social justice. This links with a cultural politics that challenges disabling stereotypes and the notion of an 'able-bodied/minded' normality and seeks ways to affirm a positive disabled identity. In this way the movement supplements its concern with economic and social inequalities with the danger that this stance falls short of a comprehensive denial of core capitalist values.

Another key feature in new social movements in general and the politicization of disability in particular has been internationalization (Driedger, 1989). Disabled activists formed Disabled People's International (DPI) in 1981. Its first world congress was held in Singapore in the following year and attracted 400 delegates from around the world. They agreed on a common programme: the empowerment of disabled people through collective political action (DPI, 1982). For DPI, the prerequisite for change lay in the promotion of grassroots organizations and the development of public awareness of disability issues. Its slogan, 'Nothing about is without us' (Charlton, 1998), has been embraced by disabled people's organizations around the world.

As indicated earlier, the impact of the disabled people's movement at the international level has had a major influence on international and global politics as witnessed by the attention given to disability issues within trans-national organizations such as the United Nations, World Health Organization, the International Monetary Fund, and the World Bank.

Overall, the disabled people's movement has utilized both radical and conventional politics. The balance between the two has varied historically; currently those committed to wide-ranging social change have lost ground to those supporting political involvement in the established political institutions and trying to break down disabling barriers from within the system. Of course, there is no single 'royal road' to 'independent living' or 'empowerment', and no user's manual, overarching set of political tactics or universally applicable form of self-organization; nor can there be. The approach taken by the disabled people's movement in different countries demonstrates considerable variation in their political analyses and strategies. Yet, for most disabled people, what is important is not whether disabled people's struggle is categorized as either 'new' or 'old' style politics but that it sustains and enhances the extraordinary vitality and impact of disability politics built up over recent decades.

Conclusion

Elsewhere in this book we have traced the rise of the disabled people's movement and how it originated in their adverse material circumstances. We have also discussed the movement's achievements in improving the living conditions of some disabled people and suggested that recently, many of the issues raised by the movement have been incorporated into the agenda of global capitalism.

Despite these developments, clearly we were over-optimistic about the role of new social movements in producing significant social change. Yet many of the emergent movements operating in the last century have either been absorbed into government or become marginal to the political process. Regrettably, we would suggest, this has become the temporary fate of the disabled people's movement. Most significantly, there has been no coming together of the disabled people's movement and other political groups, such as the lesbian and gay movement (Shakespeare, Gillespie-Sells & Davies, 1996) or perhaps more significantly the anti-capitalist movement (Horsler, 2003), for example, to create more powerful alliances. And in some respects the social divisions that characterized British society in the twentieth century, such as ethnicity, race, and religion, for instance, have widened.

Most importantly, the prohibition of racism, sexism, ageism and disablism by law has done little to eliminate these problems. By the same token, the singular focus on disability as a rights issue will not solve the problem of disability discrimination and oppression. At best, it will benefit only a very small minority of the disabled population: those with plenty of money to spend and those employed in the legal and related professions. At worst, it will legitimize further the rhetoric of those who support an inherently unjust and inequitable society and hamper further the struggle for meaningful equality and justice.

We still believe that the only viable long-term political strategy for disabled people is to be part of a far wider struggle to create a better society for all. It is a struggle that must take on board the fact that twenty-first century Britain is a society near the top of world league tables for illiteracy, teenage pregnancy, childhood obesity, school exclusions and relative poverty. All of this must be contextualized within a global society characterized by an exploding human population, growing cultural conflict, climatic change and environmental degradation. These are the issues that today's generation will almost certainly have to address if the struggle for a society fit for all is to be achieved.

Like Peters, Gabel and Symeonidou (2009) we agree that 'notions of resistance are intended to offer hope and possibilities that inform and globalise the struggle to overcome the oppression of disabled people' (p. 555). However, we wish to add that the oppression of disabled people will only end when the oppression of all is overcome and that will only happen with major structural, economic, political and cultural transformation as well as resistance.

9

Doing Disability Studies

Introduction

We began by describing our own personal and professional backgrounds which have obviously influenced our writing in general, and this book in particular. When we began our careers as sociologists, we were introduced to the dominant tradition of 'scientific objectivity' which stressed the need to distance ourselves from our own personal experiences in our professional work. We wore this cloak of objectivity during our initial studies but soon experienced 'cognitive dissonance' in pursuing our own areas of interest. Influenced by both the interactionist sociologies of the 1960s, Marxism and feminism and the writings of some disabled individuals, we soon came to realize that scientific objectivity was a very partial way of viewing the world which distorted our personal experiences of impairment and denied the politics of our material circumstances.

We were not interested in sociology as an objective and value-free discipline, but as a committed and contested subject which, to paraphrase Marx, was more concerned with changing the world than understanding it. Rejecting the notions of objectivity and value freedom did not mean we rejected the discipline of sociology. Instead we sought to use our own experiences to revise our sociological understandings of both impairment and disability. This part of our journey is described mainly in Chapter 2 but also appears elsewhere in this book. We do not propose to return to this here but instead to look at the emergence of disability studies, its status, its position within academia and its potential and influence on political and social change.

Disciplining Disability Studies

While the emergence of disability studies was originally dominated by sociology and writers drawing extensively on that discipline, there is no doubt that in recent times it has drawn upon much wider sources and influences, as one recent text describes:

> Disability studies is an emergent field with intellectual roots in the social sciences, humanities, and rehabilitation sciences. The theoretical and conceptual armamentaria of these disciplines provide frameworks to address the persistent themes addressed in the volume, raise the critical issues in need of attention, better understand the problems of the field, and suggest integrative approaches to uniting the field. Equally important to the conception of disability studies is the inclusion of the disability community and those with disabilities who do not actively participate in the community or discourse. (Albrecht, Seelman & Bury, 2001, p. 2)

Given this plethora of influences and sources it raises the issue of whether disability studies is a discipline in its own right or a sub-discipline of something else. If it is the latter sociology can no longer claim to be the parental discipline, as in recent years psychology, economics, history, cultural studies and humanities have all made significant contributions to the field. This perhaps raises the question of whether disability studies can properly be called a discipline at all or should be called something else. It is certainly true that in recent times the disciplinary terrain within academia has become increasingly complex and contested for all disciplines.

The current situation of disability studies fits in well within a recent description of this:

> The rise and fall of disciplinary regimes are consequences of powerful alliances which marshall the distribution of rewards within a field of academic practice. Disciplines are periodically fragmented and dispersed by internal intellectual studies and by external conflicts with adjacent disciplines. Some disciplines never get fully accepted into the academy, while certain area studies may disappear. Disciplines through internal specialization may fragment and divide, and as a consequence disciplines which are held together by the requirements of an external professional body may be more resistant to internal fragmentation. (Turner, 1999, p. 276)

Locating Disability Studies

Theoretical analyses of disability in Britain, as in America, have their roots in the political activities of disabled people in the late 1960s and 1970s, including specific campaigns for greater autonomy and control by disabled people in residential institutions (Finkelstein, 1991) and for a comprehensive disability income and new living options (Oliver & Zarb,1989). In this climate of social and political change the unprecedented politicization of disabled people runs parallel to the formulation of radical social analyses of disability.

The early American literature, however, differs in that it references the changing status of disabled people in other parts of the world, but ignores the debates about developing a social model or social understanding of disability in Europe or elsewhere. A further contrast is that disability studies in America were dominated by academic writers, whereas in Europe disabled activists outside academia provided a significant input (Barnes, Oliver & Barton, 2002). Thus the early work in Britain offered a more comprehensive and, in many ways, more accessible examination of the economic, political and cultural phenomena that gave rise, and continue to shape the process of disablement in capitalist societies.

We would also suggest that the emergence of disability studies in Britain and Europe drew on very different theoretical traditions than in America. Here we relied on a materialist perspective stemming from the work of Finkelstein (1980), Oliver (1990), Barnes (1997) and Gleeson (1999). In America disability studies initially drew on functionalist and phenomenological perspectives (Safilios-Rothschild, 1970; Albrecht, 1976; Zola, 1982) but later were influenced by the various theoretical developments loosely termed 'postmodernism' or 'poststructuralism' (Davis, 1995; Thomson, 1996; Mitchell & Snyder, 1997).

Debating Disability Studies

While the materialist perspective remains a key part of disability studies, there is little doubt that it is the postmodernist/poststructuralist perspectives which have come to dominate not just in America, but also in the work of British academics (see, for example, Corker & Shakespeare, 1998; Shakespeare & Watson, 2001; Goodley, 2011). Part of this is understandable with the collapse of Soviet-style communism, the changing political climate of the 1980s and 90s, and the associate abandonment of radical theorizing generally within the social sciences and economics in particular (Harvey, 2010). The result was a widespread retreat from radical sociology into applied disciplines like criminology and/or the dead

end of philosophy. Notwithstanding that, the dominance of postmodernist/
poststructuralist perspectives has profound implications for those of us committed
to developing an emancipatory and transformative disability studies.

During the late 1990s this major challenge to the dominance of materialist
analyses of disablement was particularly evident in the work of North American
and Scandinavian writers (see for example, Davis, 1995; Wendell, 1996;
Mitchell & Snyder, 1997; Thomson, 1997, 2006; Linton, 1998; Snyder &
Mitchell, 2001; Kristiansen, Velmas & Shakespeare, 2009). These approaches
moved away from an emphasis on the primacy of material factors in the creation
of disability toward a more nuanced focus on culture, language and discourse.

Central to these accounts is a deconstruction of the concept of normality or
'normalcy' and its discursive impact on societal responses to impairment as
provided by Davis(1995). This analysis of changing cultural responses to
impairment provides a useful addition to materialist accounts of the emergence
of the disability category discussed earlier. Davis argues that 'the social processes
associated with disabling cultural environments arrived with industrialisation as
a new set of discourses and practices'. This is not very different from materialist
accounts except for the emphasis given to the cultural rather than the economic.

It is constructions of the body rather than the economic and social relations
of capitalism that are given primacy. The construction of the 'disabled' individual
and group was an inevitable outcome of the displacement of the 'ideal' by the
'normal/abnormal' dichotomy. Consequently, the dominant discourses around
notions of the 'grotesque' and the ideal body in the Middle Ages were
completely overturned by the normalizing gaze of modern science. This
established a hierarchical standard for pronouncing some bodies and minds as
abnormal and inferior – in terms of appearance and performance. Standards of
physical health, mental balance and moral soundness became closely linked, so
that defective bodies and minds were associated with 'degeneracy' (Young,
1990).

Postmodernist accounts have also sought to analyse how the categories of
'impairment' and 'disability' are being constantly rewritten as part of a wider
politics of the body. An attempt to generate an embodied notion of disability is
evident in the work of Thomson (1997) when she challenges the widespread
belief that 'able-bodiedness' and 'disability' are 'self-evident physical conditions'.
Instead, she explores how the 'physically disabled body' becomes 'a repository

for social anxieties'. Her objective is to remove the disabled body from medical discourse and recast disabled people as a disadvantaged minority in the tradition of American writings.

The postmodernist critique of materialist disability studies is not simply concerned with the primacy of discourse and deconstruction but also launches an assault on the social model of disability (Tremain, 2002, 2005; Shakespeare & Watson, 2001; Shakespeare, 2006). Whilst it is acknowledged that the social model has proved invaluable in mobilizing the disabled people's movement and opened up new areas of academic enquiry, especially in the UK, it is now considered to have outgrown its usefulness within disability studies. The crux of this assault hinges on the impairment/disability distinction upon which the social model rests. For postmodernists this distinction is not tenable as it represents nothing less than a new impairment/disability dualism synonymous with a modernist world view.

Hence, for postmodernists, the social model explains disability as a universal construct that has generated a 'totalizing historical metanarrative' that excludes important dimensions of disabled people's lived experience and knowledge. Further, Shakespeare (2006) suggests that the social model is an outdated ideology because the distinction between impairment and disability and its emphasis on barrier removal is untenable. Disability studies in the UK is criticized for its failure to concentrate on subjective meanings of impairment and the British disabled people's movement is accused of being unrepresentative of the disabled population as a whole.

For us, whilst postmodernist accounts have reaffirmed the importance of cultural responses to disability, their arguments sidestep the material reality of the social production of culture, the reality of impairment, and provide little or no insight into how the problem of disablism might be resolved in terms of politics, policy or practice. Furthermore, if the postmodernist denial of agency is taken to its logical conclusion then disability activism and politics are inconceivable: 'Impaired people might as well lie down to the discrimination and exclusion that disables their lives' (Hughes, 2005, p.90). Certainly Shakespeare's work (2006) can be seen as supportive of the social relations of capitalism with his apparent endorsement of disabling corporatism and his uncritical support for the involvement of medicine in the lives of disabled people (Oliver, 2007, 2009).

As the problems with postmodernism/poststructuralism have become more apparent, there have been various attempts to import critical realism into the picture:

> impairment and disability are interrogated as a phenomena [*sic*] enacted at the levels of the psyche, culture and society. While critical disability studies might start with disability, they never end with it, remaining ever vigilant of political, ontological and theoretical complexity. And in order to analyse disablism we need to be mindful of the complementary hegemony of ablism. Critical disability studies contest dis/ablism. (Goodley, 2011, p. 157)

As yet the precise relationship between postmodernism/poststructuralism and critical disability studies remains unclear but as the above quote illustrates, they both use academic language in a way that disables rather than enables those without an academic background (Swain, 2011). This is not an 'anti-intellectual' stance, though we are sometimes accused of taking such a position. In fact we believe that a great deal of intellectual work is necessary if we are to really understand, challenge and change the disabling society. Further we believe that intellectuals have an absolute responsibility to communicate their ideas in a way that enables others to use them for the betterment of all. For us, postmodernist, poststructuralist and critical disability studies have yet to demonstrate their inclusivity or their usefulness in this endeavour.

Politicizing Disability Studies

Earlier we pointed to the possible division of disability studies into two overtly hostile camps and, according to one commentator, this is already the case:

> In the materialistic perspective disability is seen as socially created by socio-economic factors, barriers and discrimination. In the narrow definition disability studies is also seen as tightly connected to the political activism of disabled persons. In the wider definition disability studies refers to research about disability in the social sciences and humanities. In this wider definition no reference is made to any particular meta-theoretical assumptions or relation to activism. The wider definition is sometimes separated from disability studies by being named disability research. (Soder, 2009. p. 67)

For us this is a matter of some regret and we would not like to see disability studies become exclusively a matter of academic in-fighting and career advancement. We do not shy away from the fact that doing disability studies is inherently political, however. This warrants challenging the disability knowledge base which uses methodological individualism and investigatory foundationalism; taking responsibility for the new disability politics produced by those who want impairment and the body to be central components of the disability studies agenda; and forging and maintaining links with disabled people, their experiences and their organizations.

For us, as unrepentant materialists, we would like to see the postmodernists and critical theorists respond to the new political challenges that are emerging from the recent crisis in global capitalism rather than provide yet more spurious and unfounded critiques of the social model of disability in the guise of theoretical progress and make yet further calls for the incorporation of the body into social theory. This newly emerging politics is drawing upon impairment and the body in ways that they might come to regret.

For example, in Britain at the time of writing disability seems to be back on the government's political agenda and its plans have attracted a great deal of attention. Responding to global capitalism's latest crisis, it has decided that disabled people's benefits and services are to be severely cut back as a key part of its plans to reduce public expenditure. The last time the British government had similar aims was in response to an earlier crisis in capitalism some thirty years ago when the then government had similar plans for disabled people.

The response of the disabled people's movement then was very different from today. It rejected society's stereotype that disabled people were tragic victims of unfortunate circumstances and instead promoted the social model, anti-discrimination legislation and independent living as ways to respond to the crisis. The movement also promoted positive images of disabled people and was not afraid to reinforce its demands and messages by taking to the streets in non-violent direct action.

The political response to the current crisis seems very different and much more muted. Led by the leaders of disabling corporatism, disability pride seems to have disappeared and there are no new ideas about what to do being promoted. Protests are much more orderly and often confined to the internet or carefully controlled marches. The limit of disabling corporate responses to government plans seem to be to ask politely for the benefits and services for disabled people to be protected.

There are obviously a number of reasons for these different responses, many of which we have discussed in various parts of this book and we do not propose to go over this ground again here. However the calls of postmodernists, post-structuralists and critical theorists for impairment and the body to be a central plank of disability studies have clearly influenced the recent re-affirmation of the traditional view that disabled people are weak and vulnerable and in need of protection. These discourses have in many ways provided academic justification for politicians and policy makers to legitimate their cost-cutting measures while continuing to promise to protect people with impairments and 'long term health conditions' unable to help themselves. It also provides a rationale for disabling corporatism to continue to represent disabled people because disabled people need help and protection. And so far, these approaches have provided no new ideas or platform for action for disability politics, no matter how it is constituted.

We make this link between ideas and action not to score points against advocates of these perspectives, but in the hope that a constructive dialogue might emerge not about the nature of reality but what might be done in response to the ongoing economic crisis and the effects it is having on disabled people. Whether disability studies is a discipline, subject, area of studies or whatever is of little importance. For us it is an emancipatory project and its effectiveness, as such, would be much diminished if it were to fracture into two hostile camps. The dangers of this have recently been spelled out:

> However if we are to begin to go beyond a position where we fail to read each others' work in full and adopting clichéd stands on the 'perceived essences' of these works then we need to understand the full range of points being made and the context for these writings ... The shift towards a more diverse and arguably academicised disability studies risks overlooking the fundamental issues of importance for disabled people; poverty, unemployment, lack of access to benefits, increasingly severe rationing of social support all characterise the early 21st century. (Roulstone, 2011, p. 380)

Rescuing Disability Studies: The Wind is Still Blowing

Whether we are academics, activists or both we believe that disability studies has played an important part in recent changes in the lives of disabled people and this can and should continue along the lines we suggest below:

> There is a sense in which this book can be read both pessimistically and optimistically. The argument suggests that the dominant view of disability as an individual, medical problem is created by the productive forces, material conditions and social relations of capitalism. The chances of transcending these forces, conditions and relations are therefore intrinsically bound up with the possibilities of capitalism itself being transcended. These possibilities do not appear to be likely to materialize in the foreseeable future, for, even allowing the idea of post-capitalist society, such a society appears more as an extension of capitalist forces, conditions and relations than as a transition on the road to socialism.
>
> However, disability does not appear as an individual, tragic and medical problem in all societies that have existed historically nor in some that exist currently. So it may be that the material conditions and social relations of disability can be improved without waiting upon the possibility of the transcending of the productive forces of capitalism itself. Thus there are grounds for optimism from this more limited view. (Oliver, 1990, p. 132)

The above two paragraphs were the first two paragraphs of the Postscript to the first edition. We went on to conclude that the disabled people's movement offered grounds for optimism that the material conditions and social relations of capitalism could be improved without transforming capitalism itself. Indeed, we would argue that this has in varying degrees been the case for some disabled people in both rich and poor countries, and especially so in wealthy states. However the world is now a very different place from twenty years ago in two main respects relevant to this book.

To begin with, it is all too evident that over the last decade inequality within and across nation states has escalated, and global capitalism has experienced the worst economic crisis in recorded history (Harvey, 2010). Additionally, in common with other radical social movements, the disabled people's movement appears to be in decline rather than ascendancy.

The inevitable outcome of this unfortunate situation is the systematic introduction of austerity measures and cutbacks in public services and support by national governments and trans-national agencies for what are traditionally seen as 'weak' and 'vulnerable' groups: disabled people, children, women, older people, minority ethnic communities and unemployed people. All of which will mean a lowering of living standards in some form or another. Without strong and organized voices to defend them, the outcome for these groups could be catastrophic, especially in the poorer nations of the world where abject poverty is the norm rather than the exception for those at the foot of the social hierarchy. In these changed circumstances we urgently need

> a political analysis which is inspired by a desire for transformative change and that constitutes hope at the centre of struggles ... At both the individual and collective level a crucial task is to develop a theory of political action which also involves the generation of tactics or strategies for its implementation. This is a difficult but essential agenda. (Barton, 2001, p. 3)

We sincerely hope that this revised edition of the politics of disablement will make a contribution to this agenda.

Bibliography

Aail-Jilek. L. M. (1965) 'Epilepsy in the Wapagoro Tribe in Tanganyika', *Acta Psychiatr Neurol Scand*, 41, 57–86.

Abberley, P. (1987) 'The Concept of Oppression and the Development of a Social Theory of Disability', *Disability, Handicap and Society*, 2 (1), 5–19.

Abberley, P. (1988) 'The Body Silent: A Review', *Disability, Handicap and Society*, 3 (3), 306–7.

Abberley, P. (1993) 'Disabled people and 'normality'', in J. Swain, V. Finkelstein, S. French, and M. Oliver (eds) *Disabling Barriers – Enabling Environments* (London: Sage, in association with the Open University).

Abberley, P. (1995) 'Disabling ideology in health and welfare profession – the case of occupational therapy', *Disability and Society*, 10 (2), 221–32.

Abberley, P. (1997) 'The Limits of Classical Social Theory in the Analysis and Transformation of Disablement: (can this be the end, to be stuck inside of Mobile with the Memphis Blues again?)', in Oliver, M. and Barton, L. (eds) *Disability Studies: Past, Present and Future* (Leeds: The Disability Press. Available at: http://www.leeds.ac.uk/disability-studies/archiveuk/Abberley/chapter%202.pdf, accessed 10 June 2010).

Abberley, P. (2004): 'A critique of professional support and intervention', in J. Swain, S. French, C. Barnes and C. Thomas (eds) *Disabling Barriers – Enabling Environments*, 2nd edn (London: Sage).

Abrams, P. (1968) *The Origins of British Sociology 1834–1914* (Chicago: University of Chicago Press).

Abrams, P. (1982) *Historical Sociology* (London: Open Books).

ADAPT (1993) *Asian and Disabled: A Study into the Needs of Asian People with Disabilities in the Bradford Area* (West Yorkshire: Asian Disability Advisory Project Team, The Spastics Society and Barnardos).

ADD (2005) *Election Monitoring and Disabled People's Right to Vote*. Available at: Action on Disability and Development http://www.add.org.uk/downloads/Election%20Monitoring.pdf, accessed 10 March 2008.

Albert, B. (ed.) (2006) *In or Out of the Mainstream? Lessons from research on disability and development cooperation* (Leeds: The Disability Press).

Albert, B. and Harrison, M. (2006) 'Lessons from the Disability Knowledge and Research Programme', in B. Albert (ed.) *In or Out of the Mainstream? Lessons from research on disability and development cooperation* (Leeds: The Disability Press).

Albrecht, G. L. (1992) *The Disability Business: Rehabilitation in America* (London: Sage).

Albrecht, G. (ed.), (1981) *Cross National Rehabilitation Policies: A Sociological Perspective* (London: Sage).

Albrecht, G. and Levy, J. (1981) 'Constructing Disabilities as Social Problems', in G. Albrecht (ed.) *Cross National Rehabilitation Policies: A Sociological Perspective* (London: Sage),

Albrecht, G. L., Seelman, K. D. and Bury, M. (eds) (2001) *Handbook of Disability Studies* (London: Sage).

Allen, P. (2009) 'Cancer survival estimates: how they have changed', *Society Guardian*, Friday 20 March. Available at: http://www.guardian.co.uk/society/interactive/2009/mar/20/cancer-survival-rates-no-impact accessed 17 January 2011.

Althusser, L. (1971) *Lenin and Philosophy and Other Essays* (London: New Left Books).

Andreski, S. (ed.) (1975) *Herbert Spencer* (London: Nelson).

Anspach, R. (1979) 'From stigma to identity politics: political activism among the physically disabled and former mental patients', *Social Science and Medicine*, 13A, (6), 765–73.

Åsbring, A. and Närvänen, P. (2002) 'Women's Experience of Stigma in Relation to Chronic Fatigue Syndrome and Fibromyalgia', *Qualitative Health Research*, 12 (2), 148–60.

Audit Commission (1986) *Making a Reality of Community Care* (London: HMSO).

Azmi, S., Emerson, E., Caine, A. and Hatton, C. (1996) *Improving Services for Asian People with Learning Difficulties and their Families* (Manchester: Hester Adrian Research Centre/The Mental Health Foundation).

Barnes, C. (1990) *Cabbage Syndrome: The Social Construction of Dependence* (Lewes: Falmer Press).

Barnes, C. (1991) *Disabled People in Britain and Discrimination* (London: Hurst and Co., in association with the British Council of Organisations of Disabled People).

Barnes, C. (1992a) 'Qualitative Research: Valuable or Irrelevant', *Disability and Society*, 7 (2) 115–24.

Barnes, C. (1992b) *Disabling Imagery and the Media: An Exploration of Media Representations of Disabled People* (Belper: The British Council of Organisations of Disabled People).

Barnes, C. (1996a) 'Disability and the Myth of the Independent Researcher', *Disability and Society*, 10, (4), 107–11.

Barnes, C. (1996b) 'The Social Model of Disability: Myths and Misrepresentations', *Coalition: the Magazine of the Greater Manchester Coalition of Disabled People*, August, 25–30.

Barnes, C. (1996c) 'Forward', in J. Campbell and M. Oliver (eds) *Disability Politics: Understanding our Past, Changing our Future* (London: Routledge).

Barnes, C. (1997) 'A Legacy of Oppression: a history of disability in western culture', in L. Barton and M. Oliver (eds) *Disability Studies: Past, Present and Future* (Leeds, The Disability Press).

Barnes. C. (2003a) 'Rehabilitation for Disabled People: A Sick Joke?' *Scandinavian Journal for Disability Research*, 5 (1), 7–24.

Barnes, C. (2003b) 'Work is a Four Letter Work: Disability Work and Welfare', invited presentation, 'Working Futures: Policy, Practice and Disabled People's Employment', University of Sunderland, Seaburn, 3 December. Available at: http://www.disability-archive.leeds.ac.uk/authors_list.asp?AuthorID=8&author_name=Barnes%2C+Colin, accessed 12 June 2011.

Barnes, C. (2008) 'An Ethical Agenda in Disability Research: Rhetoric or Reality?'in D. M. Mertens and P. E. Ginsberg (eds) *The Handbook of Social Research Ethics* (London: Sage).

Barnes, C. and Mercer, G. (eds) (1996)*Exploring the Divide: Illness and Disability* (Leeds: The Disability Press.Available at: http://www.leeds.ac.uk/ disability-studies/archiveuk/Barnes/exp%20the%20divide%20CONTENTS.pdf, accessed 7 September 2009).

Barnes, C. and Mercer, G. (2003) *Disability: An Introduction* (Cambridge: Polity Press).

Barnes, C. and Mercer, M. G. (2005) 'Disability, Work and Welfare: challenging the social exclusion of disabled people', *Work Employment and Society*, 19, (5), 527–45.

Barnes, C. and Mercer, G. (2006) *Independent Futures.* Creating user-led disability services in a disabling society (Bristol: The Policy Press).

Barnes, C. and Mercer, G. (2010) *Exploring Disability*: 2nd edn (Cambridge: Polity).

Barnes, C. and Oliver, M. (1995) 'Disability Rights: Rhetoric and Reality in the UK', *Disability and Society*, 10 (1), 111–16.

Barnes, C. and Sheldon, A. (2010) 'Disability, Politics and Policy in a Majority World Context', *Disability and Society*, 25 (7), 77 –82.

Barnes, C., Oliver M. and Barton, L. (eds) (2002) *Disability Studies Today* (Cambridge: Polity).

Barnett, E., Scott, R. and Morris, G. (2007) *Polls Apart Cymru 2007* (London: Scope Cymru).

Barron, T. and Ncube, J. M. (2010) *Poverty and Disability* (London: Leonard Cheshire International).

Bartlett, P. and Wright, D. (1999) *Outside the Walls of the Asylum: The history of care in the community* (London: The Athlone Press).

Bartley, M. (2004) Health inequality: *Theories, concepts and methods* (Cambridge: Polity).

Barton, L. (ed.) (2001) *Disability Politics and the Struggle for Change* (London: David Fulton).

Battye, L. (1966) 'The Chatterley Syndrome', in P. Hunt (ed.) *Stigma* (London: Geoffrey Chapman).

Bauman, Z. (1990) *Thinking Sociologically* (Oxford: Blackwell).

Baxter, C. (1995) 'Confronting colour blindness: developing better services for people with learning difficulties from Black and ethnic minority communities', in T. Philpot and L. Ward (eds) *Values and Visions: Changing Ideas in Services for People with Learning Difficulties* (Oxford: Butterworth-Heinemann).

Baxter, C., Poonia, K., Ward, L. and Nadirshaw, Z. (1990) *Double Discrimination: Issues and services for people with learning difficulties from black and ethnic minority communities* (London: King's Fund Centre).

Baylies, C. (2002) 'Disability and the notion of human development: questions of rights and responsibilities', *Disability and Society*, 17 (7), 725–39.

BCODP (1986) *Disabled Young People Living Independently* (London: British Council of Organisations of Disabled People).

Beard, M. (2008) *Pompeii* (London: Profile Books).

Becker, H. (1963) *Outsiders: Studies in the Sociology of Deviance* (New York: Free Press).

Beckett, A., Ellison, N., Barrett, S., and Shah, S. (2010) 'Away with the Fairies? Disability within primary age children's literature', *Disability and Society*, 25 (3) 373–86.

Begum, N. (1992) 'Disabled Women and the Feminist Agenda', *Feminist Review*, 40 (Spring), 70–84.

Begum, N. (1994) 'Mirror, mirror on the wall', in N. Begum, M. Hill and A. Stevens (eds) *Reflections: Views of Black disabled people on their lives and community care* (London: Central Council for Education and Training in Social Work).

Begum, N. (1996) 'General Practitioners' Role in Shaping Disabled Women's Lives', in C. Barnes and G. Mercer (eds) *Exploring the Divide* (Leeds: The Disability Press).

Bell, D. (1960) *The End of Ideology: on the exhaustion of political ideas in the fifties* (Illinois: Glencoe).

Beresford, P. (2002) 'Thinking about 'mental health': towards a social model', *Journal of Mental Health*, 11 (6), 581–4.

Beresford, P. (2004) 'Treatment at the hand of professionals', in J. Swain, S. French, C. Barnes and C. Thomas (eds) *Disabling Barriers – Enabling Environments*, 2nd edn (London: Sage).

Beresford, P. (2011) *Supporting People* (Bristol: The Policy Press).

Berthoud, R. (2011) *Trends in the Employment of Disabled People in Britain* (Colchester: Institute for Social and Economic Research: University of Essex).

Bickenbach, J. E. (2009) 'Disability, non-talent, and distributive justice' in Kristiansen, K., Velmas, S. and Shakespeare, T. (eds) *Arguing About Disability: philosophical perspectives* (London: Routledge).

Biklen, D. and Bogdana, R. (1977)'Media portrayals of disabled people: a study of stereotypes', *Interracial Books for Children Bulletin*, 8 (6 & 7), 4–7.

Blaxter, M. (1976) *The Meaning of Disability* (London: Heinemann).

Blumer, H. (1969) *Symbolic Interactionism: perspective and method* (Englewood Cliffs, NJ: Prentice Hall).

Bogdan, R. and Taylor, S. J. (1982) *Inside out: the social meaning of mental retardation* (Toronto: University of Toronto Press).

Borsay, A. (1986) *Disabled People in the Community* (London: Bedford Square Press).

Borsay, A. (2005) *Disability and Social Policy in Britain since 1750* (Basingstoke: Palgrave Macmillan).

Bowe, F. (1978) *Handicapping America* (New York: Harper & Rowe).

Bracking, S. (1993) 'Independent Living: a brief overview', in C. Barnes (ed.) *Cashing in on Independence* (Derby: the British Council of Organisations of Disabled People. Available at: http://www.leeds.ac.uk/disability-studies/archiveuk/Barnes/making%20our%20own%20choices.pdf, accessed on 10 December 2011).

Braedley, S. and Luxton, M. (2010) *Neoliberalism and Everyday Life* (Montreal and Kingston: McGill-Queen's University Press).

Brault, M. (2008) *Americans with Disabilities: 2005, Current Populations Reports, P70–117* (Washington, DC: US Census Bureau).

Brechin, A. Liddiard and JSwain (1981): *Look at it this Way: new perspectives in rehabilitation* (Sevenoaks: Hodder & Stoughton in association with the Open University).

Bredberg, E. (1999)'Writing disability history: problems, perspectives and sources', *Disability and Society*, 14 (2), 189–201.

Bretton Woods Update(2009) 'Bank Health Work Flawed: still pushing privatisation of services', *Bi-monthly Digest of Information and Action on the World Bank and IMF*, 10 July, 1–3. Available at: http://www.brettonwoodsproject.org/update/66/bwupdt66.pdf, accessed 27 June 2011.

Brisenden, S. (1986) 'Independent living and the medical model of disability', *Disability, Handicap and Society*, 1 (2), 173–8.

Brisenden, S. (1989) 'A Charter for Personal Care In Disablement Income Group', *Progress London*, 16, 9–10.

Bulmer, M. (1984) *The Chicago School of Sociologists: Institutionalization, Diversity and the Rise of Sociological Research* (London: University of Chicago Press).

Burchardt, T. (2000) Enduring Economic Exclusion: Disabled People, Income and Work (York: The Joseph Rowntree Foundation. A summary version is available at: http://www.jrf.org.uk/Knowledge/findings/socialpolicy/060.asp, accessed 12 November 2010).

Burchardt, T. (2005) *The Education and Employment of Disabled Young People* (Bristol: The Policy Press/JRF).

Burleigh, M.(1994) *Death and Deliverance: Euthanasia in Germany 1900–1945* (Cambridge: University Press).

Burton, M. (1983) 'Understanding mental health services; theory and practice', *Critical Social Policy*, 3 (7), 54–74.

Bury, M. (1982) 'Chronic Illness as Biographical Disruption', *Sociology of Health and Illness*, 4 (2), 167–82.

Bury, M. (1991) 'The Sociology of Chronic Illness: A review of research and prospects', *Sociology of Health and Illness*, 13 (4), 451–68.

Bury, M. (1996) 'Defining and researching disability: challenges and responses', in C. Barnes and G. Mercer (eds) *Exploring the Divide: Illness and Disability* (Leeds: The Disability Press).

Bury, M. (1997) *Health and Illness in a Changing Society* (London: Routledge).

Bury, M. (2000) 'A Comment on the ICIDH2', *Disability and Society*, 15 (7), 1073–7.

Bury, M. (2001) 'Illness narratives: fact or fiction?' *Sociology of Health and Illness*, 23 (3), 263–85.

Butt, J. and Mizra. K. (1996) *Social Care and Black Communities*, (London: HMSO).

Bynoe, I., Oliver, M. and Barnes, C. (1991) *Equal Rights and Disabled People* (London: Institute of Public Policy Research).

Bynum, W. F. (2008) *The History of Medicine: A very short introduction* (Oxford: Oxford University Press).

CAB (2010) *Not Working: CAB evidence on the ESA work capability test* (Citizens Advice Bureau. Available at: http://www.citizensadvice.org.uk/ not_working accessed 22nd Nobverber4, accessed 14 December 2010).

Cabinet Office (2005) *Improving the Life Chances of Disabled People: Final Report* (London: The Cabinet Office. Available at: http://www.strategy.gov.uk/downloads/work_areas/disability/disability_repor t/index.htm., accessed 23 November 2010).

Calhoun, C., Gerteis, J., Moody, J., Pfaff, S. and Virk, I. (2002) *Contemporary Sociological Theory* (Oxford: Blackwell).

Cameron, C. (2010) 'It's all about Conforming', presentation at MeCCA (Media, Communication and Culture Association), Currents in the Mainstream: Media and Disability Conference. Leicester: De Montforf

University, 22 September. Available at: http://currentsinthemainstream. co.uk/conference-abstracts/ accessed 28 June 2011.

Campbell, J. (2009) 'Assisted Dying: not in Our Name', *The Guardian online*, 7 July. Available at: http://www.guardian.co.uk/commentisfree/2009/jul/07/ assisted-dying-disabled-terminally-ill, accessed 12 February 2011.

Campbell, J. and Oliver, M. (1996) *Disability Politics: understanding our past, changing our future* (London: Routledge).

Campling, J. (1979) *Better Lives for Disabled Women* (London: Virago).

Campling, J. (1981) *Images of Ourselves: Women with Disabilities Talking* (London: Routledge and Kegan Paul).

Carter, J. (1981) *Day Services for Adults: Somewhere to go* (London: George Allen and Unwin).

Chappell, A. L. (1998) 'Still out in the cold: people with learning difficulties and the social model of disability', in T.Shakespeare (ed.) *The Disability Reader: Social Science Perspectives* (London: Cassell).

Charlton, J. I. (1998) *Nothing About Us Without Us: Disability Oppression and Empowerment* (Berkeley, CA: University of California Press).

Chivers, S. and Marcotic, N. (eds) (2010) *The Problem Body: Projecting Disability on Film* (Ohio: The Ohio State University Press/Columbus).

Christie, L. (2000) 'Where have all the activists gone?', *Coalition: The Magazine of the Greater Manchester Coalition of Disabled People*, Special Issue: Where have all the Activists Gone, Part 2, October, 28–32.

Clark, D. and Seymour, J. (1999) *Reflections on palliative care: sociological and policy perspectives* (Buckingham: Open University Press).

Clark, L. (2003) *Leonard Cheshire Vs the Disabled People's Movement: A review.* Available at: http://www.leeds.ac.uk/disability-studies/archiveuk/ Clark,%20Laurence/leonard%20cheshire.pdf accessed 12 December 2010.

Clark, L. and Marsh, S. (2002) *Patriarchy in the UK: The language of Disability.* Available at: http://www.leeds.ac.uk/disability-studies/archiveuk/ Clark,%20Laurence/language.pdf, accessed 5 July 2010.

Clarke, J. (2004) *Changing welfare, changing states: new directions in social policy* (London: Sage).

Clements, L. and Read, J. (2008) *Disabled People and European Human Rights* (Bristol: The Policy Press).

Cohen, S. (1985) *Visions of Social Control: Crime, punishments and classification* (Cambridge: Polity Press).

Cole, S. and Lejeune, R. (1972) 'Illness and the legitimation of failure', *American Sociological Review*, 37, 347–56.

Coleman, L. M. (1997) 'Stigma: An enigma demystified', in Davis, L. J. (ed.) *The Disability Studies Reader* (London: Routledge).

Coleridge, P. (1993) *Disability, Liberation and Development* (Oxford: Oxfam Publications).

Coleridge, P. (2000)'Disability and Culture', in M. Thomas and M. J. Thomas (eds) *Selected Readings In community Based Rehabilitation*, Series 1 (Bangalore: Asia Pacific Disability Rehabilitation Journal).

Coleridge, P. (2006)'CBR as part of community development and poverty reduction' in S. Hartley (ed.) *CBR as part of Community Development: A Poverty Reduction Strategy* (London: Centre for International Child Health, University College London).

Comte, A. (1987) *The Positive Philosophy* (New York: AMS Press).

Confederation of Indian Organisations (1987) *Double Bind: To be disabled and Asian* (London: Confederation of Indian Organisations).

Conrad, P. (1975) 'The Discovery of Hyperkinesis: Notes on the Medicalisation of Deviant Behaviour', *Social Problems*, 23 (1), 12–21.

Conrad, P. (2005) 'The Shifting Engines of Medicalisation', *Journal of Health and Social Behaviour*, 46 (1), 3–14.

Conrad, P. and Leiter, V. (2004) 'Medicalisation, Markets and Consumers', *Journal of Health and Social Behaviour*, 45 (Supplement 1), December, 158–76.

Conrad, P. and Potter, D (2000)'From Hyperactive Children to ADHD Adults', *Social Problems*, 47 (3), 559–82.

Conrad, P. and Schneider, J. (1992) *Deviance and Medicalisation: From Deviance to Badness*, 2nd edn (Philadelphia: Temple University Press).

CORAD (1982)*Report of the Committee on Restrictions against Disabled People* (London: HMSO).

Corker, M. (1998) *Deaf and Disabled, or Deafness Disabled?* (Buckingham: Open University Press).

Corker, M. and Shakespeare, T. (2002) (eds) *Disability/Postmodernity: Embodying disability theory* (London: Continuum).

Cox, R. H. (1998) 'The Consequences of Welfare Reform: How conceptions of social rights are changing', *Journal of Social Policy*, 27 (1), 1–8.

Crawford, R. (1977) 'You are Dangerous to Your Health: the Ideology and Politics of Victim Blaming', *International Journal of Health Services*, 7 (4), 663–80.

Crow, L. (1996) 'Including all of our lives: renewing the social model of disability', in C. Barnes and G. Mercer (eds) *Exploring the Divide: Illness and Disability* (Leeds: The Disability Press).

Crowther, N. (2007)'Nothing About us or nothing without us', *Disability and Society*, 21 (7), 791– 4.

CSCI (2006) *The State of Social Care in England 2004/05* (London: Commission for Social Care Inspection).

Cumberbatch, G. and Negrine, R. (1992) *Images of Disability on Television* (London: Routledge).

Cumberbatch, G. and Gauntlett, S. (2006) *On Screen Representations of Disability* (London: Broadcasting and Creative Industries Disability Network).

Dalley, G. (ed.) (1988) *Ideologies of Caring: rethinking community and collectivism* (Basingstoke: Macmillan).

Darke, P. (2004) 'The changing face of representations of disability in the media', in J. Swain, S. French, C. Barnes and C. Thomas (eds) *Disabling Barriers – Enabling Environments*, 2nd edn (London: Sage).

Darwin, C. (1922) *The Descent of Man and Selection in Relation to Sex* (New York: Appleton).

Darwin, C. (ed. G. Beer) (1996) *The Origin of Species* (Oxford: Oxford University Press).

Davis, K. (1990) *A Social Barriers Model of Disability Theory into Practice – The Emergence of the Seven Needs* (Derby: Derbyshire Coalition of Disabled People. Available at: http://www.leeds.ac.uk/disability-studies/archiveuk/DavisK/davis-social%20barriers.pdf, accessed 10 December 2010).

Davis, K. and Mullender, A. (1993) *Ten Turbulent Years: A Review of the Work of the Derbyshire Coalition of Disabled People.* (Nottingham: University of Nottingham Centre for Social Action. Available at: http://www.leeds.ac.uk/disability-studies/archiveuk/DavisK/TEN%20TURBULENT%20YEARS.pdf, accessed 10 December 2010).

Davis, L. J. (1995) *Enforcing Normalcy: Disability, Deafness, and the Body* (London and New York: Verso).

Davis, L. J. (2006) 'The Bell Curve, the Novel, and the Invention of the Disabled Body in the Nineteenth Century', in L. J. Davis (ed.) *The Disability Studies Reader*, 2nd edn (London: Routledge).

Davis, L. J. (2008) *Obsession: A History* (Chicago and London: University of Chicago Press).

Davis, L.J. (ed.) (2010) *The Disability Studies Reader*, 3rd edn (London: Routledge).

Deacon, A. (2002) *Perspectives on Welfare: Ideas, Ideologies and Policy Debates* (Buckingham: The Open University Press).

De Jong, G. (1979a) *The Movement for Independent Living: Origins, Ideology and Implications for Disability Research* (Michigan: University Centre for International Rehabilitation, Michigan State University).

De Jong, G. (1979b) 'Independent Living: From Social Movement to Analytic Paradigm', *Archives of Physical Medicine and Rehabilitation*, 60, 435–46.

De Jong, G. (1981) 'The Movement for Independent Living: Origins, Ideology and Implications for Disability Research', in A. Brechin, P. Liddiard and J. Swain (eds) *Handicap in a Social World* (Sevenoaks: Hodder & Stoughton, in association with the Open University Press).

De Jong, G. (1983) 'Defining and Implementing the Independent Living Concept', in N. Crewe and I. Zola (eds) *Independent Living for Physically Disabled People* (London: Jossey-Bass).

Denzin, N. (1997) *Interpretive Ethnography: Ethnographic practices for the 21st Century* (London: Sage).

Derrida, J. (1990) *Writing and Difference*, trans. A. Bass (London: Routledge and Kegan Paul).

Deshen, S. and Deshen, H. (1989) 'On social aspects of the use of guide dogs and white canes', *Sociological Review*, 37 (1), 89–103.

DfID (2000) *Disability, Poverty and Development* (London: Department for International Development Available at: http://www.dfid.gov.uk/pubs/files/disabilitypovertydevelopment.pdf, accessed 12 April 2007).

DH (2010) *Personalisation* (London: Department of Health. Available at: http://webarchive.nationalarchives.gov.uk/+/www.dh.gov.uk/en/SocialCare/Socialcarereform/Personalisation/index.htm, accessed 7 December 2010).

Dickens, P. (2000) *Social Darwinism* (Buckingham: Open University Press).

Dingwall, R. (2003) *Aspects of Illness*, 2nd edn (Aldershot: Ashgate).

DPI (1982) *Disabled Peoples' International: Proceedings of the First World Congress* (Singapore: Disabled Peoples' International).

DPI (2000) *Disabled People Speak on the New Genetics: DPI Europe position statement on bioethics and human rights* (Disabled Peoples' International, DPI Europe. Available at: http://freespace.virgin.net/dpi.europe/ downloads/bioethics-english.pdf, accessed 23 October 2007).

Directgov (2007) *Disability and the Equality and Human Rights Commission.* Available at: http://www.direct.gov.uk/en/DisabledPeople/RightsAnd Obligations/DisabilityRights/DG_10023457, accessed 22 November 2010.

Directgov (2010) 'What are Special Educational Needs?' Directgov: Public Services all in one place. Available at: http://www.direct.gov.uk/en/Parents/ Schoolslearninganddevelopment/SpecialEducationalNeeds/DG_4008600, accessed 22 November 2010.

Disability Rights Task Force (1999) *From Exclusion to Inclusion: Report of the Disability Rights Task Force on Civil Rights for Disabled People* (London: The Disability Rights Task Force. Available at: http://www.disability-archive.leeds.ac.uk/authors_list.asp?AuthorID=68&author_name=Disability +Rights+Task+Force, accessed 30 December 2010).

Disabled World (undated) *British Sign Language Information.* Available at: http://www.disabled-world.com/disability/types/hearing/communication/ british-sign-language.php, accessed 23 February 2010.

Douglas, M. (1966) P*urity and Danger: An Analysis of the Concepts of Pollution and Taboo* (London: Routledge).

Doyle, B. (2008) *Disability Discrimination: Law and Practice*, 6th edn (Bristol: Jordans).

Drake, R. F. (1999) *Understanding Disability Policy* (Tavistock; Macmillan).

Driedger, D. (1989) *The Last Civil Rights Movement: Disabled People's International* (London: Hurst & Co.).

Duncan Smith I. (2010) *Welfare for the 21st Century (Direct Gov).* Available at: http://www.dwp.gov.uk/newsroom/ministers-speeches/2010/27-05-10.shtml, accessed 18 November 2010.

Dutton, K. R. (1996) *The Perfectible Body: The western ideal of physical development* (London: Cassell).

Dwyer, P. (2000) *Welfare Rights and Responsibilities: Contesting Social Citizenship* (Bristol: The Policy Press).

Dwyer, P. (2004) 'Creeping Conditionality; From Welfare Rights to Creeping Entitlements', *Canadian Journal of Sociology*, 263–87.

Eide, A. H. and Loeb, M. E. (2006) 'Reflections on disability data and statistics in developing countries', in B. Albert (ed.) *In or Out of the Mainstream: Lessons from research on disability and development cooperation* (Leeds: The Disability Press).

Elias, N. (1978) *The Civilising Process*, vol. 1 (Oxford: Blackwell).

Engels, F. (1969) *The Condition of the Working Class in England* (St Albans, Granada Publishing).

Erlanger, H., and Roth, W. (1985) 'Disability Policy: The Parts and the Whole', *American Behavioural Scientist*, 28 (3), 211–32.

Esping-Andersen, G. (1990) *The Three Worlds of Welfare Capitalism* (New Jersey: Princeton University Press).

Ettorre, E. (2006) 'Reproductive Genetics, Gender and the Body: "Please doctor may I have a normal baby"?' *Sociology*, 34 (3) 403–20.

Evans-Pritchard, E. E. (1937) *Witchcraft, Oracles and Magic among the Azande* (Oxford: The Clarendon Press).

Exworthy, M. and Halford, S. (1999) 'Professionals and Managers in a Changing Public Sector: Conflict, Compromise and Collaboration?', in M. Exworthy and S. Halford (eds) *Professionals and the New Managerialism in the Public Sector* (Buckingham: Open University Press).

Fagan, T. and Lee, P. (1997) 'New Social Movements and Social Policy: a case study of the disability movement', in M. Lavalette and A. Pratt (eds) *Social Policy: A Conceptual and Theoretical Introduction* (London: Sage)

Farber, B. (1968) *Mental Retardation: Its Social Context and Social Consequences* (Boston: Houghton Mifflin).

Fawcett, B. (2000) *Feminist Perspectives on Disability* (Harlow: Prentice Hall)

Fiala J. and Lewis, O. (2008) 'Human rights aspects of deaths of institutionalised people with disabilities in Europe', in L. Clements and J. Read (eds) *Disabled People and the Right to Life: The protection and violation of disabled people's basic human rights* (London: Routledge).

Fielder, L. A. (1981) *Pity and Fear: Myths and Images of the Disabled in Literature and the Popular Arts* (New York: International Centre for the

Disabled. Available at: http://www.eric.ed.gov.proxy.lib.wayne.edu/
PDFS/ED256133.pdf, accessed 15 January 2011).

Fielder, L. A. (1996) *Tyranny of the Normal: Essays in Bioethics, Theology and Myth* (London: Barnes and Noble).

Finch, J. (1984) 'Community care: developing non-sexist alternatives', *Critical Social Policy*, 3 (9), 6–18.

Finch, J. and Groves, D. (eds) (1983) *A Labour of Love: Women, Work and Caring* (London: Routledge).

Findlay, B. (1995) 'From Charity to Rights: A disabled person's journey', in G, Zarb, (ed.) *Removing Disabling Barriers*, (London: Policy Studies Institute).

Fine, Michael and Glendinning, C. (2005) 'Dependence, independence or interdependence? Re-visiting the concepts of "care" and "dependency"', *Ageing and Society*. 25 (4), 601–21.

Fine, Micheline and Asch, A. (1988) *Women with Disabilities: Essays in Psychology, Culture, and Politics* (Philadelphia: Temple University Press).

Finger, A. (1992) 'Forbidden fruit', *New Internationalist*, 233, 8–10.

Finkelstein, V. (1980) *Attitudes and Disabled People: Issues for Discussion* (New York: World Rehabilitation Fund. Available at: http://www.disability-archive.leeds.ac.uk/, accessed 26 June 2010).

Finkelstein, V. (1991) 'Disability: An Administrative Challenge (The Health and Welfare Heritage)', in M. Oliver (ed.) *Social Work: Disabled People and Disabling Environments* (London: Jessica Kingsley).

Finkelstein, V. (1993) 'The commonality of disability', in J. Swain, V. Finkelstein, S. French, and M. Oliver (eds) *Disabling Barriers – Enabling Environments* (London: Sage, in association with the Open University).

Finkelstein, V. (1996) 'Outside: Inside Out', *Coalition: the Magazine of the Greater Manchester Coalition of Disabled People*, April, 31–6. Available at: http://www.disability-archive.leeds.ac.uk/, accessed 26 June 2010.

Finkelstein, V. (1998) 'Rethinking Care in a Society Providing Equal Opportunities for All', a Discussion Paper prepared for the World Health Organization's Disability and Rehabilitation Team. Available at: http://www.leeds.ac.uk/disability-studies/archiveuk/finkelstein/finkelstein2.pdf, accessed 2 March 2009.

Finkelstein, V. (1999) *Professionals Allied to the Community* (PACs) 11. Available at: http://www.leeds.ac.uk/disability-studies/archiveuk/finkelstein/pacall.pdf, accessed 12 June 2011.

Finkelstein, V. (2002) 'The Social Model of Disability Repossessed', *Coalition: the Magazine of the Greater Manchester Coalition of Disabled People*, February, 12–13. Available at: http://www.disability-archive.leeds.ac.uk/, accessed 26 June 2010.

Forder, A. Caslin, T. Ponton, T and Walklate, S. (1984) *Theories of Welfare*, London: (Routedge and Kegan Paul).

Foucault, M. (1967) *Madness and Civilisation: A history of madness in the age of reason* (London: Tavistock).

Foucault, M. (1972) *The Archaeology of Knowledge*, trans. A, M. Sheridan (London: Tavistock).

Foucault, M. (1976) *The Birth of the Clinic* (London: Tavistock).

Foucault, M. (1977) *Discipline and Punish* (Harmondsworth: Peregrine).

Foucault, M. (1980)'The Eye of Power', in C. Gordon (ed.) *Power/ Knowledge: Selected Interviews and other writings 1972–1977* (Brighton: Harvester Press).

Fraser, N. (1997) *Justice Interruptus: Critical Reflections on the 'Postsocialist' Condition* (New York and London: Routledge).

Fraser, N. (2000) 'Rethinking recognition', *New Left Review*, (second series) 3 (May–June), 107–20.

French, S. (1993) 'Disability, Impairment or Something In-between', in J. Swain, V. Finkelstein, S. French and M. Oliver (eds) *Disabling Barriers – Enabling Environments* (London: Sage, in association with the Open University).

French, S. and Swain, J. (2008): *Understanding Disability: A guide for health professionals* (London: Churchill Livingstone, Elsevier).

French, S. and Vernon, A. (1997) 'Health care for people from ethnic minority groups', in S. French (ed.) *Physiotherapy: A Psychosocial Approach*, 2nd edn (Oxford: Butterworth-Heinemann).

Gallagher, H. (1995) *By Trust Betrayed: Patients, physicians and the licence to kill in the Third Reich* (Arlington, VA: Vandamere Press).

Garfinkel, H. (1967) *Studies in Ethnomethodology* (Eaglewood Cliffs, New Jersey: Prentice Hall).

Garland, R.R.J. (1995) *The Eye of the Beholder: Deformity and Disability in the Graeco-Roman World* (London: Duckworth).

Gartner, A. and Joe, T. (eds) (1987) *Images of the Disabled. Disabling Images* (New York: Praeger).

George, V. and Wilding, P. (1994) *Welfare and Ideology* (London: Harvester Wheatsheaf).

Gerhardt, U. (1989) *Ideas about Illness: An Intellectual and Political History of Medical Sociology* (London: Macmillan).

Ghai, A. (2001) 'Marginalisation and disability: experiences from the Third World', in M. Priestley (ed.) *Disability and the Life Course* (Cambridge: Cambridge University Press).

Giddens, A. (1982) *Sociology. A brief but critical introduction* (London: Macmillan).

Giddens, A. (1989) *Sociology* (Cambridge: Polity).

Giddens, A. (1991) *Modernity and Self-Identity: Self and Society in the Late Modern Age* (Cambridge: Polity).

Giddens, A. (1998) *The Third Way: The Renewal of Social Democracy* (Cambridge: Polity).

Giddens, A. (2000) *The Third Way and its critics* (Cambridge: Polity).

Giddens, A. (2001) *Sociology*, 4th edn (Cambridge: Polity).

Giddens, A. 2006: *Sociology*, 5th edn (Cambridge: Polity).

Gillespie-Sells, K. and Campbell, J. (1991) *Disability Equality Training: Trainers Guide* (London: Central Council for Education and Training in Social Work. Available at: http://www.leeds.ac.uk/disability-studies/archiveuk/index.html, accessed 24 May 2010).

Gillespie-Sells, K., Hill, M. and Robbins, B. (1998) *She Dances to Different Drums: Research into disabled women's sexuality* (London: King's Fund).

Gilman, M. (2008) 'In practice from the viewpoint of a social worker', in J. Swain and S. French (eds) *Disability on Equal Terms* (London: Sage).

Giroux, H. A. (1997) *Pedagogy and the Politics of Hope: theory, culture and schooling* (Bolder, Colorado: Westview Press).

Gleeson, B. J. (1997): 'Disability Studies: a historical materialist view', *Disability and Society*, 12 (2), 179–202.

Gleeson, B. J. (1999) *Geographies of Disability* (London: Routledge).

Glendinning, C., Halliwell, S., Jacobs, S., Rummery, K. and Tyrer, J. (2000) 'New Kinds of Care, New Kinds of Relationships: How Purchasing Services Affects Relationships in Giving and Receiving Personal Assistance', *Health and Social Care in the Community*, 8 (3), 201–11.

Goble, C. (2003) 'Controlling Life', in J. Swain, S. French and C. Cameron (eds) *Controversial Issues in a Disabling Society* (Buckingham: Open University Press).

Goffman, E. (1961) *Asylums* (Garden City, NY: Doubleday/ Anchor).

Goffman, E. (1968) *Stigma: Notes on the management of a spoiled identity* (Harmondsworth: Penguin).

Goggin, G. and Newall, C. (2004) 'Uniting the Nation: Disability stem cells and the Australian media', *Disability and Society*, 19 (1), 147–60.

Goodley, D. (undated) 'Towards socially just pedagogies: Deleuzogauttarian critical Disability studies'. Available at: http://www.leeds.ac.uk/disability-studies/archiveuk/goodley/Dan%20Goodley%20revised%20submission%20for%20IJIE%20special%20issue.pdf, accessed 11 February 2011.

Goodley, D. (2000) *Self-advocacy in the Lives of People with Learning Difficulties* (Buckingham: Open University Press).

Goodley, D. (2001) 'Learning Difficulties, the Social Model of Disability and Impairment: challenging epistemologies', *Disability and Society*, 16 (2), 207–31.

Goodley, D. (2011) *Disability Studies: An Interdisciplinary introduction* (London: Sage).

Gordon, B.O. and Rosenblum, K. E. (2001) 'Bringing Disability Studies into the Sociological Frame: a comparison with disability, race, sex and sexual orientation statuses', *Disability and Society*, 16, (1), 5–19.

Gordon, C. (1966) *Role Theory and Illness: A Sociological Perspective* (New Haven, Connecticut: College and University Press).

Gordon, D., Parker, R., Loughran, F. with Heslop, P. (2000) *Disabled children in Britain: A re-analysis of the OPCS Disability Surveys* (London: HMSO).

Gough, I. (1979) *The Political Economy of the Welfare State* (Tavistock: Macmillan).

Gould, S, J. (1980) *The Panda's Thumb: More reflections on natural history* (Harmondsworth: Penguin).

Gouldner, A. (1970) *The Coming Crisis of Western Sociology* (New York: Avon).

Gramsci, A. (1985) *Selections from the Cultural Writings*, edited and translated by D. Forgacs and G. Nowell-Smith (London: Lawrence & Wishart).

Graves, R. (1960) *The Greek Myths: Complete Edition* (London: Penguin).

Griffiths, R. (1988) *Community Care: Agenda for Action* (London: HMSO).

Gustavsson, A. (2004) 'The role of theory in disability research – springboard or strait-jacket?', *Scandinavian Journal of Disability Research*, 6 (1), 55–70.

Haber, L. and Smith, R. (1971) 'Disability and Deviance, normative behaviour and role behaviour', *American Sociological Review*, 36, 87–97.

Hahn, H. (1985) 'Towards a Politics of Disability: Definitions, Disciplines and Policies'. *Social Science Journal*, 22 (4), 87–105.

Hahn, H. (1986) 'Public Support for Rehabilitation Programmes; the analysis of US disability Policy', *Disability, Handicap and Society*, 1 (2), 121–38.

Hall, S. (1980) 'Encoding/decoding', in S. Hall et al., (eds) *Culture, Media, Language: working papers in cultural studies 1972–79* (London: Hutchinson, in association with Centre for Contemporary Cultural Studies, University of Birmingham).

Hall, S. (ed.) (1997) *Representation: Representation and signifying practices* (London: Sage in association with the Open University).

Haller, B. A. (1995) 'Rethinking Models of Media Representations of Disability', *Disability Studies Quarterly*, 15 (2), 26–30.

Haller, B. A. (2009) 'Disability Visibility in US Entertainment TV in 2008', *Media dis&dat*. Available at: http://media-dis-n-dat.blogspot.com/ 2009/01/disability-visibility-in-us.html, accessed 28 June 2011.

Hammersley, M. (2000) *Taking Sides in Social Research* (London: Routledge).

Hanks, J. and Hanks, L. (1948) 'The Physically Handicapped in Certain Non-Occidental Societies', *Journal of Social Issues*, 4 (4), 11–20.

Harbert, W. (1988) 'Dignity and Choice', Insight, 25, March, cited in Oliver, M. (1990) *The Politics of Disablement* (London: Macmillan).

Harris, A., Cox, E. and Smith, C. (1971) *Handicapped and Impaired in Great Britain, Part 1* (London: HMSO).

Harris, J. (1995) *The Cultural Meaning of Deafness: Language, identity and power relations* (Aldershot: Avebury).

Harvey, D. (2010) *The Enigma of Capital* (London: Profile Books).

Harwood, R. (2005) *The End of the Beginning – An analysis of the first decade of the Disability Discrimination Act employment provision 1995–2005*. (London: Public Interest Research Unit. Available at: http://www.disability-archive. leeds.ac.uk/, accesed 26 June 2010).

Harwood, R. (2006) *Teeth and their use: Enforcement action by the three equality commissions* (London: Public Interest Research Unit. Available at: http://www.disability-archive.leeds.ac.uk/, accessed 26 June 2010).

Hattersley, J. (1991) 'The future of normalisation', in S. Baldwin and J. Hattersley (eds) *Mental handicap: Social science perspectives* (London: Tavistock/Routledge).

Held, D., McGrew, A., Goldblan, D. and Perraton, J. (1999) *Global Transformation: Politics, Economics and Culture* (Cambridge: Polity).

Henderson, L. and Zimbardo, P. G. (2005) The Shyness Home Page (from The Shyness Institute, Palo Alto, California). Available at: http://shyness.com/encyclopedia.html, accessed 15 September 2009.

Hevey, D. (1992) *The Creatures that Time Forgot: Photography and Disability Imagery* (London: Routledge).

Hill, M. (1994) 'They are not our brothers: the disability movement and the black disability movement', in N. Begum, M. Hill and A. Stevens (eds) *Reflections: Views of Black Disabled People of their Lives and Community Care*, Paper 32.3 (London: Central Council for Education and Training in Social Work).

Hill-Collins, P. (1990) *Black Feminist Thought: Knowledge, Consciousness and the Politics of Empowerment* (Oxford: UnwinHeinemann).

Hirst, P. and Woolley. P. (1982) *Social Relations and Human Attitudes* (London: Tavistock).

Hobbes, T. (1660) *Leviathan*. Available at: http://oregonstate.edu/instruct/phl302/texts/hobbes/leviathan-contents.html, accessed on 10 June 2011.

Hobsbawm, E. J. (1995) *The Age of Revolution 1789–1848* (London: Weidenfeld & Nicolson) '

Hoggart, R. (1995) *The Way we Live Now* (London: Chatto & Windus).

Holden, C. and Beresford, P. (2002) 'Globalization and Disability', in C. Barnes, M. Oliver and L. Barton (eds) *Disability Studies Today* (Cambridge: Polity).

Hooks, B. (1984) *Feminist Theory: From margins to centre* (Boston, MA: South End).

Horstler, J. (2003): *Bridging the Divide: An investigation into relations between the disabled people's movement and the anti capitalist movement* (Leeds: School of Sociology and Social Policy, MA dissertation. Available

at: http://www.disability-archive.leeds.ac.uk/authors_list.asp?AuthorID
=87&author_name=Horsler%2C+Julian, accessed 12 February 2011).

Hudson, M. (2000) 'Where have all the activists gone? deadlock or division', *Coalition: The Magazine of the Greater Manchester Coalition of Disabled People*, Special Issue: Where have all the Activists Gone? Part 1, August, 13–15.

Hughes, B. (2005) 'What Can a Foucauldian Analysis Contribute to Disability Theory?', in S. Tremain (ed.) *Foucault and the Government of Disability* (Ann Arbor: The University of Michigan Press).

Humphries, S. and Gordon, P. (1992) *Out of Sight: The Experience of Disability 1900–1950* (London: Northcote House).

Hunt, P. (1966) 'A critical condition', in P. Hunt (ed.) *Stigma: The Experience of Disability* (London: Geoffrey Chapman. Available at: http://www.disability-archive.leeds.ac.uk/, accessed 26 June 2010).

Hurst, R. (2000) 'To revise or not to revise?', *Disability and Society*, 15 (7), 1083–7.

Hurst, R. and Albert, B. (2006) 'The Social Model of Disability: human rights and development cooperation', in B. Albert (ed.) *In or Out of the Mainstream? Lessons from research on disability and development cooperation* (Leeds: The Disability Press).

Ignatieff, M. (1983) 'Total institutions and the working classes: A review essay', *History Workshop Journal*, 15 (1) 167–73.

Ignatieff, M. (1985) 'State, Civil Society and Total Institutions',. in Cohen, S. and Scull, A. (eds) *Social Control and the State* (London: Basil Blackwell).

Illich, I., Zola, I. K., McKnight, J., Caplan, J. and Shaiken, H. (1977) *Disabling Professions* (London: Marion Boyars).

ILO (2003) *Time for equality at work* (Geneva: International Labour Organization).

Inclusion Europe (2008) *The Specific Risks of Discrimination against Persons in Situations of Major Dependence or with Complex Needs* (Brussels: Inclusion Europe. Available at: http://www.inclusion-europe.org/documents/CNS%20Volume%203.pdf, accessed 13 April 2010).

Ingleby, D. (1985) 'Mental Health and Social Order', in Cohen, S. and Scull, A. (eds) *Social Control and the State* (London: Basil Blackwell).

Inglehart, R. (1990) 'Values, Ideology and Cognitive Mobilisations in New Social Movements', in R.J. Dalton and M.Kuechler (eds) *Challenging the Political Order* (Cambridge: Polity).

Ingstad, B. (1999) 'The myth of disability in developing nations', *Lancet*, 354 (9180), 757–8.

Ingstad, B. (2001) 'Disability in the Developing World', in G. L. Albrecht, K. D. Seelman and M. Bury (eds) *Handbook of Disability Studies* (London: Sage).

Ingstad, B. and Whyte, S.R. (eds) (1995) *Disability and Culture* (Berkeley: University of California Press).

Janowitz, M. (1966) (ed.) *W.J. Thomas on Organisation and Social Personality* (Chicago: University of Chicago Press).

Jewson, N. (1976) 'The disappearance of the sick man from medical cosmology 1770–1870', *Sociology*, 10, 225–44.

Johnstone, M. (2001) 'Stigma, social justice and the rights of the mentally ill: Challenging the status quo', *Australian and New Zealand Journal of Mental Health Nursing*, 10, 200–209.

Jolly, D. (2010) *Pilot Stuidy: The UN Convention on the Rights of Persons with Disabilities* (Valencia: European Network for Independent Living).

Jones, K. and Fowles, J. (1984) *Ideas on Institutions* (London: Routledge & Kegan Paul).

Jones, K. and Tillotson, A. (1965) *The Adult Population of Epileptic Colonies* (London: British Epilepsy Association and International Bureau for Epilepsy).

Jones, K., Brown, J. and Bradshaw, J. (1978) *Issues in Social Policy* (London: Routledge & Kegan Paul).

Jones, M. and Marks, L. (eds) (1999) *Disability, Divers-ability and Legal Change* (The Hague: Kluwer Law International/ Martinus Nijhoff Publishers).

Karpf, A. (1988) *Doctoring the Media* (London: Routledge).

Kassebaum. G. and Baumann, B. (1965) 'Dimensions of the Sick Role in Chronic Illness', *Journal of Health and Social Behaviour*, 6, 16–25.

Katsui, H. (2006) 'Human Rights and Disabled People in the South', in A. Teittinen (ed.) *Vammaisten Ihmisoikeuksista Etäiiä* (Helsinki: Vliopistopaino. Available at: http://www.disability-archive.leeds.ac.uk, accessed 17 November 2010).

Keeley, H., Redley, M., Holland, A. J. and Clare, I. (2008) 'Participation in the 2005 general election by adults with intellectual disabilities', *Journal of Intellectual Disability Research*, 52 (3), 175–81.

Kelly, M. P. (1992) *Colitis* (London: Routledge).

Kerr, A. and Shakespeare, T. (2002) *Genetic Politics: From eugenics to genome* (Cheltenham: New Clarion Press).

Kerr, A., Cunningham-Burley, S., Amos, A. et al., (1998) 'Eugenics and the New Genetics in Britain, Examining contemporary professional accounts', *Science, Technology and Human Values*, 23 (2), 175–98.

Kevles, D. J. (1985) *In the name of eugenics: genetics and the uses of human heredity* (New York: Knopf).

Kisanji, J. (1995) 'Attitudes and beliefs about disability', in B. O'Toole and R. McConkey (eds) *Innovations in Developing Countries for People with Disabilities* (Chorley: Liseaux Hall).

Kittrie, N. (1971) *The Right to be Different: Deviance and Enforced Therapy* (Baltimore: Johns Hopkins).

Kristiansen, K., Velmas, S. and Shakespeare, T. (eds) (2009) *Arguing About Disability: philosophical perspectives* (London: Routledge).

Lapper, A. (2005) *My Life in My Hands* (London: Simon & Schuster).

Law I. (2010) *Racism and Ethnicity* (London: Longman).

Ledbetter, C. (2004) *Personalisation through Participation: A New Script for Services* (London: Demos).

Lemert, E. (1951) *Social Pathology* (New York: McGraw-Hill).

Leonard, P. (1984) *Personality and Ideology: Towards a Materialist Understanding of the Individual* (London: Macmillan).

Lévi-Strauss, C. (1958) *Anthropologie Structurale* (Paris: Librarie Plon).

Lévi-Strauss, C. (1983) *Structural Anthropology*, translated from the French by Monique Layton (Chicago, Ill.: University of Chicago Press).

Linton, S. (1998) *Claiming disability: knowledge and identity* (New York: New York University Press).

Liu, T. S. and Miller, T. A. (2008) 'Economic Analysis of the future growth of cosmetic surgery procedures', *Cosmetic Surgery and Reconstruction*, 121 (6), 404e–412e, June.

Locker, D. (1983) *Disability and Disadvantage* (London: Tavistock).

Longmore, P. K. and Omansky, L. (eds) (2001) *The New Disability History: American Perspectives* (New York: New York University Press).

Lonsdale, S. (1990) *Women and Disability* (London: Macmillan).

Lord, G. (1981) *The Arts and Disabilities: A Creative Response to Social Handicap* (Edinburgh: MacDonald).

Lukes, S. (1973) *Individualism* (Oxford: Basil Blackwell).

Lupton, D. (1994) *Medicine as Culture* (London: Sage).

Macfarlane, I. (1978) *The Origins of English Individualism* (Oxford: Basil Blackwell).

McLean, S. M. (2007) *Assisted Dying: Reflections on the Need for Law Reform* (London: Routledge Cavendish).

Manion, M. and Bersani, H. (1987) 'Mental Retardation as a Western Sociological Construct: A cross cultural analysis', *Disability, Handicap and Society*, 2 (3), 231–46.

Mann, K. (1992) *The Making of an English 'Underclass': The social division and labour* (Milton Keynes: The Open University Press).

Marconis, J.J. and Plummer, K. (1998) *Sociology a Global Introduction* (London: Prentice-Hall Europe).

Marin, B., Prinz, C. and Queisser, M. (eds) (2004) *Transforming Disability Welfare Policies: Towards World and Equal Opportunities* (Avebury: Ashgate).

Marshall, T. H. (1950) *Citizenship and Social Class* (Cambridge: Cambridge University Press).

Martin, J., and White, A. (1988) *OPCS Surveys of Disability in Great Britain: Report 2 – The financial circumstances of disabled adults living in private households* (London: HMSO).

Martin, J., Meltzer, H. and Elliot, D. (1988) *OPCS Surveys of Disability in Great Britain: Report 1 – The prevalence of disability among adults* (London: HMSO).

Marx, K. (1904 [1859]) *A Contribution to the Critique of Political Economy: Translated from the Second German edition by N. I. Stone, with an Appendix Containing Marx's Introduction to the Critique Recently Published among his Posthumous Papers* (Chicago: Charles H. Kerr & Company 1918).

Marx, K. and Engels, F. (1976) *Collected Works: Karl Marx and Friedrich Engels, Vol, 6 1845–1848* (London: Lawrence & Wishart).

Mason, M. (1990) 'Internalised oppression', in R. Rieser and M. Mason (eds) *Disability Equality in the Classroom: A Human Rights Issue* (London:

Inner London Education Authority, 27–8. Available at: http://www.leeds.ac.uk/disability-studies/archiveuk/Mason,%20Michelene/mason.pdf, accessed on 10 June 2011).

Mason, M. (2000) *Incurably Human* (London: Working Press).

Mason, T., Carlisle, C., Watkins, C. and Whitehead, E. (eds) (2001) *Stigma and Social Exclusion in Healthcare* (London: Routledge).

Mead, G. H. (1934) *Mind, Self and Society from the standpoint of a Social behaviourist*, edited by C. W. Morris (Chicago: Chicago University Press).

Meekosha, H. and Dowse, L. (1997) 'Distorting images, invisible images: gender, disability and the media', *Media International Australia*, 84 (May), 91–101.

Meltzer, H., Gatward, R. with Goodman, R. and Ford, T. (2000) *Mental Health of children and adolescents in Great Britain* (London: ONS).

Merton, R. K. (1957) *Social Theory and Social Structure* (Free Press: New York).

Merton, R. K. and Nisbet, R. A. (eds) (1966) *Contemporary Social Problems*, 2nd edn (New York: Harcourt, Brace & World).

Miles, M. (1995) 'Disability in an Eastern Religious Context: Historical perspectives', *Disability and Society*, 10 (1), 49–69.

Miles, M. (2001) 'ICIDH meets Postmodernism, or "incredulity toward meta-terminology"', *Disability World*, (March–April), unpaged. (Available at: http://www.disabilityworld.org/03-04_01/resources/icidh.html, accessed 26 July 2006).

Miles, M. (2006) 'Social responses to Disability and Poverty in Economically Weaker Countries: research, trends, critique, and lessons not usually learnt' *Annotated bibliography of modern and historical material*. Available at: http://www.independentliving.org/docs7/miles200603.html, accessed 17 December 2010.

Miller, E. J. and Gwynne, G. V. (1972) *A Life Apart* (London: Tavistock).

Miller, P., Gillinson, S. and Huber, J. (2006) *Disablist Britain: Barriers to Independent Living for Disabled People in Britain in 2006* (London: SCOPE, Disability Awareness in Action, DEMOS. Available at: http://www.demos.co.uk/ publications/disablistbritain, accessed 17 December 2010.

Mills, C. W. (1970) *The Sociological Imagination* (Harmondsworth: Penguin).

Mitchell, D.T. and Snyder, S. L. (eds) (1997) *The Body and Physical Difference* (Ann Arbor: The University of Michigan Press).

Morris, J. (1991) *Pride Against Prejudice. Transforming Attitudes to Disability* (London: The Women's Press).

Morris, J. (1992) 'Lives worth living', in *Disabled Lives: Many voices, one message* (London: BBC Education).

Morris, J. (1993) *Independent Lives, Community Care and Disabled People* (London: Macmillan).

Morris, J. (ed.) (1996) *Encounters with Strangers* (London: The Women's Press).

Morris, J. (1997) 'Care or Empowerment? A Disability Rights Perspective', *Social Policy and Administration*, 31 (1), 54–60.

Morris, J. (2011) *Independent living and government policy: triumph or tragedy*, paper presented at the Centre for Disability Studies, University of Leeds, 23 March.

Morris, P. (1969) *Put Away* (London: Routledge & Kegan Paul).

Mulcahy, F. (2005) *DPI position paper on the definition of disability*. Available at: http://v1.dpi.org/lang-en/print.php, a accessed 6 March 2009.

Murphy, R. (1987) *The Body Silent* (New York: Henry Holt & Co.).

Murphy, R. (1995) 'Encounters: The Body Silent in America', in B. Ingstad and S. R. Whyte (eds) *Disability and Culture* (Berkeley: University of California Press).

McQuail, D. (ed.) (1972) *Sociology of Mass Communications: selected readings* (Harmondsworth: Penguin).

Navarro, V. (1976) *Medicine under Capitalism* (London: Croom Helm).

Navarro, V. (1978) *Class Struggle, the State and Medicine* (London: Martin Robertson).

Neubeck, K. J. (1979) *Social Problems: A Critical Approach* (New York: Random House).

NHS (2010) *Community Care Statistics 2008–09: Social Services Activity Report, England* (Leeds: National Health Service: The Information Centre. Available at http://www.ic.nhs.uk/statistics-and-data-collections/social-care/adult-social-care-information/personal-social-services-expenditure-and-unit-costs-england-final-2008-09, accessed 26 June 2010).

Nicolaisen, I. (1995) 'Persons and Nonpersons: Disability and Personhood among the Punan Bah of Central Borneo', in B. Ingstad and S. R. Whyte (eds) *Disability and Culture* (Berkeley: University of California Press).

Nirje, B. (1969) 'The normalization principle and its human management implications', in R. Kugel and W.Wolfensberger (eds) *Changing patterns in residential services for the mentally retarded* (Washington, DC: President's Committee on Mental Retardation).

Norden, M. (1994) *The Cinema of Isolation: a history of disability in the movies* (New Brunswick: Rutgers University Press).

Oakley, A. (1980) *Women Confined: Towards a Sociology of Childbirth* (Oxford: Martin Robertson).

O'Brien, M. and Penna, S. (1998) *Theorising Welfare: Enlightenment and modern society* (London: Sage).

OECD (2003) *Transforming Disability Into Ability: Policies to Promote Work and Income Security for Disabled People* (Paris: Organisation for Economic Co-operation and Development. Available at: http://213.253.134.43/oecd/pdfs/ browseit/8103021E.PDF, accessed 26 April 2010).

OECD (2006) *Sickness, Disability and Work: Breaking the Barriers (Vol. 1), Norway Poland and Switzerland* (Paris: Organisation for Economic Co-operation and Development. Available at: http://titania.sourceoecd.org/vl=2065797/cl=32/nw=1/rpsv/ij/oecdthemes/99980142/v2006n11/s1/p1l, accessed 26 April 2010).

OECD (2010) *Sickness Disability and Work: Breaking the barriers: A synthesis of findings across OECD countries* (Paris: Organisation for Economic Co-operation and Development. Available at: http://www.oecd-ilibrary.org/social-issues-migration-health/sickness-disability-and-work-breaking-the-barriers_9789264088856-en, accessed 17 December 2010).

Oliver, M. (1979) *Epilepsy, Self and Society: A Study of Three Groups of Adolescent Epileptics*, Ph.D. thesis, University of Kent.

Oliver, M. (1981) 'A New Model in the Social Work Role in Relation to Disability', in J. Campling (ed.) *The Handicapped Person: A New Perspective for Social Workers* (London: RADAR. Available at: http://www.leeds.ac.uk/disability-studies/archiveuk/Campling/handicppaed.pdf, accessed 28 September 2009).

Oliver, M. (1986) 'Social Policy and Disability: some theoretical issues', Disability, Handicap and Society, 1(1) 5–17.

Oliver, M. (1990) *The Politics of Disablement* (London: Macmillan. Available at: http://www.disability-archive.leeds.ac.uk/ accessed 26 June 2010).

Oliver, M. (1992) 'Changing the Social Relations of Research Production?', *Disability, Handicap and Society*, 7 (2), 101–14.

Oliver, M. (1996) *Understanding Disability: From Theory to Practice* (London: Macmillan).

Oliver, M. (1997) 'Emancipatory disability research: Realistic goal or impossible dream', in C. Barnes and G. Mercer (eds) *Doing Disability Research* (Leeds: The Disability Press. Available at: http://www.disability-archive.leeds.ac.uk/, accessed 26 June 2010).

Oliver, M. (2002) 'Using Emancipatory Methodologies in Disability Research', presentation at the 1st Annual Disability Research Seminar hosted by the National Disability Authority and the Centre for Disability Studies, University College Dublin, 3 December. Available at: http://www.disability-archive.leeds.ac.uk/, accessed 26 June 2010.

Oliver, M. (2004) 'The Social Model in Action: If I had a Hammer?', in C. Barnes and G. Mercer (eds) *Implementing the Social Model of Disability: Theory and Research* (Leeds: The Disability Press. Available at: http://www.disability-archive.leeds.ac.uk/, accessed 26 June 2010).

Oliver, M. (2007) 'Disability Rights and Wrongs: A review', *Disability and Society*, 22 (2), 230–4.

Oliver, M. (2009) *Understanding Disability: From Theory to Practice*, 2nd edn (Tavistock: Palgrave).

Oliver, M. and Barnes, C. (1998) *Social Policy and Disabled People: From Exclusion to Inclusion* (London: Longman).

Oliver, M. and Barnes C. (2006) 'Disability Politics: Where did it all go wrong?', *Coalition: the Magazine of the Greater Manchester Coalition of Disabled People*, August, 8–13. Available at: http://www.disability-archive.leeds.ac.uk/, accessed 26 June 2010.

Oliver, M. and Hasler, F. (1987) 'Disability and Self-help: A Case Study of the Spinal Injuries Association', *Disability, Handicap and Society*, 2 (2), 113–25.

Oliver, M. and Sapey, M. (2006) *Social Work and Disabled People*, 3rd edn (Basingstoke: Palgrave).

Oliver, M. and Zarb, G. (1989) 'The Politics of Disability: a new approach', *Disability, Handicap and Society*, 4 (3), 221–40.

Oliver, M. and Zarb, G. (1992) *Greenwich Personal Assistance Schemes: An evaluation* (Greenwich: University of Greenwich. Available at: http://www.disability-archive.leeds.ac.uk/, accessed 26 June 2010).

Oliver, M., Zarb, G., Silver, J., Moore, M. and Sainsbury, V. (1988) *Walking Into Darkness: The experience of Spinal cord Injury* (London: Macmillan).

ONS (2005) *National Statistics: Special Educational Needs in England* (London:Office of National Statistics). Available at:. http://dfes.gov.uk/rsgateway/DB/SFR/s000584/SFR24-2005.pdf

ONS (2006) *Labour Force Survey, April–June, 2005* (London: Office of National Statistics. Available at: http://www.statistics.gov.uk/statbase/product.asp?vlnk=14248, accessed 3 November 2010).

NS (2010) *Statistical Bulletin: Labour Market Statistics, December* (London: Office of National Statistics. Available at: http://www.statistics.gov.uk/statbase/product.asp?vlnk=1944, accessed 15 December 2010).

Oxfam (2009) *Blind Optimism: Challenging the myths about private health care in poor countries* (Oxford: Oxfam). Available at: http://www.oxfam.org.uk/resources/policy/health/downloads/bp125_blind_optimism_private_health_care.pdf, accessed 27 June 2011).

Oxlade, P. (2010) 'Economy watch: What next for Britain?', 28 October 2010. Available at: http://www.thisismoney.co.uk/credit-crisis, accessed 3 November 2010.

Oyen, E. (ed.) (1986) *Comparing Welfare States and Their Futures* (Aldershot: Gower).

Parker, G. (1993) *With this Body: caring and disability in marriage* (Buckingham: Open University Press).

Parker, R. (1988) 'A Historical Background', in I. Sinclair (ed.) *Residential Care: The Research Reviewed* (London: HMSO).

Parsons, T. (1951) *The Social System* (New York: Free Press).

Pasternak, J. (1981) 'An analysis of social perceptions of epilepsy: increasing rationalisation as seen through the theories of Comte and Weber', *Social Science and Medicine*, 15E (3), 223–9.

Peck, S. (2009) 'Rieser's Reservations on Ratification', *Disability Now*, April, 7.

Pernick, D. (1997) 'Defining the Defective – Eugenics, Aesthetics and Mass Culture in Early Twentieth Century America', in D.T. Mitchell and S.

L.Snyder (eds) *The Body and Physical Difference* (Ann Arbor: The University of Michigan Press).

Perrin, B. and Nirje, B. (1989) 'Setting the Record Straight: A Critique of some Frequent Misconceptions of the Normalisation Principle', in A. Brechin and J. Walmsley (eds) *Making Connections: Reflecting on the Lives and experiences of People with Learning Difficulties* (London: Hodder & Stoughton).

Peters, S., Gabel, S. and Symeonidou, S. (2009) 'Resistance, transformation and the politics of hope: imagining a way forward for the disabled people's movement', *Disability and Society*, 24 (5) 543–556.

Pfieffer, D. (2000) 'The devil is in the detail', *Disability and Society*, 15 (7), 1079–82.

Pilgrim, D. and Rogers, A. (1993) *A Sociology of Mental Health and Illness* (Buckingham: Open University Press).

Pilgrim, D. and Treacher, A. (1992) *Clinical Psychology Observed* (London: Routledge).

Potts, M. and Fido, R. (1991) *A Fit Person to be Removed* (Plymouth: Northcote House).

Prideaux, S. J. (2005) *Not so New Labour: A sociological critique of New Labour's policy and practice* (Bristol: The Policy Press).

Prideaux, S. J. (2010) 'The Welfare Policies of Charles Murray are Alive and Well, in the *International Journal of Social Welfare*, 19 (3), 293–302.

Priestley, M. (1998a) 'Constructions and Creations: idealism, materialism and disability theory', *Disability and Society*, 13 (1), 75–95.

Priestley, M. (1998b) *Community Care or Independent Living* (Cambridge: Polity).

Priestley, M. (2003) *Disability: A life course approach* (Cambridge: Polity).

Priestley, M. (2004) 'Tragedy Strikes Again: Why Community Care Still Poses a Problem for Integrated Living', in J. Swain, S. French, C. Barnes and C. Thomas (eds) *Disabling Barriers: Enabling Environments*, 2nd edn (London: Sage).

Priestley, M., Woodin, S., Matthews, B. and Hemingway, L. (2009) *Choice and Control: A Rapid evidence assessment (RAE), for the Office of Disability Issues* (London: Office of Disability Issues and the Department of Work and Pensions).

Quick, J.1985: *Disability in Modern Children's Fiction* (London: Croom Helm).

Radford, J. P. (1994) 'Intellectual disability and the heritage of modernity', in M. Rioux and M. Bach (eds) *Disability Is Not Measles: New Research Paradigms in Disability* (North York, Ontario: Roeher Institute).

Rabiu, M. M. (2001) 'Cataract blindness and barriers to uptake of cataract surgery in a rural community in northern Nigeria,', *British Journal of Ophthalmology*, 85, 778–80.

Rae, A. (1989) 'What's in a Name', *Worldview*, International Rehabilitation Review. Available at: http://www.leeds.ac.uk/disability-studies/archiveuk/ Rae/Whatsname.pdf, accessed 28 September 2009.

Rae, A. (1993) 'Independent Living, Personal Assistance and Disabled Women', in C. Barnes (ed.) *Making Our Own Choices: Independent Living, Personal Assistance and Disabled People* (Derby: British Council of Organisations of Disabled People).

Rae, A. (1996) 'Social model under attack', *Coalition: the Magazine of the Greater Manchester Coalition of Disabled People*, August 37–40.

Ramesh, R. (2010) 'Healthy living is cut short by 17 years for poorest in Britain', *The Guardian Online*, Society, 1–11. Available at: http://www.guardian.co.uk/society/2010/feb/10/equality-poverty-health-society, accessed 17 February 2010.

Ramon, S. (1996) *Mental Health in Europe: ends, beginnings, and rediscoveries* (London: Macmillan).

Rapley, M. (2004) *The Social Construction of Intellectual Disability* (Cambridge: Cambridge University Press).

Rasmussen, K. J. (1908) *People of the Polar North* (London: K. Paul, Trench Trubner). Available at: http://www.archive.org/stream/ peopleofpolarnor00rasmuoft/peopleofpolarnor00rasmuoft_djvu.txt, accessed June 25 2009).

Reeve, D. (2006) 'Towards a Psychology of Disability: The emotional effects of living in a disabling society', in D. Goodley and R. Lawthom (eds) *Disability and Psychology: Critical Introductions and Reflections* (Basingstoke: Palgrave Macmillan).

Riddel, S. and Watson, N. (eds) (2003) *Disability, Culture and Identity* (London: Pearson, Prentice Hall).

Rieser, R. (1990) 'Internalised Oppression: How it Seems to Me', in R. Rieser and M. Mason (eds) *Disability Equality in the Classroom: A Human Rights Issue* (London: Inner London Education Authority).

Rieser R. and Mason M. (eds) (1990) *Disability Equality in the Classroom: A Human Rights Issue* (London: Inner London Education Authority).

Rogers, L (2006) 'Babies with club foot are aborted', *The Sunday Times*, 28 July .

Rose, N. (1989) *Governing the Soul. The shaping of the private self*, 2nd edn (London: Free Association Books).

Ross, K. (1997) *Disability and Broadcasting: A View From The Margins* (Cheltenham: Cheltenham and Gloucester College of Higher Education).

Rothman, D. J. (1971) *The Discovery of the Asylum* (Boston: Little, Brown).

Roulstone, A. (1998) *Enabling Technology: Disabled People, Work and Welfare* (Milton Keynes: Open University Press).

Roulstone, A. (2011) 'Review: *Exploring Disability:* Second Edition, *Understanding Disability: From theory to practice*, Second Edition, *Disability and Society*, 26 (3), 3375–81.

Roulstone, A. and Barnes, C. (eds) (2005) *Working Futures: Disabled People*, Policy and Social Inclusion (Bristol: The Policy Press).

Russell, M. (1998) *Beyond Ramps: Disability at the End of The Social Contract – a warning from an uppity crip* (Monroe, Maine: Common Courage Press).

Russell, M. (2002) 'What Disability Civil Rights Cannot Do: employment and political economy', *Disability and Society*, 17 (2), 117–137.

Ryan, J. and Thomas, F. (1987) *The Politics of Mental Handicap* Harmondsworth: Penguin).

Safilios-Rothschild, C. (1970) *The Sociology and Social Psychology of Disability and Rehabilitation* (New York: Random House).

Safilios-Rothschild, C. (1976) 'Disabled Persons' Self-Definitions and Their Implications for Rehabilitation', in G. Albrecht (ed.) *The Sociology of Physical Disability and Rehabilitation* (Pittsburgh: University of Pittsburgh Press).

Sainsbury, S. (1973) 'Measuring Disability', occasional Papers on Social Administration. No. 54 (London: Bell).

Sancho, J. (2003) 'Disabling Prejudice: Attitudes towards disability and its portrayal on television'. Available at: http://www.leeds.ac.uk/disability-studies/archiveuk/sancho/disability.pdf, accessed 16 February 2010.

Sapey, B. (2004) 'Impairment, disability and loss: reassessing the rejection of loss', *Illness, Crisis and Loss*, 12 (1), 1–12.

Saupe, M. (2008) 'Unheard voices: human rights issues of disabled youngsters from Rumanian institutions', in L. Clements and J. Read (eds) *Disabled People and the Right to Life: The protection and violation of disabled people's basic human rights* (London: Routledge).

Sayce, L. (2000) *From Psychiatric Patient to Citizen* (London: Macmillan).

Scambler, G. (1989) *Epilepsy* (London: Tavistock and Routledge).

Scambler, G. (2004) 'Re-framing Stigma: Felt and Enacted Stigma and Challenges to the Sociology of Chronic and Disabling Conditions', *Social Theory and Health*, 2 (1), 29–46.

Scambler, G. and Hopkins, A. (1986) 'Being epileptic: coming to terms with stigma', *Sociology of Health and Illness*, 8 (1), 26–43.

Scheer, J. and Groce, N. (1988) 'Impairment as a Human Constant: cross cultural and historical perspectives', *Journal of Social Issues*, 44 (1), 23–37.

Scheff, T.J. (1966) *Being Mentally Ill* (New York: Aldine).

Scheper-Hughes, N. (1992) *Death without Weeping: The Violence of Everyday Life in Brazil* (Berkeley: University of California Press).

Schutz, A. (1970) *Alfred Schutz on phenomenology and social relations with an introduction by Helmut R. Wagner* (Chicago: University of Chicago Press).

Scotch, R. (1989) 'Politics and Policy in the History of the Disability Rights Movement', *Milbank Quarterly*, 67 (Supplement 2, Part 2), 380–400.

Scott, A. (1990) *Ideology and New Social Movements* (London: Unwin Hyman).

Scott, R. and Crooks, A. (2005) *Polls Apart 4: Campaigning for Accessible Democracy* (London: Scope).

Scull, A. (1978) *Museums of Madness* (London: Allen Lane).

Scull, A. (1984) *Decarceration*, 2nd edn (Cambridge: Polity Press).

Shakespeare, T. W. (1994) *Conceptualising Impairment and Disability in Sociological Perspective*, unpublished Ph.D. thesis, University of Cambridge.

Shakespeare, T. W. (1995) 'Back to the future? New genetics and disabled people', *Critical Social Policy*, 44 (5), 22–35.

Shakespeare, T. W. (2006) *Disability Rights and Wrongs* (London: Routledge).

Shakespeare, T. W. (2009) 'A Choice for Dignity in Dying', *The Guardian online*, 7 July. Available at: http://www.guardian.co.uk/commentisfree/2009/jul/07/ assisted-dying-terminally-ill-disabled, accessed 12 February 2011.

Shakespeare, T. W. and Watson, N. (2001) 'The Social Model of Disability: An Outdated Ideology?', in S. N. Barnartt and B. M. Altman (eds) *Exploring Theories and Expanding Methodologies: Where Are We And Where Do We Need To Go? Research in Social Science and Disability*, Vol. 2 (Amsterdam: JAI Elsevier).

Shakespeare, T. W., Gillespie-Sells, K. and Davies, D. (1996) *The Sexual Politics of Disability* (London: Cassell).

Shearer, A. (1981) *Disability: Whose Handicap?* (Oxford: Basil Blackwell).

Sheldon, A. (1999) 'Personal and perplexing: Feminist disability politics evaluated', *Disability and Society*, 14 (5), 645–59.

Sheldon, A. (2004a) 'Changing Technology', in J. Swain, S. French, C. Barnes and C. Thomas (eds) *Disabling Barriers: Enabling Environments*, 2nd edn (London: Sage).

Sheldon, A. (2004b) 'Women and Disability', in J. Swain, S. French, C. Barnes and C. Thomas (eds) *Disabling Barriers: Enabling Environments*, 2nd edn (London: Sage).

Sheldon, A. (2005) 'One World, One People, One Struggle? Towards the global implementation of the social model of disability', in C. Barnes and G. Mercer (eds) *The Social Model of Disability: Europe and the Majority World* (Leeds: The Disability Press).

Shilling, C. (1993) *The Body and Social Theory* (London: Sage).

Shilling, C. (2003) *The Body and Social Theory*, 2nd edn (London: Sage).

Sieglar, M, and Osmond, M. (1974) *Models of Madness: Models of Medicine* (London: Collier Macmillan).

Silverman, D. (1998) 'Research and Social Policy', in C. Seale (ed.) *Researching Society and Culture* (London: Sage).

Smith, N. (2010) 'Is welfare reform doomed to fail?' BBC Radio 4: News Politics, 11 November. Available at http://www.bbc.co.uk/news/uk-politics-11732919, accessed 12 November 2010.

Snyder, S. L. and Mitchell, D. T. (2001) 'Re-engaging the Body: Disability Studies and the Resistance to Embodiment', *Public Culture*, 13 (3), 367–89.

Soder, M. (1984) 'The Mentally Retarded: Ideologies of care and surplus population',. in L. Barton and S.Tomlinson (eds) *Special Education and Social Interests* (London: Croom Helm).

Soder, M. (2009) 'Tensions, perspectives and themes in disability studies', *Scandinavian Journal of Disability Research*, 11 (2), 67–81.

Sokolowska, M., Ostrowska, A., and Titkow, A. (1981) 'Creation and Removal of Disability as a Social Category: The Case of Poland', in G. Albrecht (ed.) *Cross National Rehabilitation Policies: A Sociological Perspective* (London: Sage).

Stammeringlaw (2010) 'Equality Law 2010 (Equality Bill)'. Available at: http://www.stammeringlaw.org.uk/changes/sea.htm, accessed 27 June 2010.

Stiker, H. J. (1999) *A History of Disability* (Michigan: University of Michigan Press).

Stone, D. A. (1984) *The Disabled State* (London: Macmillan).

Stone, E. (ed.) (1999) *Disability and Development: Learning from action and research on disability in the majority world* (Leeds: The Disability Press. Available at: http://www.disability-archive.leeds.ac.uk/ authors_list.asp?AuthorID=159&author_name=Stone%2C+Emma, accessed 5 July 2010).

Stuart, O. (1993) 'Double Oppression: An appropriate starting point', in J. Swain, V. Finkelstein, S. French and M. Oliver (eds) *Disabling Barriers – Enabling Environments* (London: Sage).

Sullivan, D. A. (2001) *Cosmetic Surgery: The Cutting Edge of Commercial Medicine in America* (New Brunswick, NJ: Rutgers University Press).

Sutherland, A. (1981) *Disabled we Stand* (London: Souvenir Press. Also available at http://www.disability-archive.leeds.ac.uk/authors_list.asp? AuthorID= 160&author_name=Sutherland%2C+Allan, accessed 12 November 2010).

Sutherland, A. (2006) 'The Other Tradition; From Personal Politics to Disability Arts', presentation at the Disability Association Conference, Lancaster University, 19 September. Also available at http://www.disability-archive.leeds.ac.uk/authors_list.asp?AuthorID= 160&author_name=Sutherland%2C+Allan, accessed 12 November 2010.

Swain, J. (2004) 'International Perspectives on Disability', in J. Swain, S. French, C. Barnes and C. Thomas (eds) *Disabling Barriers: Enabling Environments* (London: Sage).

Swain, J. (2011) 'Review; Goodley, D., 2011: Disability Studies: An Interdisciplinary Introduction', *Disability and Society*, 26 (4), 503–5.

Swain, J. and Cameron, C. (1999) 'Unless otherwise stated: discussions of labelling and identity in coming out', in M. Corker and S. French (eds) *Disabling Discourse* (Buckingham: Open University Press).

Swain, J. and French, S. (2000) 'Towards an Affirmative Model of Disability', *Disability and Society*, 15 (4), 569–82.

Swain, J. and French, S. (2008) *Understanding Disability: a Guide for Professionals* (London: Churchill Livingstone Elsevier).

Swain, J., French, S. and Cameron, C. (2003) *Controversial Issues in a Disabling Society* (Buckingham: Open University Press).

Swain, J., French, S., Barnes, C. and Thomas, C. (eds) (2004) *Disabling Barriers: Enabling Environments*, 2nd edn (London: Sage).

Sweeney, B. and Riddell, S. (2003) 'Mainstreaming Disability on Radio 4', in S. Riddell and N. Watson (eds) *Disability, Culture and Identity* (London: Pearson Prentice Hall).

Sykes, W. and Groom, C . (2009) *Developing Standard Disability Survey Questions: A report on cognitive testing* (Canterbury: Canterbury Personal Social Services Research Unit).

Szasz, T. S. (1961) *The Myth of Mental Illness* (New York: Harper & Row).

Takamine, Y. (2006) *History of the Global Disability Movement* (Okinawa: University of the Ryukyus. Available at: http://www.jicafriends.jp/leaders/gi2006/material/lecture/img/1023amhistory.pdf, accessed 29 November 2008).

Talle, A. (1995) 'A Child is a Child: Disability and Equality among the Kenya Masai', in B. Ingstad and S. R. Whyte (eds) *Disability and Culture* (Berkeley: University of California Press).

Taylor, B. (2001) 'HIV, stigma and health: integration of theoretical concepts and the lived experiences of individuals', *Journal of Advanced Nursing*, 35 (5), 792–8.

Taylor, S. J. and Bogden, R. (1989) 'On Accepting Relationships between People with Mental Retardation and Non-disabled People: toward and understanding of acceptance', *Disability, Handicap and Society*, 4 (1), 21–36.

The Economist (2010) 'Getting it Right; Lessons in welfare reform for

Britain's coalition government', 11 November. Available at:
http://www.economist.com/ node/17463433?story_id=17463433, accessed
16 November 2010.

Thomas, C. (1997) 'The baby and the bath water: disabled women and
motherhood in social context'. *Sociology of Health and Illness*, 19 (5),
622–43.

Thomas, C. (1999) *Female Forms: Experiencing and Understanding Disability*
(Buckingham: Open University Press).

Thomas, C. (2004a) 'How is disability understood? An examination of
Sociological approaches', *Disability and Society*, 19 (6), 569–83.

Thomas, C. (2007) *Sociologies of Disability and Illness: Contested ideas in
Disability Studies and Medical Sociology* (Basingstoke: Palgrave
Macmillan).

Thomas, D. (1982) *The Experience of Handicap* (London: Methuen).

Thomas, K. (1977) 'The place of laughter in Tudor and Stuart England', *Times
Literary Supplement*, 21 January, 77–81.

Thomson, R. G. (1997) *Extraordinary Bodies: Figuring Physical Disability in
American Culture and Literature* (New York: Columbia University Press).

Thomson, R. G. (2006) 'Ways of Staring', *Journal of Visual Culture*, 5 (2),
173–92.

Titmuss, R. (1968) *Commitment to Welfare* (London: Allen & Unwin).

Tomlinson, S. (1996) 'Conflicts and dilemmas for professionals in special
education', in C. Christensen and F.Rizvi (eds), *Disability and the
Dilemmas of Education and Justice* (Buckingham: Open University Press).

Topliss, E. (1979) *Provision for the Disabled*, 2nd edn (Oxford: Blackwell with
Martin Robertson).

Topliss, E. (1982) *Social Responses to Handicap* (Harlow: Longman).

Touraine, A. (1981) *The Voice and the Eye: an analysis of social movements*
translated by Alan Duff (Cambridge: Cambridge University Press).

Townsend, P. (1979) *Poverty in the United Kingdom* (Harmondsworth:
Penguin).

Tremain, S. (2002) 'On the subject of impairment', in M. Corker and T.
Shakespeare (eds) *Disability/Postmodernity: Embodying Disability Theory*
(London: Continuum).

Tremain, S. (2005) 'Foucault, Governmentality and Critical Disability Theory:

An Introduction', in S. Tremain (ed.) *Foucault and the Government of Disability* (Ann Arbor: The University of Michigan Press).

Truman, C. (2005) 'The autonomy of professionals and the involvement of patients and families'. *Current Opinion in Psychiatry*, 18 (5), 572–5.

Turner, B. (1987) *Medical Power and Social Knowledge* (London: Sage).

Turner, B. (1999) *Classical Sociology* (London: Sage).

Turner, V. (1967) *The Forest of Symbols: Aspects of Ndembu Ritual* (New York: Cornell University Press).

UN (1948) *Universal Declaration of Human Rights* (New York: United Nations.

UN (1971) *Declaration of the Rights of Mentally Retarded Person* (New York: United Nations).

UN (1975) *Declaration of the Rights of Disabled Persons* (New York: United Nations).

UN (1993) *Standard Rules on the Equalisation of Opportunities for Persons with Disabilities* (New York: United Nations. Available at: http://www.un.org/esa/socdev/enable/dissre00.htm, accessed 17 November 2010).

UN (2006) *Convention on the rights of persons with disabilities and optional protocol* (New York: United Nations. Available at: http://www.un.org/disabilities/documents/convention/convotprot-e/pdf, accessed 17 November 2010).

UN (2010) *Including the rights of person with disabilities in United Nations programming at country level: A Guidance Note for United Nations Country Teams and Implementing Partners* United Nations Development Group/Inter-Agency Support Group for the CRPD Task Team (New York: United Nations).

UNDP. (2005) *Human Development Report: International cooperation at a crossroads* (United Nations Development Programme New York: Oxford University Press).

UN Enable (undated) *Convention and Optional Protocol: Signatures and Ratifications'* (New York: United Nations. Available at: http://www.un.org/disabilities/ countries.asp?id=166, Accessed 11 June 2011).

Ungerson, C. (1997) 'Social politics and the commodification of care', *Social Politics*, 4 (3), 362–81.

Ungerson, C. (2004) 'Whose empowerment and independence? A cross-national perspective on 'cash for care' schemes', *Work, Employment and Society*, 13 (4), 583–600.

UPIAS (1976) *Fundamental Principles of Disability* (London: Union of the Physically Impaired Against Segregation).

Üstün, T. B., Chatterji, S., Bickenbach, J. E., Trotter, R. T., Room, R., Rehm, J. and Saxena, S. (2001) *Disability and Culture: Universalism and Diversity* (Seattle: Hogrefe & Huber, for World Health Organization).

Vasey, S. (1992) 'A Response to Liz Crow', *Coalition: the Magazine of the Greater Manchester Coalition of Disabled People*, September, 42–4.

Vellacot, P. (1971) *Sophocles and Oedipus: A study of 'Oedipus and Turranus' – with a new translation* (London: Macmillan).

Verbrugge, L. M. (1985) 'Gender and Health: An update on hypotheses and evidence', *Journal of Health and Social Behaviour*, 26, 156–82.

Vernon, A. and Swain, J. (2002) 'Theorising Divisions and hierarchies: Towards a commonality or diversity', in C. Barnes, M. Oliver and L. Barton (eds) *Disability Studies Today* (Cambridge: Polity).

Wachman, R. (2011) 'Southern Cross strikes deal with landlords in bid to stave off collapse', *Guardian online*. Available at: http://www.guardian.co.uk/business/2011/jun/16/southern-cross-care-landlords-deal, accessed 16 June 2011.

Walker, A. (1984) the political economy of privatisation, in J. Le Grand and R. Robinson, (eds) *Privatisation and the Welfare State* (London: Allen & Unwin).

Wallerstein, I. (1990) *The Modern World System II* (New York: Academic Press).

Walmsley, J. (1991) 'Talking to Top People: Some issues relating to the citizenship of people with learning difficulties', *Disability, Handicap and Society*, 6 (3), 219–31.

Walmsley, J. (1997) 'Including People with Learning Difficulties: Theory and Practice', in L. Barton and M. Oliver (eds) *Disability Studies: Past, Present and Future* (Leeds: The Disability Press).

Wates, M. and Jade, R. (eds) (1999) *Bigger than the Sky: disabled women on parenting* (London: The Women's Press).

Watson, N. (2002) '"Well, I know this is going to sound very strange to you, but I don't see myself as a disabled person": identity and disability', *Disability and Society*, 17 (5), 509–27.

Watters, E, (2011) *Crazy Like Us: The globalisation of the American psyche*
(London: Robinson Publishing).

Weber, M. (1994) *The Protestant Ethic and the Spirit of Capitalism; translated
by Talcott Parsons; Introduction by Anthony Giddens* (London:
Routledge).

Wendell, S. (1996) *The Rejected Body: feminist philosophical reflections on
disability* (London: Routledge).

WHO (1976) *International Classification of Disease*, 9th Revision (Geneva:
World Health Organization).

WHO (1980) *International Classification of Impairments, Disabilities and
Handicaps* (Geneva: World Health Organization).

WHO (2001a) *International Classification of Functioning, Disability and
Health* (Geneva: World Health Organization).

WHO (2001b) *Rethinking Care from the Perspective of Disabled People*
(Geneva: World Health Organization's Disability and Rehabilitation Team.
Available at: http://www.who.int/inf-pr-2001/en/note2001-16.html,
accessed 4 August 2007).

WHO (2002) *Towards a Common Language for Functioning, Disability and
Health* (ICF) (Geneva: World Health Organization. Available at:
(http://www3.who.int/icf/icftemplate.cfm?myurl=beginners.html&mytitle=
Beginner%27s%20Guide, accessed 19 February 2007).

WHO (2010) Disability and Rehabilitation Team Homepage (Geneva: World
Health Organization. Available at: http://www.who.int/disabilities/en/,
accessed 17 November 2010).

WHO (2011) *World Report on Disability* (Geneva: World Health
Organization. Available at:
http://whqlibdoc.who.int/publications/2011/9789240685215_eng.pdf,
accessed on 10 June 2011).

World Bank (2007) *Social Analysis and Disability: A Guidance Note*
(Washington: World Bank). Available at:
http://siteresources.worldbank.org/DISABILITY/ Resources/280658-
1172606907476/SAnalysisDis.doc accessed 28 November 2008).

Wilde, A. (2009) 'Alison Wilde Reviews six episodes of 'Cast Offs' Available at:
http://www.disabilityartsonline.org.uk/?unique_name= Alison-
Wilde&item=509&itemoffset=7, accessed 28 June 2011.

Wilding, P. (1982) *Professional Power and Social Welfare* (London: Routledge & Kegan Paul).

Wilson, S. (2003) *Disability, Counselling and Psychotherapy: challenges and opportunities* (New York: Palgrave Macmillan).

Winkler, F. (1987) 'Consumerism in Health Care: beyond the Supermarket Model', *Policy and Politics* 15 (1), 1–15.

Wilkin, D. (1987) 'Conceptual Problems in Dependency Research', *Social Science and Medicine*, 24 (10), 867–73.

Williams, G. H. (1998) 'The Sociology of Disability: Towards a Materialist Phenomenology', in T. Shakespeare (ed.) *The Disability Reader: Social Science Perspectives* (London: Cassell).

Williams, G. H. (2001) 'Theorising Disability', in G. L. Albrecht, K. D. Seelman and M. Bury (eds) *Handbook of Disability Studies* (London: Sage).

Williams, R. (1981) *Culture* (Glasgow: Fontana).

Williams, R. (1989) *Resources of Hope* (London: Verso).

Williams, S. J. (1999) 'Is anybody there? Critical realism, chronic illness and disability debate', *Sociology of Health and Illness*, 21 (6), 797–819.

Williams, S. J. (2001) 'Sociological Imperialism and the medical profession: Where are We Now?', *Sociology of Health and Illness*, 23 (2), 135–58.

Williams, S. J. (2003) *Medicine and the Body* (London: Sage).

Wolfensberger, W. (1972) *The principle of normalisation in human services* (Toronto: National Institute on Mental Retardation).

Wolfensberger, W. (1989) 'Human Service Policies: The Rhetoric versus the Reality', in L. Barton (ed.) *Disability and Dependence* (Lewes: Falmer).

Wolfensberger, W. and Thomas, S. (1983) *Program Analysis of Service Systems Implementation of Normalisation Goals: Normalisation and Ratings Manual*, 2nd edn (Toronto: National Institute of Mental Retardation).

Wood, R. (1991) 'Care of Disabled People', in G. Dalley (ed.) *Disability and Social Policy* (London: Policy Studies Institute).

Wrigley, E. A. and Souden, D. (eds) (1986) *The Works of Thomas Robert Malthus* (London: Pickering and Chatto).

Wrong, D. (1970) *Max Weber* (New Jersey: Prentice Hall).

Yeo, R. (2001) 'Chronic Poverty and Disability', Background Paper No. 4. (Chronic Poverty Research: Centre for Action on Disability and

Development. Available at: http://www.chronicpoverty.org/pdfs/04Yeo.pdf, Accessed 16 November 2007).

Yeo, R. (2006) 'Disability poverty and the New Development Agenda', in B. Albert (ed.) *In or Out of the Mainstream? Lessons from research on disability and development cooperation* (Leeds: The Disability Press).

Yeo, R. and Bolton, A. (2008) *'I don't have a problem, the problem is theirs'. The lives and aspirations of Bolivian disabled people in words and pictures* (Leeds: The Disability Press).

Young, I. M. (1990) *Justice and the Politics of Difference* (Princeton: Princeton University Press).

Zimonjic, P. (2006) 'Church supports baby Euthanasia', *Times online*, 12 November . Available at: http://www.timesonline.co.uk/tol/news/uk/article634486.ece, accessed 16 January 2010.

Zola, I. K. (1972) 'Medicine as an Institution of Social Control', *Sociological Review*, 20 (4), 487–504.

Zola, I. K. (1973) 'Pathways to the Doctor: from Person to Patient', *Social Science and Medicine*, 5, 977–89.

Zola, I. K. (1982) *Missing Pieces: A Chronicle of Living with a Disability* (Philadelphia: Temple University Press).

Zola, I. K. (1991) 'The medicalisation of ageing and disability', in G. L. Albrecht and J. A. Levy (eds) *Advances in Medical Sociology*, Vol. 2 (Greenwich, Connecticut: JAI Press).

Index

240   *Index*